FUNDAMENTALISM
in
American Religion
1880 - 1950

A forty-five-volume facsimile series
reproducing often extremely rare material
documenting the development of one of the
major religious movements of our time

■ *Edited by*
Joel A. Carpenter
Billy Graham Center, Wheaton College
■ *Advisory Editors*
Donald W. Dayton,
Northern Baptist Theological Seminary
George M. Marsden,
Duke University
Mark A. Noll,
Wheaton College
Grant Wacker,
University of North Carolina

A GARLAND SERIES

Fighting Fundamentalism: Polemical Thrusts of the 1930s and 1940s

Edited by
Joel A. Carpenter

Garland Publishing, Inc.
New York & London 1988

For a list of the titles in this series, see the final pages of this volume.
The facsimile of *Facts for Baptists to Face* has been made from a copy
in the Cedarville College Library; the facsimile of *The Growing
Menace of the Social Gospel* is from of copy in the Billy Graham
Center of Wheaton College; that of *The Conflict of Christianity* is
from the Moody Bible Institute, and that of *The Case Against
Modernism* is from the Wheaton College Library.

Introduction copyright © 1988 by Joel A. Carpenter.
All rights reserved.

Library of Congress Cataloging in Puiblication Data

Fighting Fundamentalism : polemical thrusts of the 1930s and 1940s/
   edited with an introduction by Joel A. Carpenter.
   p. cm. -- (Fundamentalism in American religion, 1880-1950)
   Reprint of works originally published 1936-1949.
   Bibliography: p.
   Contents: Facts for Baptists to face/Robert T. Ketcham -- The
growing menace of the "social gospel"/J. E. Conant -- The conflict
of Christianity with its counterfeits/W. B. Riley -- The case
against modernism/Chester E. Tulga.
      ISBN 0-8240-5034-7 (alk. paper)
      1. Modernist-fundamentalist controversy. 2. Baptists--United
States--Doctrines. I. Carpenter, Joel A. II. Series.
BT82.3.F54 1988
   273'.9--dc19

                                                      88-22722

Design by Valerie Mergentime
Printed on acid-free, 250-year-life paper.
Manufactured in the United States of America

CONTENTS

■ *Introduction*

■ *Facts for Baptists to Face*
Robert T. Ketcham

■ *The Growing Menace of the "Social Gospel"*
J. E. Conant

■ *The Conflict of Christianity with Its Counterfeits*
W.B. Riley

■ *The Case Against Modernism*
Chester E. Tulga

INTRODUCTION

Fundamentalists' offensives against theological liberalism in the major denominations had ceased in failure by the mid-1930s, but in the aftermath of these defeats, many militants waged guerilla campaigns and formed resistance movements. Modernist theology continued to be their prime target, but as the four pieces republished here will show, liberal church leaders' left-wing politics drew fire also. These selections are drawn from the first two decades of fundamentalists' sojourn in the hinterlands of the American religious landscape. They illustrate the alarmist rhetoric and combativeness that became the hallmark of "fighting fundamentalism."

These pieces also reflect fundamentalism's changed circumstances as the movement entered a new phase during the early 1930s. It was ceasing to function as a militantly conservative faction in denominational disputes, because no one wished to argue with them any more. No one needed to argue with them, either, since fundamentalists were losing their access to a hearing in both the religious and secular presses. Beginning with the Scopes Trial debacle at Dayton, Tennessee, fundamentalism became increasingly discredited as a public voice to be taken seriously.[1]

At the same time, fundamentalism was becoming more of an independent, sectarian movement, with its own identity and distinctive institutions. The movement's most alienated leaders formed a variety of small fellowships in the early and mid-1930s. These separatists argued that the old-line denominations were beyond hope of reform, and they aggressively recruited other conservatives to "come out from among them"[2] and join the new fellowships. Among the church groups fundamentalists founded during these years were the Independent Fundamental Churches of America (1930), the General Association of Regular Baptist Churches (1932), the Orthodox Presbyterian Church (1936), and the Bible Presbyterian Church (1937). Many separatists avoided even these options, however, and affiliated with totally independent local congregations.[3]

Other fundamentalists remained nominally a part of the older denominations but developed parachurch networks of fellowship and ministry. This fundamentalist network, which served separatists and nonseparatists alike, was comprised of influential urban congregations, such as Calvary Baptist Church in New York; Bible schools, most notably the Moody Bible Institute in Chicago; and a variety of other independent religious agencies, such as *The Sunday School Times*, a religious weekly with a circulation of over 200,000; the Sudan Interior Mission, with headquarters in Toronto; and Charles E. Fuller's radio ministry, which was based near Los Angeles.[4]

In part because of this welter of new sects and non-denominational agencies, fundamentalism was fragmented in its loyalties and affiliations. The backgrounds of the four authors in this volume show this very clearly. Each was a Baptist, with roots in the Northern Baptist Convention. Yet each one had chosen a different path in response to the controversies of the 1920s.

Robert T. Ketcham (1889–1978) was one of the founders of the General Association of Regular Baptist Churches, formed in 1932 by congregations coming out from the Northern Baptist Convention. William Bell Riley (1861–1947), on the other hand, was a prominent militant who remained within the denomination. Over time, Riley was able to achieve a semi-separate status by becoming the "boss" of the Minnesota state convention of the Northern Baptists. He eventually parted company with the denomination in 1947, just before his death. Chester E. Tulga (1896–) was a member of the Fundamentalist Fellowship of the Northern Baptist Convention. The Fellowship's denominational loyalism rankled the likes of Riley and Ketcham and prompted them to part ways with it. But by the 1940s, Tulga and many of his colleagues were moving toward separatism themselves as the Fellowship became embroiled in a controversy over modernism and missions. Fellowship fundamentalists formed the Conservative Baptist Foreign Mission Society in 1943, and when this agency was denied official denominational status, several hundred of its supporting churches founded the Conservative Baptist Association in 1947. Judson E. Conant (1867–1955) was as much a fundamentalist as the others, but he had become a freelance evangelist and Bible conference speaker by the 1920s, with friendly ties to the Moody Bible Institute. So denominational issues became pretty much irrelevant to his work.[5]

One might expect that with their own religious enterprises to carry forward, fundamentalists might grow less interested in lashing out at the liberals. Over time, this proved to be true, at least for a moderate wing of the movement. But as historian George M. Marsden has pointed out, anti-modernism was the distinctive ideological core of fundamentalism.[6] Continuing a line of anti-modernist criticism, then, became vitally important for maintaining the movement's identity. Since fundamentalists were now largely deprived of a hearing outside of their own circles, much in these four works seems aimed at the already-convinced, to bolster their morale. These works functioned as show trials of the modernists *in absentia*; they were designed to set the record straight and to persuade the faithful that the modernists had *not* gotten the upper hand.

It is also very clear that these works were aimed at other conservatives who were still largely uncritical of their denominations. If things are as bad as we show them to be, the authors argued, how can "Bible-believing" Christians continue to go about their business as if nothing is wrong? Even for non-separating fundamentalists like Riley and Conant, such anti-modernist consciousness-raising was vital for recruitment. Fundamentalist leaders were continually challenged and frustrated by the great numbers of traditional, non-ideological, and denominationally loyal evangelicals whom they had not yet mobilized behind their banner.

Facts for Baptist to Face (Gary, Indiana: by the author, 1936) was Robert Ketcham's attempt to scandalize and mobilize other "Bible-believing" Baptists. He argued that the situation in the Northern Baptist Convention was hopeless, and that "back of the scenes is a deliberate program . . . which is destined to land the Baptists of this country completely in the camp of Modernism and a rank Communistic Socialism" (p. 2). This fiery booklet, filled with documented accusations of modernism and friendliness to communism among Baptist officials, was compiled from a series of "cases" that Ketcham had presented in the *Baptist Bulletin*, the new monthly magazine of the General Association of Regular Baptist Churches (GARBC).[7]

Ketcham was the most powerful champion the Regular Baptists had. He was by rearing and experience a fighter from the rough-and-tumble mining towns of western Pennsylvania. He was converted at age twenty-one, and became the pastor two years later of a Baptist church in the village of Roulette, Pennsylvania, where, Ketcham later claimed, there were more Socialists than church members. Ketcham was largely self-taught, with no formal pastoral education, but he was a voracious reader in spite of a serious sight disability; and his eloquent, impassioned preaching and relentless energy quickly propelled his career forward.

Early on in his ministry Ketcham grew alarmed at modernist trends in his denomination, which he encountered first-hand during an abortive enrollment at Crozier Theological Seminary. A later incident, while he was a pastor in Butler, Pennsylvania, turned Ketcham into a bitter foe of the Convention's officials. In 1919, some state Baptist leaders, who were incensed over Ketcham's opposition to the Interchurch World Movement fund-raising campaign, had a shouting and shoving match with him in his parlor after threatening him with blacklisting if he didn't line up with the program. Thereafter, "Fighting Bob" Ketcham prowled relentlessly in search of modernism in Northern Baptists' schools, missions, publications boards, and state secretaries' offices. He joined the militant Baptist Bible Union in 1923, and when the denominational fight seemed lost, he helped to found the GARBC in 1932. In 1948 he became the denomination's national representative. But from the early thirties until his retirement in 1966, Ketcham's main calling was as chief controversialist and recruiter for the Regular Baptist movement.[8]

Facts for Baptists to Face was aimed at Ketcham's main objective in the GARBC's early years, which was to convince wavering congregations to leave the Northern Baptist Convention and join the Regular Baptists. Ketcham led many sorties into the pulpits of sympathetic congregations from Pennsylvania to Iowa, charging Northern Baptist leaders with the sins enumerated in this booklet. Baptist churches had the right to withdraw from the Convention, Ketcham argued, and they could take their property and legal standing as

Baptists with them (pp. 38–9). Evidently, hundreds of Baptist congregations acted accordingly, and the GARBC received many of them. From a tiny sect with some 84 churches and 22,000 members in 1936, the Regular Baptists grew to some 468 churches by the time Ketcham became the group's National Representative in 1948. At the time of his retirement eighteen years later, the GARBC included some 1,200 churches and 165,000 members.[9] Most of this postwar growth came from the birth of new congregations, but in its earlier years, the GARBC was very much at war with the Northern Baptist Convention. In 1960, Ketcham estimated that some 400 of the GARBC's congregations had come out of the Convention.[10]

Relatively little, however, of the fundamentalists' controversial writing of the 1930s and 1940s had the same purpose as *Facts for Baptists to Face*. Rather than promoting ecclesiastical separatism, most of this literature was aimed more at expressing a fundamentalist perspective on particular issues, or more broadly, a fundamentalist world view. The other three documents in this volume fall into this genre.

The Growing Menace of the Social Gospel (Chicago: Bible Institute Colportage Association, 1937), by free-lance Baptist evangelist, author, and Bible conference speaker Judson E. Conant, was occasioned by a major revival of the Social Gospel movement in the 1930s. Under the influence of economic upheaval, an encouraging climate for collectivist social thought during the New Deal, and a major intellectual tilt toward the left, many prominent church leaders were making cooperative Christian socialism the major agenda item for the Kingdom of God.[11]

Fundamentalists had of course criticized the Social Gospel movement in its earlier incarnations, but what made it seem particularly ominous to Conant at the time he wrote was that it was converging with what he considered to be an insidious collectivist direction on the part of the State. The current attempts of the Roosevelt administration to increase the size of (and thus liberalize) the Supreme Court was the most immediately threatening example of that trend, which Conant perceived to be part of a worldwide collectivization movement. Those nations where the process had gone farthest—Nazi Germany and the Soviet Union—were places where freedom had died. Of the several alarming trends in the United States, Conant believed that the Social Gospel was "by far the most serious and menacing"; for when Christians should have been contending for freedom and true faith, this movement was "giving aid and comfort to the enemies of our faith and the forces that would destroy our freedom." This was not simply a practical application of the old Gospel, but the program of "Modernistic" church leaders "who are friendly to the Russian system and who even have words of praise for Communism" (p.51).

Conant's pamphlet is more than an alarmist attack on the Left, however. It is also perhaps the most complete expression available of fundamentalists' conservative and individualistic bent in theology and social thought. Conant took his readers back to Creation, and asserted that God's purpose for creating humans was to show His love. Because God loved humankind, He endowed our ancestors with the freedom to choose to follow His will, or to rebel. Adam and Eve rebelled, and ever since, humans have had a built-in preference for their own will, and have defied outside authority. This willful abuse of freedom, claimed Conant, was the sole source of humanity's political, social, and economic woes. Throughout history, under a great variety of systems of government, commerce, and society, injustice and oppression have cropped up again and again. So Conant was skeptical of socialists' prescription of yet another reconstruction of the social order to bring an end to injustice.

God's will for human government, Conant argued further, is for the State to minimize injustice by restraining violence and exploitation, and by protecting basic human rights. This principle was based, he claimed, on God's covenant with Noah in Genesis chapter nine, in which God instituted capital punishment for murder, which is the ultimate violation of humans' right to live out their lives as they choose. Conant then added an interesting twist, a distinctly evangelical variation on classic natural rights theory. He argued that since worship of God is the primary divinely intended use of human freedom, the right to worship freely is the most fundamental of human rights. Following from this basic religious right are the rights to free speech and free assembly; implied from these is the right to pass on one's faith to the next generation (the basis for the right to maintain a home); and to secure all of the above, the right to own and control private property follows; and from this, the right to private profit. Conant's scheme gave religious rights priority, but in effect it also provided a religious sanction for property rights and the profit motive as the God-ordained means of securing religious freedom. From this he argued that any collectivist plan ultimately was an attack on religious freedom, and thus the work of the enemies of God.

This last point reveals what Conant found to be so menacing about the Social Gospel. By a unique providence, he claimed, the United States Constitution had established and protected this God-ordained system of human freedom. But the American Left, those "sworn enemies of our Constitution," were in their passion for power and plunder striving to destroy the American system (p. 41). Conant turned next to the political left's partners in the Social Gospel movement. These ministers' motives may have been altruistic, he allowed, but they were mistakenly trying to institute the Kingdom of God on earth through Christian socialism. The Kingdom, Conant insisted, following the dispensationalist theology that pervaded fundamentalism,[12] was not the program for this age, but for the next, when Christ would return and personally reign on earth. In this age, he concluded, "the whole mission of the Church is to be summed up in the word 'witness'" (p. 60). When the Church takes up "social righteousness" and neglects its evangelistic task, too often the result is the freedom-crushing union of Church and State and the moral decay of society where Christian conversion grows scarcer. Given the ominous signs he saw in the United States, Conant concluded that it was high time that true Christians preached the gospel of individual redemption, stayed away from Social Gospel programs, and warned others of these programs' dire consequences.

Conant's work reflects the fundamentalist movement's nearly total abandonment of social or political reform. Yet the reader will note a strong tension in this piece between its argument for an apolitical stance on the part of the Church on the one hand, and its heated calls for Christians to oppose collectivist trends on the other. Fundamentalists' cultural alienation and separatism in the 1930s masked deeply conservative social and political values and an entrenched belief that America was an elect nation. Both of these items held potential for fueling political action. The rise of the New Religious Right in the late 1970s, with fundamentalists playing prominent roles, was in fact a release of the movement's latent political energy.[13]

William Bell Riley sounds many of the same themes in his small book, *The Conflict of Christianity with Its Counterfeits* (Minneapolis: Irene Woods, 1940), which is the third offering in this volume. At age 79, Riley was near the end of a long and distinguished tenure as the pastor of the First Baptist Church of Minneapolis, having served there since 1897. He was the dominant force among fundamentalists in Minnesota and neighboring states, largely by virtue of the network of alumni from his Northwestern Bible and Missionary Training School (founded in 1902). Riley had been a leader in national fundamentalist organizations as well, notably the World's Christian Fundamentals Association (WCFA), and the Baptist Bible Union—until the latter's demise in 1928. A gifted orator and a formidable debater, Riley had toured widely during the 1920s on behalf of the WCFA, challenging evolutionists to debate. He claimed never to have lost a match.

By the time that this little book was published, however, Riley's hopes of turning back the modernist tide in either the Northern Baptist Convention or society more generally had been nearly drowned. Filled with discouragement and bitterness, he was now toying with some of the most paranoic and anti-Semitic conspiracy theories available during those years.[14] *The Conflict of Christianity with Its Counterfeits* conveys a little of that conspiratorial thinking, and some of Riley's bitterness, for that matter, but its major function is as a shadow-boxing ritual, aimed at showing the old warrior's determination "never to run up the flag of surrender, or even to hint a truce with the enemies of God or His Word" (p. 6). Unlike his earlier works, which were produced by reputable religious publishers and presumably achieved fairly wide circulation, *The Conflict* was a virtual self-publication, comprised of minimally edited chapters that betray their origins as occasional sermons and addresses.

Riley's premise for the book was that the Church's historic career was marked by constant warfare with satanic or "antichristian" counterfeits. In the current era, religious modernism had become the latest of these fakeries, and it was the greatest menace ever to true Christianity. The ensuing chapters focus on much the same subject as Conant's *Growing Menace*, the rejuvenation of the the Social Gospel in the 1930s. Riley's book includes his attacks on the Interchurch World Movement of twenty years earlier, and on its perceived successors in the 1930s: the Committee of Nine on Social Action of the Northern Baptist Convention, Toyohiko Kagawa's movement to establish "Christian Cooperatives," E. Stanley Jones's call for social reconstruction to embody the Kingdom of God envisioned in the Bible, and for good measure (though not fitting the rubric very well), the "Oxford Movement" to bring faith to the fashionable set. The book then closes with a ringing testimony to fundamentalism, "the true coin of the Christian realm"—as represented by Riley's WCFA (p. 129).

While the book is officially aimed at modernism and the "Red" Social Gospel, it gives evidence throughout of not being intended for any genuine polemical exchanges with the opposition, or even, as in the case of Ketcham's *Facts*, to prompt a particular sort of antimodernist action. Rather, Riley is re-certifying himself as a red-blooded, militant, fighting fundamentalist. Aggressiveness had by this time become an important self-identifying badge of fundamentalism, and aggressive posturing before a congregation of the already-convinced was a way of ritually enacting the movement's emotive trademark and encouraging the followers to "fight the good fight"[15] in their own lives. Such sermons were also important ways of telling parishioners what to think about various contemporary religious and social trends, for as fundamentalism became increasingly sectarian, its leaders sought to nail down hard and fast ideological boundaries, a strong sense of "us and them."

Chester E. Tulga's *The Case Against Modernism* (Chicago: Conservative Baptist Fellowship, 1949) has much the same implied purpose as Riley's work, but it came at a different sort of moment. It was part of a multi-volume series of "Case" booklets which Tulga wrote in service of a new separatist movement out of Northern Baptist ranks. At the very time that William Bell Riley was on his deathbed, the majority of churches in the Minnesota Baptist Convention were in the process of leaving the Northern Baptist Convention. They were part of the Conservative Baptist movement, which resulted in a new fundamentalist denomination, the Conservative Baptist Association (CBA), begun in 1947.

Tulga, who had ministered for two decades in small-town congregations throughout the Midwest before becoming the pastor of the Norwood Park congregation in Chicago, was hired in 1946 as "research director" of the Conservative Baptist Fellowship (CBF; formerly the Fundamentalist Fellowship of the Northern Baptist Convention). Tulga's job was much the same as Ketcham's had been for the Regular Baptists; he was the polemical point man for a new separatist movement. In 1948, Tulga launched a series of pocket-sized (ca. 60 page) works, called "The Case Books."[16] According to Conservative Baptist historian Bruce Shelley, the first in the series, *The Case against the Federal Council of Churches*, sold over 18,000 copies in a little over a year. By mid-1951, some 100,000 copies had been sold.[17]

Of the four works in this volume, Tulga's *Case Against Modernism* is the most clearly a ritual slaying of one's opponent for an appreciative audience. Its introduction states no purpose, other than to trace the "devious course" of modernism as it came to occupy "the strongholds of the Protestant world" (p. 8). The drift of the book, however, is to show that the older modernism of the early twentieth century has fallen into increasing disrepute, and is being replaced by a revisionist "liberalism" (Tulga doesn't distinguish between liberals and the neo-orthodox), which is in fact as seriously deficient as its predecessor. *The Case* is presented in a self-righteous, condescending, "we told you so" tone; and its rhetoric oozes with contempt for liberals' beliefs and resentment at their higher status and influence.

Tulga's work betrays a nearly total dependence upon the arguments of the disputants within the liberal tradition in American Protestantism. After marshalling quotes of neo-orthodox critics and "chastened liberals" against the older modernism, Tulga then used the criticisms of liberals and humanists to lambast "the new liberalism" (largely neo-orthodoxy). While Tulga had done an impressive amount of reading in twentieth-century liberal and neo-orthodox literature, he had no acute insights or fresh critical perspectives of his own to offer. This work clearly reflects, too, that Tulga either had a very confused understanding of what was going on over on the liberal side of the Protestant divide, or else he was so determined to maintain a posture of condescending scorn that he did not deign to betray a too-intimate understanding of his opponents.

The Conservative Baptist Fellowship and Tulga, its chief spokesman, served the Conservative Baptist movement very usefully in establishing the case for its independence and a "party line" for its constituency, but these watchdogs would cause the Conservative Baptist Association a great deal of grief in the years to come. Apparently stuck in an "attack" mode, the CBF eventually turned its critical fire on the new denomination. Tulga resigned in 1954, and the CBF became independent of the Conservative Baptist Association; but it had become a rallying point for the more militant factions within the denomination. As a result, the Conservative Baptists have experienced sporadic controversy and schisms.[18]

Fundamentalist pugnacity, suspicious vigilance, and militant conservatism became important defining features for the movement, and documents such as those reproduced herein became common to the literature of the movement's more sectarian sub-communities. But as the Tulga episode shows, this fighting mentality did not always contribute positively to these new groups once the main fight was over. Like old counter-insurgency commandos discharged from active duty, fighting fundamentalists' instinctive impulse was to distrust even their friends and to attack with deadly force any idea or person that made strange moves. Thus the history of fundamentalism after 1930 is filled with reactionary thinking, internal tensions, and splinter groups. Such a state of affairs led Ernest Sandeen to characterize this once-distinguished conservative tradition as sadly "split and stricken"; and it has led others to judge that the 1930s and 1940s marked the near-total eclipse of conservative evangelical thought.[19] Thus one cannot fully understand either the struggles of the postwar "neo-evangelical" reformers of fundamentalism to counteract this legacy, or the militantly separatistic fundamentalists' efforts to control it, without earnestly contending with the literature of fighting fundamentalism.

Joel A. Carpenter
Institute for the Study of American Evangelicals
Wheaton College

NOTES

1. George M. Marsden, *Fundamentalism and American Culture:*

The Shaping of Twentieth-Century Evangelicalism: 1870–1925 (New York: Oxford University Press, 1980), 184–195, documents this fall from public respect.

2. II Cor. 6:17.

3. For a discussion of this growing separatist trend in fundamentalism after 1930, see Joel A. Carpenter, "The Renewal of American Fundamentalism, 1930–1945" (Ph. D. dissertation, The Johns Hopkins University, 1984), chapter II, "The Separatist Impulse," 36–69.

4. Joel A. Carpenter, "Fundamentalist Institutions and the Growth of Evangelical Protestantism, 1929–1942," *Church History* 49 (March 1980): 62–75.

5. On Ketcham, see J. Murray Murdoch, *Portrait of Obedience: The Biography of Robert T. Ketcham* (Schaumberg, Illinois: Regular Baptist Press, 1979). On Riley: C. Allyn Russell, *Voices of American Fundamentalism: Seven Biographical Studies* (Philadelphia: Westminster Press, 1976), Chapter Four: "William Bell Riley, Organizational Fundamentalist," 79–106; and William Vance Trollinger, *God's Empire: William Bell Riley and Midwestern Fundamentalism* (Madison: University of Wisconsin Press, forthcoming). On Tulga: Bruce L. Shelley, *Conservative Baptists: A Story of Twentieth-Century Dissent* (Denver: Conservative Baptist Theological Seminary, 1960), 71–72, 79, 86, 102; and George W. Dollar, *A History of Fundamentalism in America* (Greenvile, S.C.: Bob Jones University Press, 1973), 227–231. Conant is a much more elusive figure. My only information on him, other than what can be gleaned from prefaces in his various publications, is the brief "Biographical Note" prepared for the *Guide to Collection 76, The Papers of Judson Eber Conant*, Archives of the Billy Graham Center, Wheaton, Illinois.

6. Marsden, *Fundamentalism and American Culture*, 3–8.

7. See, for example, R. T. Ketcham, "Is There Modernism and Apostasy in the N.B.C.? Facts for Baptists to Face," *Baptist Bulletin* 1 (February 1936): 1, 11.

8. Murdoch, *Portrait of Obedience* is a fulsome, very sympathetic biography; but see also a helpful brief account, Ruth Ryburn, "The Outworking of Obedience," *Baptist Bulletin* 31 (March 1966): 9–12.

FACTS
FOR BAPTISTS
TO FACE

By

DR. ROBERT T. KETCHAM

Published in 1936
(Second Edition 1942)

Prices

10c per copy
5c in lots of 50 or more

Order from the Author at
WALNUT STREET BAPTIST CHURCH
Waterloo, Iowa

INTRODUCTION

During the past twenty years, more particularly from the time of the New World Movement (1919), Baptist ranks have been disturbed by constant charges and rumors of Modernism. When these charges first began to appear the National and State Convention leaders everywhere were loud in their denials of the truth of such charges. Those of us who insisted that all was not well on board the Baptist ship were charged with mutiny. We were called "falsifiers," "destructionists," "religious bolshevists," etc., etc.

In more recent years another sinister element has begun to show its head in Baptist ranks. There is a constantly growing tendency in Convention circles toward a radical Socialism, and a sort of a "pink" Communism. Of course, Convention leadership denies the presence of either Modernism or Communism. Regardless of the denial, however, there are literally hundreds of Baptist Churches that know there is truth iu the charges, but how to prove it is another thing. Some of us who are in possession of the indisputable facts are constantly besieged by letters and even telegrams, to acquaint them with the evidence. This has become such a task that we can no longer take care of it by personal correspondence. We have, therefore, set ourselves the task of gathering together a few facts which we present herewith, which we trust will meet the demands of the situation.

Our difficulty has by no means been to find facts enough. On the contrary our difficulty has been the problem of selection. There is evidence enough left in my files to produce this book many times over. We have endeavored to select from this mass of evidence truly typical cases. Some of them date back through several years, some of them from the immediate present, but all of them are designed to show that back of the scenes there is a deliberate program being carried out which is destined to land the Baptists of this country completely in the camp of Modernism and a rank Communistic Socialism.

No doubt many who start to read this booklet will become indignant and will be tempted to throw it aside before it is finished. May we respectfully suggest that you read it to the end, then take one long look at Calvary, and in the light of what you see there, make your decision?

R. T. KETCHAM,
Gary, Indiana.
April 15, 1936.

CONTENTS

INTRODUCTION 2

PART ONE—MODERNISM

CHAPTER I—The Boards
(a) The Foreign Board and the Fielder Case 4
(b) The Foreign Board and the Randle Case 7
    Misrepresentation by Dr. Franklin
(c) The Foreign Board and the Burnham Case 8
    Card-playing missionary sent to the field.
(d) The Foreign Board and Evangelism 8
    Decrease in native evangelists. Increase in educational workers. Increase of schools over churches.
(e) The Boards and Waste 9
    Dr. Isaacs and Chamber of Commerce dues. Stevens Hotel. Five hundred thousand dollars squandered. Record of investments.
(f) The Boards and the Missionary Dollar 10
(g) The Foreign Board and the Layman's Missionary Appraisal Commission 10
    Fellowship with Bhudists and Christian Scientists. Fact Finders volumes sent to the foreign field. Modern Missions Movement. Dr. Pierce in defense of Board.
(h) The Foreign Board and the Inclusive Policy 11
(i) The Boards and the Designated Dollar 12
    Dr. Pierce in the Watchman-Examiner
(j) The Foreign Board and Missionary Schools 13
(k) The Foreign Board and an Outstanding Missionary 14
    Board quotes figures from Fundamentalist fields in defense of Inclusive Policy.

CHAPTER II—The Conventions and Overlordship
(a) Case Number One. The Gary Church 15
(b) Case Number Two. The Bombing Literature 16
(c) Case Number Three. Pastors to Stay at Home 17
(d) Case Number Four. Non-cooperating Pastors Immoral 17
(e) Case Number Five. Young Preacher Threatened 18
(f) Case Number Six. The Corwith, Iowa, Suit 20

CHAPTER III—Some Convention Presidents
(a) Dr. Franklin 21
    Universal fatherhood of God and brotherhood of man. Love and brotherhood sum total of all requirements. Beginning and end of the Christian religion. The cross naught but an incident in the life of Christ. Dr. Franklin and the Convention Hymn.
(b) Dr. Shaw 22
    Theistic evolutionist. Dr. Shaw and card playing. Open church membership sane. Dr. Shaw and Dr. Fosdick.
(c) Dr. Beaven 23, 24
    Dr. Beaven and the League for Industrial Democracy.

CHAPTER IV—The Conventions and Dr. Kagawa 26

CHAPTER V—Modernism and Baptist Publications
(a) "The Baptist" 27
    Jesus a converted man. Satan and "Midsummer Night's Dream."
(b) "Young People" 27
    Mary of Bethany seduced. Ghandi a preacher of the gospel.

CHAPTER VI—The Educational Situation
(a) Franklin College 28
    Dr. Spencer and the ordination of Mr. Jefferson. Refusal to answer printed questions. Dr. Spencer and moral attributes. Indiana State Convention and Franklin College.
(b) Ohio Colleges 30
    Text books advocate divorce. Bible not sufficient revelation of God's will. Only traces of Jesus meaning still left in the Gospels. The Phillipian earthquake. Paul's violent headaches.
(c) Crozier Seminary 31
    Nothing understandable in the substitutionary theory. The atonement a slander upon God.
(d) Rochester-Colgate 32
(e) Brown 32
(f) Des Moines 32
(g) Certain Harvest of Such Education 33
    A Rochester student wrestles with the problem of too many fish. Professor Webster Communistic birth control advocate.

CHAPTER VII—Modernism an Organized System of Deliberate Dishonesty 33
    Dr. Milton G. Evans and the tact of Modernists.

CHAPTER VIII—The Conventions and Hypocrisy
(a) Case Number One, Indiana Convention and Confession of Faith 34, 35
(b) Case Number Two, The Baptismal Amendment 35
    Doctors Virgin, Masse, Boynton and Brougher defend open membership. Resolution a gesture toward Rockefeller millions.
(c) Case Number Three, The Wolfkin Amendment 37

CHAPTER IX—In Conclusion on Modernism
(a) Aiding Atheism 38
(b) Baptist Churches Can Withdraw Fellowship 38
    Withdrawal from Conventions does not affect Denominational standing. Dr. Parsons agrees.
(c) Correction from Within Hopeless 39
    Disfranchising salaried servants. Salaried servants hold balance of power.
(d) Convention Versus Denomination 40

PART TWO—COMMUNISM

CHAPTER I—What Is Communism? 43
    Description of poster.

CHAPTER II—Communism in Baptist Ranks
(a) Rochester-Colgate 43
(b) Rochester Baptists 44
(c) Dr. Albert W. Beaven 44
(d) Commission on Christian Social Action 44
(e) The Famous Brown Envelope 45
(f) Mr. Frederick J. Libby 46
(g) The Federal Council of Churches 46
(h) Brooks House in Hammond, Ind. 46
(i) Sunday School Literature 47
(j) In Conclusion on Communism 48

PART ONE

MODERNISM

In the presentation of facts revealing the presence of Modernism in Baptist ranks, it will be necessary for us to bring forward as evidence several cases which reach back into the years. We desire to show that while all of these things were transpiring in our midst, our leaders were constantly denying the presence of Modernism. We also desire to show that this is not something that has come suddenly upon us or that it will pass in a moment. Modernism is so thoroughly entrenched in the machinery of the Northern Baptist Convention, that it can never be eliminated and at the same time save the machinery.

We call attention also to the fact that while in two or three instances the particular Modernist referred to has been removed, yet such would not have been the case had not some of us who are called "destructionists" raised our voices in protest. We are constantly met with the argument that when anything wrong is pointed out, the leaders make every effort to correct it. The point at issue which I raise here is, why should we have to constitute ourselves a denominational police force to force our leaders to behave themselves? Fielder and Randle would have been on the mission field today, and Communists would have been meeting in Brooks House still, had such "destructionists" as we are called, said nothing about the situation.

I

THE FOREIGN BOARD AND THE FIELDER CASE

The present Board will never live long enough to convince a Baptist who thinks twice in the same place that they are not guilty of permitting missionaries to teach Modernism when the facts of the Fielder Case are known. Mr. Fielder was a missionary in Assam. While there he wrote a long confession of his faith, and sent it to the Board in New York. We have the entire article in our possession and it is before us as we write. Here are a few quotations from the same:

"Jesus definitely disclaims any intention of placing Himself on a level with God the Father."

"But the unique element of Jesus' nature does not lie in His being the 'only begotten' Son of God. He is not that, by His own teaching. Rather, He is the only perfect one among the countless millions of sons of God who have been born into our heavenly Father's home."

"In all our life one fact we must keep uppermost in our minds—we are the children of God, and in using this term I do not mean it in the special sense in which it is sometimes used, as meaning those who have come to recognize their relationship to God through Jesus. I mean that every human being, no matter what his condition, is inalienably a child of God."

"The account of the creation given in Genesis is wonderful, and I have great reverence for an explanation which has been so satisfying for thousands of years. Without the new knowledge of our growth which God has blessed us with in these recent years, I do not see how a finer explanation of our creation and of our unhappy condition under sin could have been made than that. But now that we have the theory of evolution, attested by so much convincing evidence, I believe we have an explanation ever so much more satisfying and joyous, since it clearly sets forth God and us in our true relationship, the relationship of an unfailing and perfectly loving Father and His growing children, the perfectly normal relationship of a growing family. I rejoice in this added and detailed evidence of the relationship to God which Jesus teaches us we hold."

"I rejoice also in another great blessing which the knowledge of evolution has brought. It has released us from two dreadful ideas that have been hanging like a dark cloud over us through all these years. By it we know that at the time when we become conscious of good and evil we could not, in the nature of things, have refrained long from doing things that were wrong. It was not in us. So we did not deliberately set ourselves in opposition to the will of God when we should and could have avoided sin. There never was a time in those early days when we could have remained free from sin for any considerable period. Ought not our hearts sing with joy to know at last that we are not the culprits that we have been made out to be but that we have been doing only what people in their spiritual infancy might have been expected to do? God does not hold that against us."

"That brings us to the other idea from which we may rejoice to be free, that God, upon the commission of our first sin, drove us out in wrath from the garden of good things under a curse (of having to earn our bread by the sweat of our brow). To my mind, an age-long misrepresentation of the spirit of our God now has been done away with, and we can see clearly what the statement in Genesis has heretofore prevented us from seeing, that He never at any time has ceased loving us and providing blessings for us and caring for us in every way, as a faithful father always does for his children."

"When we see ourselves in our true position as the growing, erring children of God, is it not clear that such a thing as an atonement, a making good, for us by another could not possibly be acceptable to our Father, or even considered by Him? Surely, even in earthly families, no real father looks for an atonement for the wrong-doing of his children. He understands their short-comings and puts up with them, knowing that in time these children will show that they are true children of their father. He would take the deepest pride in an elder son who gave up all to save his brothers. But he would neither demand nor accept the gift of his life in recompense for their short-comings. That is not in harmony with loving fatherliness. A father is not looking for recompenses, he is looking for right living in his children. Seeing that we are a family together, not only is it not derogatory of God and Jesus to abandon the idea of the atonement, but it is testifying to the perfect quality of God's fatherliness. Once the idea that we were born mature is shown to be not true and the fact of God's perfect fatherly love is established, the idea of the atonement immediately loses all its force. Vicarious sacrifice remains, but the atonement cannot. It remains for us individually to make all atonement we can for our past sins by living the kind of life our Father yearns for."

"After His experience of exaltation at the time of His baptism, when He was convinced beyond doubt that it was He who was the Messiah, comes the inevitable period of depression, from which even He was not free, when He questions whether after all He is the Son of God."

"There is no man, no matter how vile, without some solid good, some of the stuff of God, in him. There is some invitation of God to which he will respond, although he may have to hear it in the next world. God will never turn His back upon His children, 'neither in this world; neither in the world to come.'"

"Neither are the life and death of Jesus necessary to bring men who do not know of Jesus into a relationship with God which He will honour and reward."

In spite of the awful character of the above statements of Mr. Fielder, it was a little over a year before he was examined by a committee of the Foreign Mission Board. The result of that examination is seen in their report of the

Board as a whole. The report is as follows:

"The committee on the case of C. G. Fielder, through its Chairman, A. C. Baldwin, introduced missionary C. G. Fielder, who addressed the Board regarding his work in Assam and in particular his service among students at Cotton College, calling particular attention to the evangelistic opportunity which this service presented. At the conclusion of his address the committee presented the following report, which was adopted unanimously:

"To the Board of Managers of the American Baptist Foreign Mission Society.

"Your committees, appointed to meet Mr. Cecil G. Fielder and inquire into his theological views and message as a missionary, desires to make the following report:

"First: Your committee are agreed that in Mr. Fielder's theological statement are declarations which are open to question and which standing alone would make it impossible to return him to the work in Assam.

"Second: Your committee faces the fact that in his work Brother Fielder has been signally blessed of God. The testimony of many of his fellow missionaries and of Dr. Witter, his predecessor in the work at Cotton College, speak in such high terms of his Christ-like character, his zeal and usefulness, his success in a position requiring peculiar qualities of spiritual equipment, that we feel he has been used of God to a marked degree.

"Nevertheless the limitations of his theological statements are real in the judgment of your committee and the criticisms which his statement has aroused cannot be ignored.

"In view of the fact, therefore, that Mr. Fielder has never had a course of theological study, we would recommend that the Board grant Mr. Fielder's request for a year of study at Newton Theological Institution, and that the question of his return to Assam be made a special order at some meeting of the Board in 1926."

ARTHUR C. BALDWIN,
W. S. ABERNETHY,
THOMAS H. STACY.

On behalf of the Board of Managers,
New York, New York,
June 10th, 1925.
(Sgd.) J. C. Robbins,
Foreign Secretary.

The Committee says that Mr. Fielder's theological statement is open to question; and that if it were to stand alone, his return to Assam would be impossible. Following that is a bit of character testimony. How in the name of common sense a man can possess peculiar qualities of spiritual equipment, and can be used of God to a marked degree, when holding a theological position which the report itself admits is practically a negation of everything for which Baptists stand, surely only a white-washing committee could discover!

Mr. Fielder pursued his course at Newton and then applied for ordination. He was ordained with thirteen voting against him. After his ordination the Board published a statement in "The Baptist" (Chicago) issue of October 16, 1926, in which they say that Mr. Fielder had "considerably changed the views expressed in the original paper prepared by him in Assam." The Board then goes on to paraphrase Mr. Fielder's new views, and then in closing dismisses all charges against him in the following language:

"Hearing this confession of faith and being convinced of Mr. Fielder's sincerity, his exceptional devotion to Christ, and his sympathetic love for all his fellow men, we felt impelled by the Spirit to dismiss the theological charges against him, leaving the question of his future service to later consideration."

Desiring to know exactly what Mr.

Fielder said in his own words, I wrote him for a copy of his last statement which he, of course, refused to produce, but did write a long letter, parts of which I now quote. Referring to the Board's published summary of his new and "considerably changed" views he says:

"I should be amazed if anyone who really knew anything about me considered that this summary indicated any radical change of view on my part."

In justification of his presence on the field he says: "This has been my basic contention from the beginning, that I represent in general a goodly part of our denomination, and that if such were the case I could serve our denomination as a missionary in all good conscience."

"So I take my stand squarely on my rights as a Baptist. Never at any time have I believed, or taught anything which it was not thoroughly proper for a Baptist to believe and teach. Many thousands of Baptists now holding positions of honour in our churches hold essentially the same views, I am sure. My contention that I represent in general a goodly part of our denomination has been abundantly proved. The statement I wrote in Assam has been read by many Baptists, persons of maturity and experience, mostly conservative in thinking, and, together with a fair presentation of the whole situation, has gained their whole-souled expressions of confidence in my fitness and right to serve as a missionary of our denomination. Persons high in the councils of our denomination have read it, without my having brought it to their attention, and later have voluntarily told me of their approval. One leading member of our denomination told me that he could not but be in favor of my return to Assam, since my point of view so closely paralleled his own."

As to any real change of views, Mr. Fielder says of his last statement: "I used the accepted theological terminology and treated some of the subjects more fully. But as I told the committee of the Board that waited on me, I felt that the considerable change mentioned in the Board's statement was rather by way of amplification and greater adequacy of statement than any radical departure from the general point of view which I had held before."

Mr. Fielder candidly admits that he changed the rough verbal dress which he used in his Assam statement for the more pleasing attire of "accepted theological terminology," but also frankly admits that this was the sole extent of his "considerably changed views" and, furthermore, that he told the Board so. Notwithstanding this they dismiss all charges and, I am convinced, had we not exposed the whole miserable affair they would have returned him to the field.

THE FOREIGN BOARD AND THE RANDLE CASE

For some time prior to the Milwaukee convention, reports had been current that Missionary Randle of Suifu, China, was unsound. The reports declared he had refused to accept the deity of Christ. At the Milwaukee convention, Dr. W. B. Riley was exposing this matter, when suddenly Dr. Franklin, then Foreign Secretary of the Board, now President of the Northern Baptist Convention, arose and flourished a letter, stating:

"God Almighty answered Dr. Riley by mail this morning." He then proceeded to read a letter from some missionary friends of Randle disproving the whole charge. Dr. Riley retired amid the hoots and jeers of the Modernist crowd. Immediately upon the conclusion of that session the pastor of the church from which Mr. Randle went to the field, came to us and stated that he had refused to participate in Randle's ordination because of just such statements before ever he went to the field. We now know that at the moment Dr. Franklin was reading from the letter before the Convention he had in his possession a letter from Randle himself addressed to the Board of Managers in which he admits the whole charge in the following language:

"I am also accused of being unwilling to answer in the affirmative the question, 'Do you believe that Christ is God?' This was a prayer meeting which I was leading and not a class in theology. Nor was it quite the proper time or place to catechize the leader because he had not expressed his faith in the phraseology which certain individuals were accustomed to use. However, to be perfectly fair to all parties concerned, I must say that I do not wish to ascribe to Jesus any higher position than that Which he claimed for himself. He did not claim to be God, but he did say that he was the Son of God. I was not asked as to my faith in the divinity of Jesus, the deity of Jesus, or His place in the Trinity. I was asked to answer categorically whether Jesus was God. Passages like the following make an affirmative answer to that question rather difficult. I Tim. 2:15; Matt. 27:46; Jno. 23:46; Col. 3:1; Luke 9:48; Matt. 3:17; 19:17; Luke 10:22."

THE FOREIGN BOARD AND MISS MARIAN BURNHAM

Miss Burnham appeared on the platform of the Northern Baptist Convention at Detroit as an outgoing missionary to India. Just before that her home church in Elmira, N. Y., on Sunday morning had publicly commissioned her, and Mr. Alden of the Board of Missionary Cooperation was present and delivered the message. Miss Burnham had been before the Board in New York, was examined and accepted, and was sent to the field, and this year (1936) is home on her first furlough.

The "Elmira Star Gazette" carried prominent news items concerning the public service in honor of Miss Burnham. Turning to the society notes of the same issue of the "Elmira Star Gazette" I quote: "The office employees of the Frostilla Company entertained Saturday evening at Elizabeth Inn with a dinner complimenting Miss Marian Burnham of Lower Maple Avenue, who is making preparations to become a missionary in India. Bridge and five hundred followed. High scores for bridge were secured by Miss Frances Custy and Miss Helen Jenkins. Five hundred favors were won by Miss Marian Burnham and Mrs. Marian Longstreet." After that date, there were still several other social notes announcing the fact that Miss Burnham had proven herself to be no novice in the art of winning at five hundred!

This young lady comes from the card table with her high score record on Saturday night, to the pulpit of the Baptist church on Sunday morning, where she is commissioned to go to India as an "evangelical" under the "inclusive policy." From the pulpit she goes to the Convention platform at Detroit and from there back to her home city to engage in a merry round of card parties, etc., from whence she departs to the mission field. Who, in this case, should have acted as denominational policeman to keep the Board from appointing such a missionary?

THE FOREIGN BOARD AND EVANGELISM

A study of the annual reports show that during the eight years from 1915 to 1923, there was a net gain on the foreign field of 311 churches and 957 schools. During this same period there was a net loss of 186 native evangelists, and a net gain of 1,480 educational workers. Someone may say, "Why go back to such ancient records?" Simply to prove that the ills from which the denomination is now suffering, began years ago and the harvest now being reaped is inevitable. Anyone can pick up the last Annual of the Northern Baptist Convention and compare its reports with those of five or ten years ago and produce substantially the same figures as we have here shown. It ought to be noted further that the decline in churches and native evangelists, and the tremendous increase in schools and educational workers, took place not during years of depression, but during the years of plenty, namely, the New World Movement. The actual period for the New World Movement, 1918 to 1923, being as follows: a net gain of 236 churches and 786 schools; a net loss of 170 native evangelists and a net gain of 853 educational workers.

THE BOARDS AND WASTE

The Foreign Board is now putting forth frantic appeals calling attention to the fact that we have cut down the force by practically two hundred missionaries within the last few years, and that seventy more must be recalled unless funds are forthcoming. It would be impossible for us to cite every case of waste on the part of the Societies, but one or two samples will suffice. The district secretary for the Rochester, New York, area, Dr. Isaacs, has some rather interesting and illuminating items in his expense account. I have before me the 1929 financial report of Dr. Isaacs in which he charges up an amount for tips at the Sagamore Hotel; also the 1931 report which shows that Dr. Isaacs received a salary including automobile expense of $4,720.00. Nevertheless, in his items of expense he charges up $25.00 for his local Chamber of Commerce dues! I have also before me, Dr. Isaacs' annual report for 1934, with a salary allottment of $4,360.00. We have another item of $37.50 charged up for the secretary's Chamber of Commerce dues. Just why executive secretaries with fat salaries and expense accounts for legitimate denominational service, should also load on to the already depleted missionary funds, their personal membership in Chambers of Commerce, and for tips to waiters in fashionable hotels, the report does not reveal.

Every year in mid-winter, the entire official family of the Northern Baptist Convention, together with the state official families, meets in Chicago for a mid-year conference. Time was, and some of us believe still is, when our paid denominational servants could have gone to Chicago, found adequate quarters in reasonable hotels, found some Baptist church that would have been glad to donate the use of its building for the conference sessions, and in such surroundings conduct the business affairs of the Convention. For such necessary overhead expenses, Baptists would be glad to pay. But instead of this, the Stevens Hotel, the most expensive hotel in the city, is always selected as the place of meeting and entertainment, and here for several days in the most expensive surroundings in the city, our Baptist official family meets at terrific expense to the missionary funds of the Convention.

This year we note that one of the speakers imported from Washington, D. C., was none other than Frederick J. Libby. Mr. Libby has been by government order denied the use of the public school buildings in Washington, and has been declared by an investigating committee of the government to be one of the enemies of our country, and yet he is brought to Chicago to address our Baptist official family on what Baptists can do to prevent war. Mr. Libby, as we will prove elsewhere in this pamphlet, is decidedly Red in some of his connections, yet his transportation from Washington to Chicago, entertainment in Stevens Hotel, and no doubt a good sized honorarium is handed over to him, while at the same time preparations are being made to bring seventy missionaries home. No doubt some one will charge us with being puerile and childish in bringing forward such small items. Our reply is that thousands of such small items scattered from Maine to California bulk large in the total!

Only a few years ago, an Advisory Committee appointed by the Northern Baptist Convention itself, reported that five hundred thousand dollars was "wastefully squandered in the work of the entire Northern Baptist Convention annually." Mark you, this is not Dr.

Ketcham's statement, this is the sober utterance of the Convention's own committee. In addition to this, we quote again from the Advisory Committee.

"We found one of the National Society's investments had 316 mortgages —maturing date of 22 not known; appraised valuation of 25—no record. In 38 cases, no assessed valuation. In 25 cases, not known when taxes were paid. In 44 cases, not known whether property was insured. In two cases, expiration of insurance not known. In 25 cases, not known how mortgage was acquired. In 18 cases, no knowledge of when the interest was last paid. Interest payment overdue in six cases. Taxes overdue in 4 cases. Principal overdue in 38 cases. And in 93 cases the amount of the mortgage was beyond what the Society's by-laws allowed. While in 86 cases the Society did not know whether the property was income bearing, or not."

THE MISSIONARY DOLLAR

According to the bulletins coming out of Baptist headquarters in New York, the missionary dollar for 1935 and 1936 is divided as follows: Foreign Missions, 31.15; Home Missions, including City Missions, 24.97; State Convention expense, 22.95; Board of Education, 9.82; Minister's and Missionary's Benefit Board, 8.44. In addition to these percentages the following flat amounts are assigned outright. State Convention Promotion, $150,000; Council of Finance and Promotion, $225,000.

Everywhere we are met with frantic appeals to give to the Unified Budget. It is called "giving to missions." In the last issue of the Indiana state paper, "The Baptist Observer," a warning is issued to every Baptist Pastor in the State, that if he wants to be considered in good standing in the State, he must swing his Church back of the Unified Budget. It is called "giving to missions." Examination of the above figures discloses some interesting information. For instance, a trifle more than 31c out of each dollar given to the Unified Budget goes to Foreign Missions. Then when we remember that the Foreign Mission Board has its tremendous overhead expense to pay out of this percentage, one can easily figure how much of this precious 31c out of each dollar given actually gets to the foreign mission field. Little wonder that 200 missionaries have been cut off in the last few years, and 70 more about to be recalled. The officers of the Foreign Board will come back immediately and say that due to returns from invested funds, which enables them to pay overhead, the entire 31c actually gets to the field, but where did these invested funds come from? Did they not come from Baptists who gave them for missions?

The Home Mission Society, including City Missions, gets practically 25c out of every missionary dollar. They, too have their overhead to pay. State Conventions get almost 23c out of each missionary dollar. This goes to keep an army of secretaries in the field to lord it over the Churches. Proof of this last statement will be found elsewhere in this booklet. The Board of Education gets almost 10c out of each missionary dollar, and when you have finished reading the item in this booklet under the heading "The Educational Situation" you can easily judge whether the 10c is well spent.

In addition to the 30c out of each missionary dollar given to the State Conventions, there is another flat $150,000 distributed among the State Conventions for promotion and then, of course, the expense of the big machine, clear at the top, called "The Council of Finance and Promotion" pulls out a cool quarter of a million, and all of this, mark you, out of the Unified Budget, which is called "giving to missions."

THE FOREIGN MISSION BOARD AND THE LAYMAN'S MISSIONARY APPRAISAL COMMISSION

I sat in the LaSalle Hotel in Chicago one day, and listened to nearly a dozen men and women, members of the Layman's Missionary Appraisal Commission, speak. It was an all-day affair, and during the entire day we heard nothing but appeals from these investigators of Missions to change the emphasis of the missionary message from the old-fashioned historic Baptist faith, in a crucified, buried, risen and regenerating Christ to some kind of a new-fangled thing called "Religion." We were to take the "best" out of Christianity, the "best" out of Mohammedanism, the "best" out of Confucianism, etc. and put them together. During the day questions could be written and sent by an usher to the platform where the speaker would answer them.

When Dr. Jones, of Haverford College, was speaking, I wrote this question; "In view of your contention that the Christian missionaries should fellowship with the Buddhist, Confucianist and Mohammedan, should not the Christian minister in the home land fellowship with Christian Scientists, Mormons, and Russelites?" Dr. Jones read the question and in a clear, ringing voice answered in one word, "Yes!" This was only one experience of many of like nature during the day.

In spite of all this our Foreign Board has never repudiated the report of this Commission, but on the other hand, according to their own report of 1934, page 22, we find that the Board has had sent to every mission station on the foreign field a complete set of the seven volumes published by this Commission. On page 23 of their report we read this significant sentence "When the constant decline of receipts which has created so many problems during recent years has finally been arrested, it will be possible to give further consideration to other of the advance steps suggested by the layman's report." We are of the distinct impression that there are a few Baptists left who will not relish any "further steps" in the direction of this conglomeration of theologies.

The Layman's Missionary Appraisal Commission disbanded and set up in its place a thing called the "Modern Missions Movement." The purpose of this new movement was to act as a clearing house for designated missionary funds, which the donors might desire to be used on such missionary projects as were described by and approved by the Layman's Missionary Appraisal Commission. Sixty-seven Mission Boards were approached by the Modern Missions Movement, asking them to cooperate with them, by listing with the Movement certain fields or sections of their foreign work which are being carried on in such a fashion as to meet with the approval of the Modern Missions Movement. They, in turn, would then send on to the Board such monies as they might have in their possession, designated to such modernized work. The last report we had was that out of 67 Mission Boards thus approached, only five had responded favorably, two of them were the American Baptist Foreign Mission Society, and the Women's American Baptist Foreign Mission Society. This fact alone is an admission that there are scattered through our foreign fields stations and institutions that fully meet the approval of this new-fangled, bloodless religion. This in spite of the fact that Dr. Earle V. Pierce, noted Convention Fundamentalist and a member of the Foreign Board, says that I am "mendacious" when I say that the Foreign Board sends Modernists to the Foreign field! Incidentally, we wonder how our good friend, Dr. Pierce, is enjoying his new-found fellowship with the Federal Council of Churches of Christ in America, of which Council he became a member last year!

THE INCLUSIVE POLICY

In the Seattle Convention of 1925, the late Dr. W. B. Hinson offered a Resolution before the Convention which, if passed, would have instructed the Foreign Board to call home at once all missionaries known to be doctrinally unsound. This Resolution in its simplicity was doctored up, changed, and amended, and left entirely in the hands of the Foreign Board to exercise its own discretion. It was at this Convention that Dr. Anderson, then President of the Foreign Board, announced the adherence of the Board to the "Inclusive Policy," under which missionaries of all shades of theological opinion should be sent to the field.

In "The Baptist", official organ of the Northern Baptist Convention, issue of June 12, 1926, we read: "The reaffirmation by President Anderson of the inclusive policy of the American Baptist Foreign Missionary Society, as that policy has been previously defined, seems to have been accepted and settled, and under the policy, graduates of some of the most divergent schools of theology in the country have accepted appointments this year."

Under date of November 15, 1923, the Foreign Board sent out a four-page folder answering charges lodged against it by those of us who believed that the Foreign Board was far too lax in its adherence to the historic faith of Baptists. I quote from that statement:

"It is charged that the Board permits the teaching of liberal doctrines by its missionaries. Our Board has frankly stated to its constituency that it gives to its officers and missionaries a considerable degree of liberty of theological opinion in accordance with the long standing policy of the Denomination, and that it firmly and kindly declines to reverse that policy. Our denomination like our individual churches, is made up of men and women of diverse views, and our Board, most appropriately made up in the same way, thinks it only right, fair and wise that our missionary force should reflect the situation in our churches at home. We have no intention of restricting our appointees and missionaries to any one group. We represent the whole Denomination and we treat all our constituency as brothers and sisters in the faith.

"This does not mean that we will appoint or retain any Baptist in good standing, regardless of what he may or may not believe. There are limits beyond which we will not go at either end of the line. We will not knowingly appoint any brother, conservative or liberal, who holds such personal views and gives such expression to them as would impair his fellowship with his colleagues on the field or obscure the vital message of the gospel of Christ.

"The exact limits of theological liberty have slowly changed in our Denomination with the years, and will doubtless further change in the future. Our Board represents the present feeling of our constituency."

According to this defense published by the Foreign Board, they frankly tell us that they will continue to send missionaries to the foreign field who are representative of the various groups in the denomination at home. This policy is no doubt satisfactory to many of the Modernists, but it is anything but satisfactory to an old-fashioned historic Baptist. The Board declares plainly that they will appoint both conservative and liberal missionaries so long as the individual missionary does not allow his personal views to impair his fellowship with his colleagues on the field. This is the Inclusive Policy.

THE BOARDS AND THE DESIGNATED DOLLAR

Much has been said about designated gifts. Many of our Fundamental churches are comforting themselves with the idea that by designating their gifts to sound missionaries, they are helping to solve the situation within the Convention. Even the optimistic Dr. Pierce admits in his article in the "Watchman Examiner" of February 27, 1936, that the designation policy is not an honest one. Quoting from the article we read:

> "For several years the plan was followed of equalizing every three years, the budgets of the various cooperating and coordinating societies of the Northern Baptist Convention because of designated gifts. This essentially defeated the will of donors who had as the purpose of their designation that certain fields of work should receive more than they otherwise would. The rule under reorganization is that when any society is brought by designations to 85% of its budget, it shall receive no more share in the Unified Budget until all other societies are up to the same level."

From a later paragraph, we quote further:

> "If a church or individual makes a designated gift to a society for the special work within the budget, it is because of the desire that that cause shall have more than it otherwise would have. But if because of this and other designations, that cause is given a smaller share of the Unified Budget to which the church may also be giving, then the will of the donor is divided. . . . Can we then blame people and churches because under these conditions they turn from our missionary projects to those where they can express themselves as they will?"

Here then is the plain simple fact that designated gifts may result in the hastening of a given society in reaching 85% of its assigned budget. From that moment on it can get no more money from the undesignated funds of the Unified Budget until ALL OTHER societies have reached 85%. It is therefore not only a possible thing, but a very probable thing that designated dollars simply continue to release so many undesignated dollars for work in other fields which do not meet the approval of the individual who designated the dollar.

THE FOREIGN BOARD AND MISSIONARY SCHOOLS

That the situation is not all that it should be in some of our schools on the foreign field, has been the contention of many of us for a long time. We have space to present one case only, namely that of Shanghai College. A missionary a few years ago, writing to the late Dr. F. J. White, president of Shanghai, says:

> "It is unfortunate that the college is hedged around by a sympathetic Board of Managers, and that nothing can be done to root out heterodox members of the faculty."

President White wrote to his chief in New York City, Dr. James H. Franklin, quoting the above statement and then continues:

> "This is a condition that must continue, or most of the members of the faculty would get out."

In this same letter President White objects to having certain orthodox conservative mission fields more largely represented on the College Board of Managers, and says:

> "To put on three men from these conservative missions, two or three of whom might be very conservative and put on especially to smell out heterodoxy, would be exceedingly unfortunate."

In another letter to Dr. Franklin, Dr. White says:

> "Dr. X has been at the head of the agitation against the theology of the institution. Have felt if we could win him the whole agitation would collapse."

Then he writes of conferring with Dr. X and telling that they proposed to elect a member of his family, and then Dr. White reports a complete change of attitude on the part of Dr. X and says:

> "Think this was brought about unconsciously to Dr. X by co-educa-

tion and the election of his——
If this is approved by the Board of Trustees, I do not see how Dr. X can relapse to the old position and oppose the college. With the defection of Dr. X the whole opposition to the college will probably collapse."

The following letter was received by a missionary in China from a young man studying at Shanghai Baptist College:

"My Dear Honored Sir:

"You are so kind to me that I often dream to talk with you in the night. I am very sorry because I cannot see you at Shanghai. At present I am sick and anxious to know some news from my church for which I have prayed. As to the conditions in our college, I am glad to say that I can pass in the lessons, but I am much troubled with teachings here. As you have told me very, very often and advised me very frequently, Christianity is indeed not good in the college. I have been told by some teacher that God spoken here is quite different from that in the church and that one's value depends totally upon the God one worships. Evolution is famous in the college, as you know. In the Biological class evolution is much emphasized. Everybody in freshman class should study biology. The examination subjects are emphasized on evolution. Moving pictures are shown in the chapel to tell how animals are made, and how a single cell can develop into a man. Secondly, I love Holy Bible though we have only two hours to study Bible every week. We are not so fortunate as the students of Nanking University where Bible is much more emphasized. They study four hours in Bible in the class room a week. I am very unhappy. This school advised me to change church. Gentlemen, you see how can I do this? You love me, help me and have good hopes for me in all respects. How can I forget you and the church? I have my duty for my church. I hope you pray for me for this reason; tell me what else i can do for my church.

Very respectfully yours."

THE FOREIGN BOARD AND AN OUTSTANDING MISSIONARY

Rev. W. M. Young, who in 1925 had served 30 years under the American Baptist Foreign Mission Board in India, and who on one tour of 70 days, together with his son, baptized 3,754 believers, 2,408 of them in eight days, writes as follows to Rev. James Wallace Jacobus, pastor of the First Baptist Church, Vassar, Mich. This letter was written while Frederick L. Anderson was still President of the Foreign Mission Board, but it reveals the truth of our general contention concerning the situation on the foreign field.

"Dear Brother Jacobus:

"Your letter of October 16 reached me while I was out on tour. . . . . I have no objection to your publishing the letter, as all statements were carefully considered before writing and I have not written stronger to others than I have written to the Board. I have sent careful discussions to the Board of the present trend of mission work for several years now. My letters have been based entirely on the Board's annual reports so they cannot object. . . . . .

"Nothing in recent years has moved me more deeply than Dr. F. L. Anderson's message at Milwaukee N. B. C. He tries to make out that Fundamentalists are demanding a radical change in methods of appointing missionaries from our time honored history, and that no doctrinal statements were required in the past. I was amazed at the statement, and more amazed that the Board should publish the address and send it out as a fact. As a matter of fact, I do not believe anyone could have been appointed as a missionary a third of a century ago when I was appointed, without a decidedly clearer and fuller doctrinal statement than Dr. Anderson gives in his homeopathic dose of theology at Milwaukee. What does Dr. Anderson mean by the vague phrase, "Within the limits of the Gospel"? Is there a Unitarian or an Universalist in the United States that would not claim to be within the limits of the Gospel? Is there an ultra Modernist in the Baptist or any other denomination that would not claim to be within the limits of the Gospel? Who is to decide what the limits are? We need men and women today on all the mission fields, not simply within the limits of the Gospel, but truly regenerated, spirit filled, men and women of prayer and a positive virile message, the fulness of the Gospel of Jesus Christ, with all its supernatural and regenerating power. . . . . . The hour has come for us to strike and to strike from the shoulder, to write and speak with no uncertain sound. The Bible Union of China and the Bible League of India are doing most effective work. I am a member of both organizations. . . . . .

"We recently returned, my oldest son and I, from a tour of 70 days. It was the most successful tour I have ever made from the standpoint of ingathering. We baptized 3754 on the tour and laid the foundation for much larger ingatherings in the future. . . . . .

"At Hsi Ken, four days west from Mong Mong, we baptized 2408 in eight consecutive days, beginning the last Sunday in January and completing the work the first day of February. In that section we ought to have 10,000 more converts in the near future. In many places we were received with sorts of ovations; but the paths were not all strewn with roses by any means. . . . . .

"We need a new emphasis on evangelism. My convictions are that 25,000 baptisms per year should be considered the minimum, with our present equipment and working staff, with present open doors on every hand. I have so written the Board at different times. Dr. Anderson in his annual addresses, gives figures from a few conservative fields with large ingatherings, then represents them as representative of all our work, and makes his plea for liberalism and an inclusive policy, but he could not point to a single field under liberalism that would support the claims made. What we want is the facts. The present trend of our work is undoubtedly toward educational work at the expense of the evangelistic work. . . . . . ."

Yours in His joyful service,

(Signed) W. M. YOUNG.

II

THE CONVENTIONS AND OVERLORDSHIP

Perhaps at no point in this disturbing situation is departure from Baptist polity more pronounced, than in connection with the individual liberty and freedom of local, independent churches and pastors. No matter what kind of work a pastor and his church may be doing for the Lord Jesus Christ, and no matter how much blessing the Lord may be pouring out upon the same, unless it all gears into the Unified Budget, that pastor and church are immediately made the objects of Convention interference, and attempted Convention control.

The Central Baptist Church of Gary, Indiana, of which I happen to be the pastor at this present writing, is the sixth largest Baptist church in the state. It is second in the amount of money given last year both for current expenses and missions, and it is first in the number of baptisms—the number last year being 114. The next largest in the state was 70. In the past three and one-half years, a few more than 500 people have united with this church. Within the last year four of its young people (two couples) have been sent to the mission fields. Missionary giving last year was well over the $4,000.00 mark. This year it bids fair to be well over the $5,000.00 mark. A few weeks ago twelve young men, members of this church, were licensed as lay-preachers at a Sunday morning service, while at the same time twenty-four more of our young people who are either day or night students in Moody Bible Institute were seated in the choir loft. At the close of the service, fourteen more gave themselves for full time, definite service. Yet only a few weeks ago, the State Baptist paper announced in boldfaced type that this church and its pastor were no longer in good standing in the state of Indiana!

On February 13, 1935, the Central Baptist Church of Gary, withdrew from the fellowship of the Northern Baptist Convention, Indiana State Convention, and the local Calumet Association. Out of a membership which was at that time eleven hundred, twenty-two votes were cast against the resolution. Unbiased review of the entire membership would indicate that had everyone of the eleven hundred actually been in the meeting, the opposition vote could not possibly have been more than thirty. Furthermore, most of the twenty-two who did vote, did so not because they did not believe that the situation was as had been presented, but for other reasons. In spite of this sovereign vote of a sovereign Baptist church, the Calumet Association nine months later, October 4, 1935, appointed a committee "to keep in touch with and work with the loyal Baptists of Gary."

In answer to all of this, we advised the executive state secretary, by telegram as follows:

"To Mr. T. J. Parsons, Executive Secretary, Indiana Baptist Convention. Re account in Baptist Observer stating hand of fellowship was withdrawn from Central Baptist Church and pastor October 4, 1935 beg to advise that Central Baptist Church and pastor withdrew hand of fellowship from Convention and Calumet Association February 13, 1935, your article therefore is reverse of the truth. Stop. Re my standing with Convention beg to advise that if I am in good standing with heaven I should worry about my standing with Indiana headquarters."

(Signed) R. T. KETCHAM.

CASE NUMBER TWO

In a certain northern Pennsylvania city, there was a small mission church pastored for eight years by an open and avowed Modernist. The church went through those years at a dying rate. At the same time the State Convention poured $500.00 a year into the pastor's salary. At the end of eight years the church asked the brother to resign, which he did. A young Fundamentalist was called and accepted the pastorate on the one condition that they cease taking the $500.00 a year aid from the state. He made no effort to pull the church out of the state, but simply insisted that he would not be under obligation to the state. The young man declared that he would take the entire responsibility, and that at the end of the year if they had not been able to pay him the stipulated salary including the $500.00, that he would cancel whatever they owed him. He was called and began to work. Prayer meetings began to jump up in attendance; preaching services well attended; several folks saved and everything in general going along fine; with salary paid in full at the end of the year.

In this same city lived another Baptist pastor who at the time was the president of the Pennsylvania State Convention. During the week of February 23, 1931, this State Convention president wrote a letter to the Rev. William G. Russell, then secretary of the Board of Missionary Promotion of the state. By a blunder on the part of the president in addressing the envelope, with another blunder on the part of the mail man, this letter fell into the hands of the young Fundamentalist pastor before it got out of the city on its way to Philadelphia. We quote two paragraphs from it, and mark you it is a state president writing to a state secretary! Not in the Roman Catholic church, not even in a Methodist church, but in a Baptist fellowship.

> "Please send me some of your Bombing Literature in the big envelope. You may need to send some of your 'Shock Troups' into this 'Sector' to line up some of the men in this territory.

> "I would advise you to keep your eye on ————. You may not have connected him up as ————— successor at —————. He is a good fellow but did not get his training at the feet of Gamaliel. The great variety of educational background of the men here in ————— is largely responsible for the failure to line up with the big things of the Denomination. But we will pray and plan and push."

The church of which the young Fundamentalist was pastor took the matter up with the good president, whereupon he offered a weak apology.

CASE NUMBER THREE

What can be said in defense of such procedure as revealed in the following Pennsylvania case. I have before me a letter announcing the coming of a denominational official to hold a conference in Meadville Baptist church. The conference is to discuss "organization and work of the local church." The church officers of an entire association are urged to be present, but all pastors are frankly requested to stay at home so that the "official" and church officers may feel no embarrassment in discussion. I quote here the two main paragraphs of the letter:

> "The conference will consist of two sessions. The first will be at 11 o'clock, at the time of the morning service, at which Brother Killian will speak. The second session will be at 2 o'clock in the afternoon, when ample time will be given for a full discussion of the organization and work of the local church. Church officers are urged to attend both sessions, and if possible make a report of the conference to their own churches at the evening service.

> "All church officers, both men and women, are urged to attend. Deacons, trustees, church clerks, financial secretaries, treasurers, Sunday School superintendents, presidents of women's missionary and ladies' aid included. Pastors are requested not to attend in order that both Brother Killian and the church officers may feel free to discuss all phases of church life. But the pastors are urged to secure as full attendance as possible of their church officers for the sake of a higher level of lay service in the churches."

Let any sound Baptist give one sane reason why the presence of pastors should be undesirable at such a conference.

CASE NUMBER FOUR

The Baptist Convention of Pennsylvania in 1934 adopted resolutions setting up a veritable ministerial inquisition. There will be two lists of preachers run in the state Annual, one of them the approved list and the other the black list. In substantiation of this charge, I quote Article 4, 5 and 6 from the resolutions adopted in 1934.

> "IV. That this Convention shall print in the State Convention ANNUAL the above statement of the requirements of ordination to be

followed immediately by the list of all such regularly ordained ministers in the Convention.

"1. The names of all men ordained in the future, not in conformity with the above requirements, shall be printed in the State ANNUAL in a separate list, so designated.

"3. Ministers coming into the fellowship of the Pennsylvania Baptist Convention from other denominations, or other State Conventions shall satisfy the Commission on Pastoral Education and Ordination that they have met the above standards of ordination before their names shall appear in the list of regularly accredited ministers of the State Convention.

"V. That each Association of the State be urged to adopt some Permanent Council form of ordination procedure, if they do not have it, wherein all candidates for ordination are required to appear before the Permanent Council or its executive committee for examination, and be approved by this Council before the regular ordination council is called.

"1. In this connection it is urged that some representative of the State Convention, in the person of one of its executive officers or a member of the Commission on Pastoral Education and Ordination be invited to sit in every ordination council.

"VI. That churches of the Pennsylvania Baptist Convention be urged to deal only with ministers whose names appear on the accredited list printed in the State Convention ANNUAL."

The joker is found in Article Six where the churches of Pennsylvania are urged to deal only with ministers whose names appear in the accredited list. If this does not mean that all the ministers appearing in the other list are on a black list, then I have lost all power to interpret the English language when I read it.

Furthermore, the Pennsylvania State Convention drew up an article which they sent out to the faculties of all theological seminaries and Bible training schools. This article describes the working of the ministerial committee and also describes the kind of preachers who will be acceptable to the state with of course, the idea in mind that these seminaries and training schools will bend every effort to produce that particular brand. The third paragraph in this article would cause Roger Williams to turn over under ground. The article goes on to say that after a man has been accepted by the "Commission" that the name then is reviewed by "the committee of nine, pastors peers, elected by the Ministers' Union and appointed by the State Convention, the review being with the purpose to accredit those with whom is found no moral derogation (which in their province includes a record for church breaking, unbaptistic practices and schismatic action in reference to our organized work.)"

Who in the wide world ever heard of a committee of nine being set up in a State Convention of Baptists calling themselves "pastors peers"? Shades of Roger Williams! Sounds like a congress of cardinals, and to all practical intents and purposes it comes mighty near being just that. Let every Baptist pastor who dares to think for himself in reference to the "organized work" bear in mind that his failure or refusal to support the organized work, is called in this paragraph "moral derogation." Since when, we would ask, has it become an immoral thing for a man to act in accordance with Christ and conscience with reference to the organized work?

CASE NUMBER FIVE

In 1919 when the New World Movement was launched, I was Pastor of the

First Baptist Church, Butler, Pennsylvania. We were asked for $17,000. After weeks of study the Church authorized me to publish a 24-page pamphlet, pointing out modernism in the beneficiary boards and societies, and the decision of the Church not to participate in the Movement.

Within two weeks after this pamphlet was released a Committee of the Pittsburgh Baptist Association called upon me in my office. They made the flat proposition that I was to recall and withdraw my pamphlet. Not one of them denied the truth of the assertions in the pamphlet. They all said, however, that it was "harmful to the Denominational Program." It didn't seem to make much difference to the Committee how harmful the Program might be to Christ.

I will remember that day throughout eternity. Just a young preacher, with my ministerial career still before me, then and there I had to decide whether my lord was to be the Lord Jesus Christ or the Denominational Program. We make no boast when we declare that we decided that day that the Christ Himself should occupy that position. There is nothing to be particularly proud of in that decision, for the simple fact of the matter is that I was afraid to make any other. It was just a question with me as to who could best take care of me in the hours of crisis which I knew would face every minister. I decided He could, and I cast my lot with Him that day, and to the praise of His everlasting glory, what a happy lot it has been.

After more than two hours of grilling, the Chairman of that Committee said "Mr. Ketcham, we may as well tell you that you must withdraw that pamphlet from circulation, or I will personally see to it that you never get another Church in the Northern Baptist Convention." My reply was "Brother, $17,000 is too much money to pay for any Baptist pulpit. I can secure a soap box for a dime." No sooner were these words out of my mouth than another member of the Committee jumped from his seat, raced across the office, grabbed me by the coat collar, and literally shook the daylights out of me, yelling into my face "You get down on your knees and tell God to forgive you for that statement."

Well, 17 years have passed since then, and God has been faithful to the trust we committed to Him that day. Three years ago, however, I had placed in my hand a letter which the Chairman of that Committee wrote to a friend in another State. He said; "For God's sake get me a church if you can. I must have something within the next six months or I shall have to crawl out of Pittsburgh on my hands and knees after dark."

Fourteen years of serving under the lordship of the Denominational Program—and the end? Crawling out of Pittsburgh on his hands and knees after dark! Seventeen years of working under the Lordship of Christ—and the end? Occupying the pulpit of one of the greatest Baptist Churches in the country; called upon North, South, East, and West for the ministry of the Word; more than 11,000 men and women having publicly confessed Christ under our ministry; more than 20 young men and women in the home and foreign mission fields in full time service for Christ, who have gone into such service under our ministry. All of this and much, much more has been our lot and all because we are some extraordinary preacher? No. But because we dared to be faithful to Him.

We cite this case not with any notion of the parade of self, but in the hope that some scared preacher who may read these lines will take courage and cast off the shackles of fear. Within the past three months I have received no less than 20 letters from pastors in the State of Indiana alone, saying in substance "God bless you Brother Ketcham. Go on with the fight, but as for me I dare not move."

One dear fellow wrote me some time

ago declaring himself to be openly on our side of the issue, and then the Convention "powers that be" began to put the screws down. Last week I received a letter from him declaring that he was ceasing all connection with our contention for the Faith, that he was going back to the N. B. C. and the Indiana State Convention. I wrote him as follows:

"Dear Brother:

"Poor fellow!

"I say this not in derision, but in heart sympathy for a Baptist preacher who can thus be scared by the 'powers that be.'

"It is just such letters as yours of March 28 which prove more and more the need for some one to arise and help break the shackles of fear from God-called ministers, and sovereign Baptist Churches.

"With every good wish, I am,

Yours and His,

(Signed) R. T. Ketcham."

RTK:LK

CASE NUMBER SIX

Another case of Convention overlordship and interference comes before us in the instance of the Corwith, Iowa, case. Some twenty years ago, the Baptist cause in Corwith, Iowa, seemed about to die out. In order that the property might be conserved for the use of Baptists in the future, in case there should be a revival of Baptist interests, the property was deeded to the Iowa State Convention for the consideration of one dollar, the expressed reason for such a transaction being that the property might be held in trust by the Convention until such time as Corwith Baptists might require the use of it again and there should be a Baptist organization of sufficient strength to carry on the work. During the years that have passed since then, the work has revived and it has developed into one of the finest smaller churches in the state. During recent years, several attempts have been made to get the State Convention to deed the property back to the church, since the purpose of transferring it to the State Convention temporarily had been fully met. This the State Convention has persistently refused to do. During these intervening years, the church had come to take a position of non-cooperation with the Northern Baptist Convention and the Iowa State Convention program. Exercising the right of conscientious judgment which hundreds had also exercised, they had decided that they could not consistently support a program so overloaded with Modernism.

Approximately a year ago, the State Convention through its secretary, Mr. Anderson, notified the church that unless they began to support the Convention programs, that they would have to give up the use of the church building. It was argued with Mr. Anderson that in the broadest ethical sense of the word, the State Convention did not own the church, but that the local congregation were the true owners of the property. The State Convention had come into possession of the deed for the sum of one dollar for very apparent reasons. Now that those reasons were eliminated, the property should have been deeded back to the local church. This the Convention refused to do, and then ordered the congregation to vacate the building or support the program. The church at a called business meeting, voted overwhelmingly not to support the program, and acting in accordance with the mandate of the state secretary, got up and walked out of the building in which some of them had worshipped for forty years. The next week they rented a building elsewhere in town and continued doing business as the First Baptist Church of Corwith, Iowa.

A few years ago, a parsonage property was purchased, which had no connection whatever with the original church property, and was not involved in the State Convention deed. A few weeks after the church voted not to support the Convention and had removed itself from the Convention owned (?) property, a minority in the church, numbering but a handful, got together under Convention instigation, called themselves the First Baptist Church of Corwith, Iowa, and served a legal notice on the pastor, Mr. Albert Rust, to vacate because the parsonage was the property of the First Baptist Church, and since the majority of the church had voted not to support the Conventions, they were therefore no longer a Baptist church. That since they, the minority, had voted to support the Conventions, they were therefore the First Baptist Church, and upon these grounds sued for possession of the parsonage. The case went to court for trial. Mr. Anderson was the star witness for the prosecution. After all the evidence was in, the judge handed down a decision in favor of Pastor Rust and the majority and ordered the State Convention minority to pay the costs. The judge's decision declared that a local Baptist church was sovereign, and that no matter what Convention program it voted not to support, it did not thereby cease to be a Baptist church. Full details of this entire proceeding may be secured by addressing Pastor Albert Rust, Corwith, Iowa.

Why should Convention officials feel that they have a right to instruct preachers to cheer for the official family simply because they happen to occupy their pulpits because a Convention official "spoke a good word" for them? When a Church has expressed itself as no longer willing to support the program of the Convention why should a Convention official or committee feel called upon to undertake to come into that church and seek to change their position? Even granting for argument's sake that the Church's position is wrong, what right has an outsider to go in to set it right?

III

SOME CONVENTION PRESIDENTS DR. FRANKLIN

The present President, Dr. James H. Franklin, published in 1935 his book "The Never Failing Light." The book throughout is an emphatic appeal for the Fatherhood of God and the Brotherhood of Man. On page 9, Dr. Franklin says "He (Jesus) told them of a Father—God who would have them all as members of one family, living together as brothers and sisters regardless of race, social status, economic privileges, or differences of belief."

On page 10 Dr. Franklin says "Truly the light was shining in dense spiritual darkness when Jesus began teaching men of all races, of all religions, and all classes to look up to the Unseen as our Father and to practice love and brotherhood as the sum total of all requirements of his children." There are thousands of people who practice the idea of love and brotherhood, and yet have no time for Jesus Christ. Such a practice is positively not the sum total of God's requirements of men. Somewhere I have read that God requires men to believe on the Lord Jesus Christ!

On page 33 Dr. Franklin says "He (Jesus) did not talk about the Fatherhood of God or the Brotherhood of Man in so many words, but He proceeded to live as if both were true. He also bade men try the experiment of living as if they were sons of God and brothers one of another." Dr. Franklin could hardly claim that Jesus said anything about the Fatherhood of God in the face of such a passage as John 8:44, "Ye are of your father the Devil." Dr. Franklin says that Jesus "lived" as though all men were sons of God, but Jesus Himself declared that all men were not the sons of God. If what Dr. Franklin claims is true then Jesus lived one thing and said another! There are some of us who still prefer to let Jesus stand as the Scriptures present Him, minus Dr. Franklin's interpretation of Him.

On page 34 Dr. Franklin quotes approvingly H. R. L. Sheppard when he says "To love God and to love your neighbor as yourself is the beginning and end of the Christian religion." Such teachings as these reduce Jesus Christ to simply a teacher who told men they were to love God and their neighbor. It is true that He told them this, but it is also true He told them something else, namely that no man could love God and his neighbor without taking Jesus Christ into account. The beginning and the end of the Christian religion is not our love for God and our neighbor, but the Lord Jesus Christ Himself who said "I am Alpha and Omega, the beginning and the end."

On page 36 Dr. Franklin says "What was the cross to Him? Naught but an incident in the life which He had already laid down for His kind." The cross may be a mere "incident" to Dr. Franklin, but you may rest assured it was far from that to Jesus! It was neither incident nor accident to Him— but the supreme consummation of all His redemptive plans.

Elsewhere we devote a chapter to some of the hypocritical actions of the Convention and Convention leaders. We pause here to discuss the hypocrisy of Dr. Franklin. The Denominational press has just released the news that Dr. Franklin has chosen as the Convention hymn, to be sung in St. Louis in May, "When I Survey The Wondrous Cross."

Thousands of Baptists will sing this precious old hymn at the next sessions of the Northern Baptist Convention, and as they sing it their hearts will be aflame with the precious message of the cross. They will know as they sing that it was there the great transaction took place, that it was there where "He who knew no sin was made to be sin for us that we might be made the righteousness of God." They will know that it was there on that cross that God dealt with His precious, Holy Son as He would have had to deal with every one of them, had Christ not gone to that Cross. Thousands of Baptists will sing this old hymn, and as they sing it they will know full well that it wasn't the life of Jesus prior to the cross which saved them, but that it was that life poured out in penal substitution in death for them, which alone gives them hope.

While thousands of Baptists will thus be singing this hymn, the President, Dr. Franklin, will be thinking of it as "naught but an incident" in the life of Christ. Baptists everywhere will be led to conclude that the old-fashioned cross is to be lifted up in the heart of the next Northern Baptist Convention because the President has selected this hymn, but let the same Baptists read Dr. Franklin's book "The Never Failing Light," and then let them wonder why he selected this particular hymn.

On page 34 Dr. Franklin declares "The teachings of Jesus support Bishop Gore in the declaration that the unaccomplished mission of Christianity is nothing less than to reconstruct Society on the basis of Brotherhood." The Lord Jesus Himself in Luke 24 reverses both Bishop Gore and Dr. Franklin when He says "Thus it is written and thus it behoved Christ to suffer, and to rise from the dead the third day; and that repentance and remission of sins should be preached in his name among all nations, beginning at Jerusalem. And ye are witnesses of these things." Getting men to act in love toward one another simply on the basis of the teachings of Jesus is a million miles from the Gospel. Something else than the Gospel may turn men to a higher plane of morals and a more civilized manner of life, but these accomplishments are far from salvation!

DR. SHAW

The Northern Baptist Convention President immediately preceding Dr. Franklin was Dr. Avery A. Shaw, President of Denison University, Granville, Ohio. A few years ago six brethren and

I spent seven hours in a hotel room in Columbus, Ohio, in conference with Dr. Shaw and fifteen or twenty other Baptist leaders of the State. We were trying to arrive at some method by which the Convention could be purged from within of these objectionable features. Dr. Shaw in the presence of all of us declared "I am a theistic evolutionist."

We confronted Dr. Shaw with several newspaper accounts of the accomplishments of his card-playing faculty in the realm of prize winning. His sole answer was "I did not know it was contrary to Christian views to play 'cards.'"

At the time of the Washington Convention Dr. Shaw was pastor of Emmanuel Baptist Church, Brooklyn, New York. It was at this Convention that it was voted two to one in favor of "Open Membership," that is, allowing Baptist Churches to receive members without Baptism, and at the same time hold full fellowship in a Baptist Convention. Dr. Shaw went home from that Convention and preached to his own people a sermon entitled "Sanity of Northern Baptists" in which he said "The sanity of northern Baptists is revealed in their settlement of the open membership question." This certainly places Dr. Shaw on that question.

When Dr. Harry Emerson Fosdick left the pastorate of a Presbyterian Church in New York City the Baptist Ministers Conference of that city, meeting in the Madison Avenue Baptist Church, appointed a Committee to send a signed statement of appreciation of his ministry to the Rev. Dr. Harry Emerson Fosdick. The statement which was sent to Dr. Fosdick follows: "The undersigned, your brethren of the Baptist Ministers Conference of New York, appreciating the remarkable ministry you have rendered, wish to express to you our fellowship with you in your attitude toward the truth of Christ, and our admiration of your kindly courage under great trial. We greatly desire and confidently hope that on your return, opportunity will open for you to exercise the great preaching gift in some pulpit in our city."

The above words were drafted by Dr. A. S. Hobart and Dr. Avery A. Shaw. Dr. Shaw has since said that it was simply an appreciation of the person of Dr. Fosdick, but what he actually wrote was "We wish to express to you our fellowship with you in your attitude toward the truth of Christ."

It is worthy of note, too, as evidence in this case, that Dr. Fosdick endorses Dr. Shaw. The Rev. Chester E. Tulga, then pastor at Niles, Ohio, wrote Dr. Fosdick stating that Dr. Shaw was passing in Ohio as a Conservative, and asked if he would advise his own personal opinion concerning the matter. Dr. Fosdick replied as follows: "I am very fond of Dr. Shaw and your letter is the first intimation I ever had that he was a Conservative in the sense which your letter seems to imply. He certainly has had very liberal associations here in greater New York, and I had supposed that he belonged to the circle of intelligent and wide awake minds that were open to all new lights. I am sure that you will find this to be the case."

DR. BEAVEN

While reference is made elsewhere in this book to Dr. Beaven's apparent sympathies for a radical Socialism, we have the following to say concerning him under the head of "Convention Presidents," since he occupied that position only recently.

The League for Industrial Democracy is one of the many Red "front" organizations which is being subsidized and propagated by Communists. In 1935, the Rochester, New York League for Industrial Democracy published a program of several meetings to be held in Rochester under its auspices. The program itself was printed on flaming red paper. On the back page of the program is a list of the sponsors, among which is the name of Dr. Albert W. Beaven, President of Colgate Rochester

Divinity School, and ex-President of the Northern Baptist Convention. In this connection, we quote herewith the entire article from the pen of Dr. Harold Strathearn in his paper "The Baptist Fellowship."

"DR. ALBERT W. BEAVEN AND HIS ASSOCIATIONS!"

"We are constantly receiving inquiries at our office concerning Dr. Beaven. The question that is always asked is: 'Do you consider Dr. Beaven a Fundamentalist?'

"To start with, there is doubt in the inquirer's mind. We always answer the inquiry in simple and positive language. 'Dr. Beaven is not a Fundamentalist!' We would remind the reader that Dr. Beaven's ability is not to be minimized. He possesses a pleasing personality. He is a political strategist to the point of keeping one guessing. His guarded phraseology leaves many people in a fog, as to what side of the fence he is on. There are those in the South who look upon him as a Fundamentalist. He is known in the North as a liberal. Dr. Beaven's influence in the Northern Baptist Convention is fully recognized which makes it all the more serious that he would lend his name to influence as a sponsor of a subversive, radical organization.

"The reader may draw his own conclusions from the following information.

"Permit us to introduce an organization known as the LEAGUE FOR INDUSTRIAL DEMOCRACY. First; its history:

"The national officers are all members of the American Civil Liberties Union.

"The League is headed by Robert Lovett, active in Communist organizations; founded by the revolutionary Jack London in 1905 heavily subsidized by the famous Garland Fund which is the financial foundation of the 'Red' movement in this country; spreads Socialistic, Communistic propaganda and literature in American Colleges; conducts student conferences each summer at Camp Tamiment, Pennsylvania; formed the Federation of Unemployed Workers Leagues of America which is under joint Communistic-Socialist I. W. W. control; its slogan is 'Education towards a new social order based on production for use and not for profit'; it boasts that 'student members of the League for Industrial Democracy have been in the thick of the miners' struggles in Harlan, Kentucky, and in West Virginia'; is the distributor of scores of pamphlets of the extreme 'Red' position. The subject of its 1931 student conference held at the University of Chicago was 'The Student in World Revolution.' The December, 1931 National Conference held in New York City was entitled, 'Guiding the Revolution' and discussed such topics as 'What Tactics Should Students Use,' et cetera. The first page of 'Students Outlook' for February, 1933, which is published by the League for Industrial Democracy says 'Wanted: Students with Guts.' Under this heading we find the following: 'If you have enlisted under the banners of Socialism you have got to carry the job through.'

Second; its objects:

"1. Abolition of private property. 'Education for a new social order based on production for use and not for profit.' 2. Recognition of Soviet Russia. 3. Disarmament of United States. This society operates through the establishment of so-called Liberal groups in colleges. IT IS RESPONSIBLE FOR THE RADICAL DISTURBANCES ON THE CAMPUS OF SYRACUSE UNIVERSITY ON FRIDAY. MAY 19, 1933; NEW YORK UNIVERSITY, MAY, 1933. And others.

"June 6, 1931, a closed meeting of the League for Industrial Democracy, The American Civil Liberties Union, Fellowship of Reconciliation, and the Committee on Militarism and Education held a New School of Social Research in New York City, admission by ticket only. In addition to the publicly announced program of this organization, the following was adopted:

> The protection of aliens.
>
> Co-operation with the working class movement.
>
> Release of Mooney and Billings.
>
> Release of I. W. W. convicts in the Centralia case.
>
> Recognition of Russia.
>
> Enactment of legislation to admit pacifists to citizenship.
>
> Repeal of Federal laws prohibiting free dissemination of birth control.
>
> Protection of political and industrial prisoners.
>
> Problems of Japanese, Philippine and Mexican radicals.
>
> Aid to strikers.
>
> Freedom of Philippine Islands.
>
> Unemployment insurance.

(Note: This program is a resume of practically every Radical propaganda.)

"Addressing the 'forum of revolution' held at Barnard College, December 27, 28, and 29, attended by the Intercollegiate Student Council of the League of Industrial Democracy, Norman Thomas, well-known radical, discussed plans for the revolution which they feel is bound to come, and envisioned a world built of, by and for the proletariat. Delegates from 29 colleges and universities were in attendance. Lewis Munford, author, Paul Blanchard, and others spoke. Birth control and other topics were discussed. THE STUDENTS WERE ASKED TO LIVE LIKE COMMUNISTS IN PREPARATION FOR THE GENERAL UPHEAVEL TO COME. (Sojourners, May 1933.)

"One of the speakers for the League is Scott Nearing, editor of the 'Revolutionary Age,' (BARRED FROM THE MAIL). He is a paid speaker under Communist auspices. He was jailed for sedition during the war. He recently said at the Play House, in Washington, D. C., when speaking on, 'The Stability of the Russian Soviet Government,' that he stood for the Soviet Government of Russia, as opposed to the capitalist government of the world. He advocated the establishment of World Communism. 'It is our business to prepare America by propaganda, to do what Russia did in 1917,' he said.

"New York State chapter headquarters, 112 East 19th Street, New York. President Reinhold Niebuhr, radical, pacifist, and labor agitator, advocate of intermingling of whites and negroes. Treasurer: Stuart Chase, member of many prominent radical societies and personal friend and associate of the notorious deported anarchist, Alexander Berkman; connected with War Registers League, Evelyn Hughes; Communist Federated Press, Frank Palmer; the Socialist Party, Paul Blanchard; the Committee on Militarism and Education, Cutler P. Smith.

"This society has organized a chapter in Rochester, through an individual known to be intimately connected with Communism and other subversive movements.

"Its second speaker this year was J. B. Matthews, Executive Secretary of the Fellowship of Reconciliation; another radical, pacifist organization. The meeting place for the Rochester organization is a building known as the Gannett House, which is the property of the Unitarian Church. Rev. David Rhys Williams is pastor of the church, and his associations are listed in 'The RED NET WORK,' a who's who and handbook of radicalism for patriots, by Mrs. Elizabeth Dilling.

"We have in our possession the 1935 program of the Rochester League for Industrial Democracy. It is worthy of note that the program is not printed in black, blue, or pink, but 'RED.' This program lists the subjects and speakers as follows:

January 29—"TWO YEARS OF ROOSEVELT!" J. B. Matthews.

February 5 — "GOVERNMENT IN BUSINESS!" Carl Thompson.

February 12—"THE MARCH OF LABOR!" Tucker P. Smith.

February 19 — "NATIONALISM IN AMERICA!" William Pickens.

February 26—"PREPARATIONS FOR WORLD WAR!" Ellen Wilkinson.

March 5—"THE COMING STRUGGLE FOR POWER!" Norman Thomas.

"On the back page of this program we find the list of sponsors and, included in that list is the name of Dr. A. W. Beaven, president of Colgate Rochester Divinity School; also the names of Professor Conrad H. Moehlman, and Professor Henry B. Robins; both teachers in the school of which Dr. Beaven is president.

"Is the above good company for Dr. Beaven to be keeping? Is he fair to Baptist interests? Is he consistent to be allied with the enemies of the Church, and the Christian Faith? Will you be led by Dr. Beaven or by the scriptural injunction:

"'Ye cannot drink the cup of the Lord and the cup of devils.'

IV

THE CONVENTIONS AND KAGAWA

Perhaps no individual has caused more comment in the religious world in recent years than has Dr. Kagawa in his tour of the United States under the sponsorship of the Federal Council of Churches of Christ in America. Dr. Kagawa spoke before a Southwide meeting of Baptist youth only recently. He also delivered a series of lectures for a week to the students of the Southern Baptist Theological Seminary of Louisville. He is also to be one of the speakers at the joint meeting of the Northern and Southern Baptist Conventions in St. Louis in May. The Indiana Baptist State paper, the "Baptist Observer" said of him, "He is the greatest force for Christ in the world today." A prominent Baptist leader said of him, "He is the greatest Christian in the world." Another Christian leader said of him, "If Kagawa is not a Christian, then there are no Christians."

Over against these statements, we place a few from Dr. Kagawa himself;

"Jesus experienced God as the forgiver of sins."—Page 32, "Religion of Jesus."

"Thus discovering the marvelous fact of an elaborate cosmic design, we cannot but feel that there exists a Being in the universe, great beyond our power to imagine. Whether this Being should be called God or not, I do not know."—Page 68, "Love the Law of Life."

"The reconstruction of human nature depends upon the power of evolution."—Page 245, "Love the Law of Life."

"Belief in evolution is faith in the progressive entrance into an ever expanding freedom, from seed to shoot, bud to flower, from anthropoid to human, from man to son of God. What a courageous faith: The Belief that there is a direct line of evolution from amoeba to man is more daring and romantic than the belief in the myth of a Creator making something out of nothing."—Page 298, "Love the Law of Life."

"Belief in evolution is a bolder faith than Abraham's belief in the promised land. His land was the lean country of Palestine; the promised land of evolution is growth from electron to divinity."—Page 299, "Love the Law of Life."

"Science is the movement preparatory to our becoming divine."—Page 272, "Love the Law of Life."

"It (faith in evolution) is convinced that though stones may not become sons to Abraham, electrons can become sons of God."—Page 300, "Love the Law of Life."

With unhesitating emphasis, we say that any man who can write the above sentences, is to an old-fashioned Baptist a long, long way from being the greatest Christian in the world, and yet he is paraded from one end of the country to the other, and everywhere our Baptist leaders are putting their approval upon him. What all of this means to a thinking young person, I am afraid to contemplate. Our leaders do not need to think that our youngsters are going to be able to "push the bones aside and take only the meat." To thousands of Baptists, young and old, what the leaders endorse must be acceptable. In a soon coming day, when our Baptist forces will reap the harvest that they have been sowing through their parading of Dr. Kagawa, let them remember that it was the leaders who led them into it.

V

MODERNISM AND BAPTIST PUBLICATIONS

"THE BAPTIST"

THE BAPTIST was originally created as the official organ of the Northern Baptist Convention. Later it was turned over to a group to edit it, and finance it. While through this arrangement it lost its "official organ" complexion, yet it was put forward as one of the great mediums of publicity and propaganda for the Convention. During its last days, Dr. U. M. McGuire was its editor, and in the issue of December 31, 1932, on page 1102, in his exposition of the Sunday School Lesson for January 8, 1933, dealing with the temptation of Jesus, Dr. McGuire says:

"Naturally, after Jesus' conversion, he faced his life work seriously. Certain problems were to be settled and choices made between goods and the Good. What was he going to be and do? The question covered a field of large and obvious options of various values. He could not dawdle with them. He must weigh and choose, in the light of his experience. A spiritual dynamo within him drove him to such a crisis. Some of his problems he must settle with and for God, without human intrusion. But what of Satan? Shall we think of him in terms of theology, as the gadfly of God sent to sting and torment men; or in terms of psychology, as the shadow demon created by human imagination, like the "shadow children" of Louise M. Alcott or Puck of "Midsummer Night's Dream," haunting all human life with leadings to error, failure and ruin?"

The page is filled with equally blasphemous statements. We understand that Dr. McGuire claims we have misinterpreted him. It is too bad that these learned gentlemen are so limited in their vocabulary that they have to use the word "conversion" if they mean something else. If I should say to you that another man, whom I called by name, did something "after his conversion" I would expect you to interpret it to mean that the man had been converted, and in view of the rest that follows on page 1102, Dr. McGuire will have a hard time convincing any thinking man that that is not exactly what he meant in reference to Jesus.

"YOUNG PEOPLE"

"Young People" is a periodical published as a story paper for Sunday Schools. In 1925 a serial ran under the title "The House of Simon" by Ambrose Bailey. I have before me the issue of November 14, 1925, which is the seventh chapter in the serial. The story goes into revolting detail of how a young man acting under orders from the Jewish leaders, inveigled Mary the sister of Martha to slip out of her room at night after everyone else was asleep to go to a dance with him. On the way to the dance he seduced Mary and the waiting guards caught her in the act of adultery and then brought her to the temple court and accused her before Jesus. This is surely taking liberty with the name and character of an ancient Bible personage, who, of course, is no longer here to defend herself against the yearning of Mr. Bailey to make a good story. I would far rather trust my reputation in the hands of Mary who could wipe the feet of Jesus with her hair, than in the hands of a modern story writer whose mind could conjure up such a revolting episode.

I have before me also a copy of the same paper, issue of June 1, 1935, which carries an article entitled "Gandhi and Imperialism" by Albert E. Bailey, with sub-title, "Go Ye Into All the World and Preach the Gospel." We quote:

> "Go preach the gospel, you little wizened Gandhi squatting defenseless and helpless before the might of an empire! You do not amount to much—only ninety-three pounds of flesh and bones! But thank God you have a weapon that will beat them yet. It is called the Sword of the Spirit. You are sharpening it now in the great dome of a head, behind those near-sighted eyes which are seeing immaterial and eternal things. Preach your gospel of non-resistance, for you have Jesus as your backer...."

> "Preach your gospel of brotherhood. Its medicine is good for your untouchable countrymen and your Brahmans as it is good for the white man. Preach your gospel of prayer for more light, of penance for the wrongs others do you, of forgiveness towards those that stone you....."
> "Oh, Hindu Gandhi, the command rests upon you as much as it does upon the whites."

And this glorification of Hinduism before the hundreds of thousands of Baptist young people. Under our item on Communism we shall have something more to say about this periodical called "Young People."

VI

THE EDUCATIONAL SITUATION

The most prolific source of Modernistic Baptist preachers is our Baptist schools. I am not in a position to bring a wholesale indictment against all our Baptist schools. I have not had time to investigate every one of them. I am prepared to say however, concerning those which I have investigated, that not one of them is thoroughly sound and true to the faith historically held by Baptists.

FRANKLIN COLLEGE

The Baptist college of the State of Indiana, known as Franklin College certainly does not appeal to orthodox Baptists. Its president, Dr. William Gear Spencer, is certainly far from clear as to his position concerning the orthodox faith. Dr. Spencer preached the ordination sermon in connection with a certain ordination within a few miles from me when I was pastor in Elyria, Ohio. In the examination of the candidate, it developed that the young man denied the authority of the scriptures, claimed the doctrine of the virgin birth was of no importance, the death of Christ was purely inspirational, and refused to acknowledge His deity. He was finally ordained by a vote of ten to four, and four not voting. In the executive session which followed the examination, Dr. Spencer, who was then with Hillsdale College, took the floor and pleaded for the young man. While the name of the young man and the place of ordination does not necessarily enter into the present argument, yet knowing the tendency of the opposition to always demand names and places, we anticipate that challenge now by declaring that the young man in question was Mr. Howard B. Jefferson, ordained December 30, 1926, in the First Baptist Church, Norwalk, Ohio.

On March 7, 1934, Dr. Spencer wrote me asking for the privilege of sending Dr. P. L. Powell, dean of Franklin College, to Gary to speak to my people in the interest of the college. I wrote Dr. Powell, as follows:

"March 13, 1934

Dr. E. L. Powell, Dean
Franklin College
Franklin, Indiana

Dear Dr. Powell:

Under date of March 7 I received a note from Dr. Spencer calling attention to "Franklin Day" on April 8, and asking for the privilege of assigning you to the pulpit of Central Baptist Church of Gary on that occasion.

You are, of course, aware that many of our Baptist churches are attempting to safeguard their testimony in relation to the historic Baptist faith. Central Church is one of them. Our Baptist schools and seminaries are at the very heart of the present day controversy touching these matters. In view of that fact I deem it wise to ask that a few questions be answered before we make any decision as to "Franklin Day" in Central Church. First of all a few personal questions as to your own views.

1. Do you believe that Jesus Christ was God, pre-existent with the Father, and born of a virgin?

2. Do you believe in the miracles of both the Old and New Testaments?

3. Do you believe that Christ's death upon the cross was substitutionary in the sense that He bore the wrath of God against our sin?

4. Do you believe in the bodily resurrection of the Lord Jesus Christ?

5. Do you believe in the bodily resurrection of believers?

6. Do you believe in the personal return of the Lord Jesus Christ to this earth, and if so is it premillennial or postmillennial?

7. Do you believe in the inspiration of the Holy Scriptures in the sense that the original manuscripts were verbally inspired?

8. Do you believe in creation by an immediate act of God, or do you accept the Evolutionary theory?

I should like also to know the general position of Franklin College as a College on the above questions.

With every good wish, I am

Yours and His,

R. T. Ketcham."

On March 18, Dr. Powell, replied and I quote the following paragraph:

"The time between now and April 8 would probably be entirely too short for us to satisfy your mind upon the controversial questions which you raise and which you might subsequently raise, even though we thought it worth while to enter upon such an undertaking. In view of these considerations, after consultation with President Spencer, we are withdrawing our request that the College be represented in your Church on the date suggested."

Surely any fair minded person will agree that as pastor of Central Baptist Church we had a perfect right under the circumstances to ask Dr. Powell where he and his school stood before we opened our pulpit to him. But instead of answering these simple questions "Yes" or "No" he takes the position that it is really none of our business what the college believes, and that really after all it is not even worth while to discuss it. I quote the last two paragraphs of my letter to Dr. Powell under date of April 8, because they briefly set forth the logical answer to such an attitude.

"Surely, Dr. Powell, we had a right, in these days especially, to ask these simple questions, particularly when the College was coming here to ask for the support of Central Church. Your refusal to answer these questions says in essence "It is none of your business what we believe." It is just such attitudes as this on the part of our denominational leaders which makes it impossible for hundreds of Baptist Churches to support Denominational programs.

"The scriptural injunction is "be ready to give an answer to everyone that asketh for the hope that lieth in you" and when a man is asked in all Christian courtesy if he believes that Jesus Christ was God, pre-existent with the Father and born of a virgin, and that His death upon the cross bore the wrath of God against our sins, and he refuses to answer, he cannot blame his questioner if he assumes that his reason for silence is due to the fact that he does not believe it."

Last November, the Michigan state B. Y. P. U. convention was held in Grand Rapids. Dr. Spencer was one of the speakers. At the close of the service, some young people interviewed him. The actual quotations of the interview are as follows:

"Question: How in your estimation can one obtain salvation?

Dr. Spencer: By accepting Christ and by trying to live up to His ideals.

Question: Then don't you believe in salvation through the blood alone?

Dr. Spencer: Shibboleth! It is just a difference of the place of emphasis. You stress the blood and we stress the moral attributes that can be developed within the individual."

In the 1935 Indiana Baptist Annual, on Page 24, the committee of seven appointed by the State Convention to investigate the entire situation in the Convention, reporting on Franklin College says the following:

"There is a strong desire all over the state that Franklin shall be so distinctively Baptist and so loyal to the Word of God in spirit and in influences, that it may receive the hearty support of all our pastors and churches. There have been severe criticisms. Many of these have not been based on facts. But wherever anything has been contrary to the truth, changes should be courageously made. We recommend that immediate steps be taken by the trustees of Franklin College and the Indiana Baptist Convention board, to make Franklin College a distinctively Baptist institution. We further recommend that as soon as this is assured, the Indiana Baptist Convention approve a launching of a campaign to increase the student body, etc."

Here then, is only a little of the evidence which can be brought forth in the case of Franklin College to cause Baptist parents to have some fears concerning the future Baptist faith of their children when once they are sent to Franklin.

OHIO COLLEGES

The text "Problems of Conduct" by Drake was used in both Baptist colleges in the State of Ohio in their course in Ethics. A few quotations from this book will show that it has no place in a Baptist College.

"How can we know what is the will of God except by considering what makes for human welfare? Our Bible is but one of a number of holy books which are held to be a revelation of God's will. Even if we grant the superior authority of the Hebrew-Christian Bible, can we rely on its teachings implicitly?" Page 161.

"Finally, we have a duty to those dumb brothers of ours, the animal species that share with us the earth." Page 232.

"It should be possible for any man or woman to find deliverance from an intolerable and apparently irremedial situation without expense, publicity, or any imputation of scandal. Divorce is always a sad matter, but is occasionally as necessary as a surgical operation and should be essentially a private arrangement. It is doubtful whether any moral end is served by requiring ''grounds'' for divorce to be shown—as proof of infidelity, cruelty, or the like; most of these alleged reasons for divorce at present are false and exaggerated pretexts offered to satisfy the law. The fundamental ground for most divorces is that the couple have found that they cannot be happy, cannot be their best selves together." Pages 227-228.

Another text used in the Ohio schools is "The Teachings of Jesus" by Stevens.

It was this very book that caused me twenty years ago to abandon my course in Crozier Theological Seminary. It is shot through and through with Modernism, a sample or two, of which is hereby given: Speaking of Jesus' teaching concerning His second coming the author takes the position that Jesus was mistaken in His notions concerning it, or that those who recorded His words deliberately wrote into them the apocalyptic viewpoint. After discussing these theories through several pages he comes to his conclusion, page 175, and says, "Traces of the original meaning of Jesus are by no means wanting."

"The Life of Paul" by Robinson is another text used in the Ohio schools.

An illustration of the attitude of the whole book is found on page 122 where the earthquake which released Paul and Silas is said to be simply one of the many natural earthquakes common in that country. In passing I would remark that it was "some NATURAL earthquake" that could shake the fetters off the wrists and ankles of prisoners, and yet leave the prisoners unhurt by the shaking! It is rather strange, too, that the jailer's home next door was not even touched by this NATURAL earthquake! We have often noticed that in doing away with the scriptural miracle our Modernist friends put themselves in the position of being forced to accept an explanation which presents a greater miracle than the one they set aside.

Another characteristic sample of the book is found on pages 39 and 40.

"In II Cor. 12:7 he speaks of a 'thorn in the flesh, a messenger of Satan to buffet me.' Many are the explanations of this thorn. Among the various explanations which most nearly fit Paul's references is that under special excitement he was subject to sudden attacks of violent headaches or dizziness, or even fainting." Who, Paul or the author?

CROZIER

Dr. Milton G. Evans, while President of Crozier said: "We have men working in the field of evangelism. Especially in the foreign fields, like China, and other countries we have already many of our Modernist men working there. We are continually gaining new ground."

When asked, "What about your prospects in America?"

Dr. Evans replied, "Very good, indeed. Why every year our leading seminaries, Colgate, Rochester, Chicago Dvinity School, Newton Center, and our own Crozier are turning out New Theology men who are speedily filling the pulpits of our land."

Dr. A. S. Hobart of Crozier in his "Transplanted Truth from Romans," page 29, says, "I cannot see anything understandable or acceptable in the theory that my guilt and my penalty were placed upon Christ, or that Christ's holiness is imparted to me, in any way that involves a substitution of His holiness for mine or His suffering for what was due me, that view of the theory of the atonement finds no foothold in my consciousness or my reason."

The late Professor Vedder of Crozier said, "Of all the slanders men have perpetrated against the Most High, this is positively the most impudent, the most insulting. No, sin cannot be escaped by a bloody sacrifice. Jesus never taught and never authorized anybody to teach in His name that 'He suffered in our stead, and bore the penalty of our sins.'"

ROCHESTER

In 1917 Rochester was deeply tainted as evidenced by the professorship of Walter Rauschenbusch, who spoke of "The Blessed Skepticism of the Age of Enlightenment." He further says, "What the death of Jesus now does for us, the death of the prophets did for Him." In addition he says, "Speaking of Democracy, we must democratize the conception of God and then, he declares, "The worst thing that could happen to God would be to remain an Autocrat while the world is moving towards democracy—he would be dethroned with the rest."

Prof. George B. Cross of Rochester says, "And now after the lapse of all intervening centuries it is still an open question whether after all it was not misleading to call Jesus the Christ."

When Prof. Cross was elected to the Rochester faculty it was none other than Dr. Strong who said, "I regard that election as the greatest calamity that has come to the Seminary. It was the entrance of an agnostic, skeptical, and anti-Christian element into its teaching, the result of which will be only evil."

BROWN

Pres W. H. P. Faunce says, "We are not absolutely sure as to just how religion came into existence any more than we are sure as to how human life itself arose."

Professor Errett Gates, Chicago University in his "The Development of Modern Christianity, sums up the training of all of these schools when he says, "It has gradually dawned upon the entire missionary management, at home and abroad, that the old approach to non-Christian peoples, on the basis of the old religious ideas, and methods, and in the old spirit, was one of the principal causes of 'The Failure of Modern Missions,' and there has recently appeared among missionary leaders an outspoken approval of and an eager resort to modern religious ideas for the solution of problems in the mission field."

DES MOINES

Another evidence of the situation within our schools was disclosed when the Baptist Bible Union took over Des Moines University. For some time charges had been made of the presence of Modernism in Des Moines. Iowa state and national leaders, however, emphatically denied the truth of the charges. In fact, several Baptist pastors in the State of Iowa lost "caste" because of their criticism of the university, but when we took over the control of the university we found as Dean of the Pharmacy Department a prominent Unitarian. He had been with the university for twenty years. We found that the head professor in the Biology Department was the rankest kind of an evolutionist with a written statement from the board of trustees that he could teach any kind of evolution he desired. We found the teacher in the Philosophy Department an atheistic evolutionist. The dean of the Bible Department was a full-blown Modernist. Others were found equally unsound, all of whom were dismissed under Bible Union control.

A booklet twice the size of this entire work could be written dealing with the educational situation in Baptist schools, but here again, as everywhere else in this booklet, we must confine ourselves to short articles from a limitless field, and present typical cases only.

THE CERTAIN HARVEST

The effects of some of this education is seen in the following instance. A Colgate Rochester Seminary student pastor, preached in the Lincoln Baptist Church New York, on Sunday evening, May 6, 1934. His subject was "Birth Control." The young student pastor, just fresh from his class room, referred to the over abundance of fish we would have in the ocean if all the eggs hatched, and so we must limit our offspring by proper methods. He then invited the young men present who wanted more advance information to see him, and the young women present could go and see his wife. This young Baptist preacher has since, by the aid and cooperation of state secretaries, been transferred to a pulpit in the state of Wisconsin.

Someone may say, "What right have we to make his school responsible for such nonsense?" The answer is at hand. On December 10, 1933, only five months before he preached this sermon, Professor Charles C. Webber, industrial secretary of the World Fellowship of Reconciliation (main purpose to work for the recognition of Soviet Russia) was brought in to Colgate Divinity School to address the student body. We quote from his address as reported in the Rochester Journal.

> "Communistic and socialistic principles will be taught by the missionaries of the future in an attempt to overthrow capitalism. Capitalism is un-Christian and unethical, and must give way to socialism and communism, and the missionaries of the future must be social revolutionists. The missionary of tomorrow will show the workers of the Orient how they can bring about the abolition of capitalism by cooperative organizations, trade unions and socialistic political parties, and the missionary of the future will allow these organizations to hold meetings in his church. He will sustain the workers in their efforts by picketing with strikers and organizing protest meetings against police interference. Missionaries should establish birth control clinics, so that workers can control the population of the world and thus better their standards of living.

> "The missionary will assist in establishing labor colleges where capitalism will be discussed pro and con, and where it will be shown that capitalism inevitably leads to international class wars. He will point out the contribution of Soviet Russia in her attempt to establish a new social order."

VII

MODERNISM AN ORGANIZED SYSTEM OF DELIBERATE DISHONESTY

We are fully conscious of the seriousness of this charge. When we say that modernism is an organized system of deliberate dishonesty we certainly should be prepared to defend ourselves. We submit herewith documentary evidence in substantiation of this claim.

I quote a letter written by Rev. C. E. Tulga, at the time pastor of the First Baptist Church, Galeton, Pennsylvania, to Dr. Milton G. Evans, then President of Crozier Baptist Theological Seminary.

> "A church near here is very anxious to secure a pastor and they want a pastor who will not fall in line with the fundamentalists of the Association. Mr. S———, at present a pastor in New Jersey, has been recommended. Some say he is a funda-

mentalist, and some say he isn't. In view of the fact that fundamentalism is on a rampage in this Association it becomes an important question.

"Could you conscientiously recommend Mr. S———— to a church that wants a liberal pastor?

Very truly yours,

(Signed) C. E. Tulga."

To this letter Dr. Milton G. Evans personally replied as follows:

"Dear Brother:

"Yours of May 17 inquiring about Mr. S———— received.

"I can conscientiously recommend Mr. S———— to any church that wants a liberal pastor. He is thoroughly modern in his approach to the Bible, and questions of Baptist church polity. I do not know a more enthusiastic and constructive pastor than Mr. S————. He has done good work wherever he has been.

"I am wondering if it is not a tribute to him that some people cannot locate him—they cannot determine whether he is a fundamentalist or a modernist. When he has occasion to speak he speaks decidedly against the fundamentalists, but he is not combative. He wins. He has won a great many disposed to be fundamental to the modernist group by his tactfulness, and by his undoubted Christian devotion to the good of his people.

"If I were a member of any church thinking of him for pastor I would unhesitatingly vote for him."

Very truly yours.

(Signed) Milton G. Evans.

Here is the signed statement of one of the most noted outstanding Baptist leaders in the Northern Baptist Convention, passing a tribute to an outright modernist who, by his tactfulness (literally dishonesty) wins many from the fundamental position to the modern position. If this is not both deliberate and dishonest then we need a new dictionary.

That this is a real system operating among modernists is demonstrated by the fact that this same language is used in many of our Baptist Schools. Several years ago when Rev. Donald J. Dunkin, now pastor of the Berean Baptist Church of Elkhart, Indiana was attending Chicago University Divinity School, one of his professors gave deliberate instruction that if one of the graduates should find himself in a fundamentalist church, he should for the most part use fundamental phraseology, with his own modernistic interpretation.

Other definite instances of such procedure are on file in my office. In this connection the passage in II Peter 2:3 is tremendously interesting. The verse reads "And through covetousness shall they with feigned words make merchandise of you." I was startled recently to discover that this word translated "feigned" in the King James Version is in the literal translated "forged." The Spirit of God, through Peter, declares that these modernistic teachers, through covetousness (for their salaries' sake) make merchandise of you, by the use of forged words. Now a forged word is a correct word used for wrong purposes, and by the wrong person. If I forge a check on John Doe I cannot do so by signing it John Smith. Here is God's divine revelation of the truth involved in the heading of this item—Modernism is an organized system of deliberate dishonesty.

VIII

THE CONVENTIONS AND HYPOCRISY

Space forbids us to cite many cases in substantiation of the assertion that our Conventions often act in a hypocritical fashion. One or two will suffice.

CASE NUMBER ONE

At the last annual meeting of the Indiana Baptist Convention held in Greensburg, October, 1935, a Confession of Faith was presented by a Committee, appointed the year before to bring in recommendations for better efficiency in the State work. The Confession of Faith which this Committee presented would satisfy the heart of any loyal Baptist. It is a clear cut declaration of the old historic Baptist position.

On Wednesday morning it was presented to the Convention for action. Five hours of hot debate followed. At a late hour in the afternoon it was finally adopted with the following amendment: "With the understanding that it is not to be used as a test of fellowship, service or membership in the Indiana Baptist Convention, nor in any of its departments."

I have shown this report to at least 50 different individuals and without a single exception they instantly look up and say "Well, why adopt it then?" That is exactly what we would like to know. However, we have a pretty thorough conviction as to why. For instance in a recent issue of the Baptist Observer Dr. Parsons says that when Dr. Ketcham says that Indiana Baptists are not orthodox he is "worthy of neither confidence nor respect" and then refers to the glorious Confession of Faith adopted by the Convention as proof of his assertion!

In another recent issue of the same paper Dr. Hillyer Straton, who signs himself "member Executive Committee Fundamentalist Movement N. B. C.", declares that "The Indiana Baptist Convention is 99 44/100% Fundamental. This was made so clear at the State Convention at Greensburg that only one who willfully desired to pervert the truth could claim otherwise. It would have been impossible for the doctrinal statement that was adopted to have been more Fundamental, and it was adopted unanimously."

The reason for the adoption of such a Confession begins to be apparent. Whenever we declare that the Convention has in it elements of Modernism the leaders can frantically pick up this Confession of Faith and wave it in the air declaring that this is what we believe, therefore anyone who declares to the contrary is a liar. I know Dr. Straton uses the more moderate term "willful perversion of the truth", but out where we come from it means the same thing. Dr. Straton's 99 44/100% of Fundamental Baptists must be reduced to a state of anemic helplessness when the other 56/100% can hold them at bay for five hours before they can pass their own Confession of Faith, and then after it is passed pull all the teeth out of it and remove all the jaw bone, so that if a Modernist should ever get his finger in the mouth of the thing it couldn't even pinch him, let alone bite him!

Under the amendment tacked onto this Confession of Faith a man who believes absolutely nothing could act as State Secretary, Director of Young Peoples Work or any other position in the State Convention, without violating the provision one iota. We unhesitatingly charge this to be an hypocritical act.

CASE NUMBER TWO

We go back to the 1925 Northern Baptist Convention held in Washington, D. C. Dr. Harry Emerson Fosdick, in his acceptance of the call to the pastorate of the Park Avenue Baptist Church of New York City, had laid down, among other conditions, that of "open membership." The membership of the church was to be open to anyone who wanted to join it, regardless of Baptism. This, of course, was an abandonment of historic Baptist practice. The Constitution of the Northern Baptist Convention, as at that time set up, would make it impossible for the Park Avenue Baptist Church to seat delegates at the annual Conventions with such a provision obtaining in their own local practice. In view of the fact that the Park Avenue Church was also Mr. Rockefeller's

Church, and in view of the fact that the Convention found itself faced with the necessity of refusing to seat delegates from the Park Avenue Church, quite obviously something had to be done.

At the Seattle Convention in 1924 a Committee was appointed to draft an amendment to the Constitution so that the Park Avenue Church might be in good standing in the Convention. This Committee met in Chicago, drafted the proposed amendment, and it was published in the Denominational papers the required length of time prior to the Washington Convention. The proposed amendment was as follows: "The Northern Baptist Convention recognizes its constituency as consisting solely of those Baptist churches in which the immersion of believers is recognized as the only scriptural baptism; and the Convention hereby declares that only immersed members will be recognized as delegates to the Convention."

We charge this amendment with being hypocritical on two counts. First, the very fact of the amendment itself puts the Convention in a hypocritical position. Through all time Baptists have insisted that the baptistry should be at the door of entrance into the local Church, and not relegated to some optional place in the rear. We have insisted that the Church is a body of baptized believers. We have insisted that the local church should be a body of baptized believers because the invisible church is exactly that. According to I Corinthians 12:12 and 13 we are all members of one body and in one Spirit are all baptized into that one body. Here we are told that the only way a believer gets into the invisible body of Christ, which is His Church, is to be baptized into it in the Spirit. As Baptists we believe, therefore, that the believer should enter the local Church which is the earthly and outward symbol of that Heavenly and invisible body, by the same method through which he entered the Spiritual reality, namely, by baptism. The symbol should not be broken. If we enter the Spiritual Body through believing and being baptized in the Spirit, we should, therefore, enter the earthly body through believing and being baptized in water.

Why should all of this glorious heritage of faith and practice be amended out of the Constitution in order to make room for a Church which no longer believes it? We have a suspicion which amounts to a certainty that had it been a poor Baptist Church, with a membership made up of poor people who had asked to have their delegates seated in the Convention, while practicing open church membership, there would have been no machinery set in motion to amend the Constitution to let them in. We unhesitatingly charge this whole affair was a miserable gesture of submission to the millions of Mr. Rockefeller. The fact that Mr. Rockefeller has since announced the withdrawal of his gifts in no wise effects the hypocrisy of the Convention's action in Washington in 1925. If it does anything at all it simply adds new emphasis to the utterance of Scripture that "Whatsoever a man soweth that shall he also reap."

In the second place, we charge the amendment with being hypocritical in its wording. Instead of wording the amendment in such a fashion that everyone understood it was opening the door to open church membership, the amendment was so adroitly worded that it has to be read several times over before even a trained mind discovers what is wrong with it. The amendment declares that the Convention considers "its constituency as consisting solely of those Baptist churches in which the immersion of believers is recognized as the only scriptural baptism." I have handed this resolution to literally dozens of men and women and almost without exception they say "Why that amendment stands for an immersed membership." And not until it is pointed out that the word used is "recognized" instead of "practiced", and that even then it doesn't require the practice to be a prerequisite to Church membership, do they suddenly realize the actual meaning of the text.

Had the amendment read as follows everyone would have understood the issue: "The Northern Baptist Convention recognizes its constituency as consisting of Baptist churches regardless of whether immersion is practiced as a prerequisite to membership, but that only immersed members will be seated as delegates to the Convention." Everybody would then have known what the amendment was actually saying, but this was exactly what the leaders of the Convention didn't want the people to know.

Over against this amendment a substitute amendment was proposed. The amendment read as follows: "The Northern Baptist Convention recognizes its constituency as consisting solely of those Baptist Churches in which the immersion of believers is recognized and practiced as a prerequisite to membership." This was simple and straightforward, nevertheless because of the fog in the original amendment, and the fine platform work of the Convention Fundamentalists, Dr. Virgin, of Chicago, Dr. Masse, Dr. Boynton and Dr. J. Whitcomb Brougher, the Convention voted for the original amendment against the substitute by an overwhelming majority of more than two to one.

Now, the Church for which the leaders went to all this trouble has even dropped the name "Baptist" from its title, and the man whose money it was designed to hold, has bidden them a fond adieu!

CASE NUMBER THREE

Another glaring instance of hypocritical action on the part of Convention leaders was the famous amendment presented at the meeting of the Northern Baptist Convention in Indianapolis. While this instance happened several years ago, yet it is constantly being referred to by Convention leaders whenever it serves their purpose to do so.

One night nearly 300 fundamental Baptists met for Conference in the Palm Room of the Claypool Hotel. After several hours of discussion and conference we decided to ask the Convention the next day to go on record as reaffirming its faith in the old New Hampshire Confession of Faith.

I shall never forget that night. Brother Joshua Gravit of Denver, Colo. stood before us and read the New Hampshire Confession throughout. The Spirit of God came upon that group and great, strong men sobbed as the glorious realization of all the precious truth involved in that Confession, gripped our hearts afresh. It was decided that Dr. W. B. Riley should read this Confession on the floor of the Convention the next day, and move that it be adopted by the Convention as a reaffirmation of their faith. Perhaps one of the most tense moments in all Northern Baptist Convention history followed Dr. Riley's reading of that document.

I shall never forget the remark made by Mr. James Colgate, a prominent Convention official. As he came to the platform to speak to the motion he said "Well, so that's the New Hampshire Confession of Faith, huh? I thought Dr. Riley was reading from the back of a Western Union Telegraph blank." Suddenly Dr. Cornelius Wolfkin arose with a substitute motion which was as follows: "Resolved that we accept the New Testament as our ground of faith and practice and that Baptists need no other Confession." This substitute motion carried by almost three to one.

The hypocricy of Dr. Wolfkin's motion was fully revealed when only a few weeks after the Indianapolis Convention, he preached a sermon in his own Park Avenue pulpit in New York City, pleading for admission to the circle of Christian fellowship of such groups as Christian Scientists and Spiritualists, etc. The old historic terminology used the words "rule of faith and practice." Dr. Wolfkin deliberately changed the word "rule" to "ground." When you use a rule you must use it all or you must use any section of it in its proper relation to the rest of the rule. But when the New Testament was put down simply as the ground of our faith and practice it meant that you could go anywhere in the New Testament, make it mean anything you wanted to, so long as you claimed justification for your position by some interpretation which you might place upon the New Testament.

Dr. Wolfkin's substitute motion also put the delegates in a position of technically voting against the New Testament if they voted against his amendment. So far as we know, there never has been such an hypocritical move made in the history of the Northern Baptist Convention, as was witnessed during that session. And yet within the past year I have had letters from Baptist leaders in the State of Indiana pointing to the professed orthodoxy of the Northern Baptist Convention because it accepted the New Testament at Indiana!

IN CONCLUSION ON MODERNISM

Perhaps no more forceful argument can be advanced for our contention that old-fashioned Baptists ought not to stay in and support such a honeycombed organization as the N. B. C. than an article taken from page 4 of the 1933 Annual Report of the American Association For the Advancement of Atheism, Inc.

"Modernists" Smoke Screen

"The Modernists seem to attack Atheism only to screen their own unbelief. No better proof of our contention that the Church is losing can be given than that the Modernists are now in control of all the larger Protestant denominations and, working from the inside, discredit the basic teachings of Christianity in the name of Christianity.

Dumb Fundamentalists

"In this grand grand farce, fortunately for us, the dumb Fundamentalists through contributions pay for the destruction of their own belief in this Bible as a superhuman, infallible book. The Modernists are superior in strategy. When recently President Smith twitted the Rev. Riley with these facts, the Fundamentalist leader boasted of what he would do at the recent annual conference in Washington of the Northern Baptists. But at that and the other denominational conventions this Spring the Fundamentalists were defeated. They are hopelessly beaten. They cannot vote the Modernists out and dare not themselves withdraw. These two groups are held together by real estate.

Acme of Absurdity

"Higher Critics within the Church, carrying on the work of Voltaire, Paine and Ingersoll, in milder language, it is admitted, have made many Christians so ashamed of their creed that we now hear of that acme of absurdity, "a creedless faith"— of persons who believe, without believing anything. Thus Christianity slowly dissolves.

Atheists Lead, Modernists Follow

"But the good work of these Modernists not only does not lessen the need of Atheist propaganda but instead serves to emphasize its importance. Though its activities are on a small scale, the Advance Guard is always the most important unit in the army. We must continue to lead the way."

BAPTIST CHURCHES HAVE A RIGHT TO WITHDRAW

In support of this assertion we quote from Hiscox Directory for Baptist Churches. This book is published by the American Baptist Publication Society, and from the publisher's note on page 3 we quote, "We commend with increased confidence the new Directory to the favor of American Baptists as a sound and scriptural exposition of New Testament Church polity as represented by our faith and practice.''

On page 4, five outstanding Baptists of former days are quoted as commending this Directory, Dr. Hovey, then President of Newton Theological Seminary, Dr. Strong, then President of Rochester Theological Seminary, Dr. Weston, then President of Crozier Theological Seminary, Dr. Corey, then President of Richmond Theological Seminary, Dr. MacArthur, then Pastor of Calvary Baptist Church, New York. This then sets Hiscox Directory squarely before us as a sound and capable guide for Baptist Churches in the matter of polity.

On page 335 speaking of Associations Dr. Hiscox says ''No Church is under obligation to affiliate with it; and any connected Church can withdraw cooperation, at any time, for any reasons which seem to itself sufficient, without prejudice to either its evangelical or its denominational reputation and standing.'' Here then is the straight out statement that a Baptist Church can withdraw from the organized work at any time and for reasons sufficient to no one but itself, without prejudice to its Denominational reputation and standing. In other words Dr. Hiscox is stating what we have been trying to present for years, namely, that the Conventions and Associations are not the Denomination. Therefore, when a Church withdraws from a Convention or an Association it does not cease to be a Baptist Church.

The Central Baptist Church of Gary, Indiana withdrew from the Conventions February 13, 1935. We are now being published all over the State as no longer a Baptist Church. Dr. T. J. Parsons, Executive Secretary, so declares. In view of this it is interesting to quote from the Indiana Baptist Observer, issue of May 12, 1921, when Dr. Parsons was the Editor and Manager. He runs an article on page 5 by M. C. Lough on ''Civil and Religious Liberty.'' At the head of the article Dr. Parsons has an editor's note in which he commends the article and says that it is so good that he is passing it on to his readers. I quote from this article: ''True, Baptist Churches form Associations, and these Associations may make up a General Association, which is a State organization, and these State Associations may unite in National Conventions, but none of these bodies possess any authority over a local Baptist Church. If a Baptist Church does not wish to affiliate with an Association it can drop out of the Association, but there is no way of keeping the congregation from going on in its own way as a regular Baptist Church so long as it observes the scriptural principles adhered to by the Denomination.''

CORRECTION FROM WITHIN HOPELESS

We believe it to be an utterly hopeless task to attempt to bring to pass any adequate correction from within of the evils either of Modernism already outlined, or of Communism which is set forth in the last section of this book. There are many reasons which lead us to this conviction, but we present one that is foremost in our mind, namely the voting power of the paid secretarial staff. My good friend, Dr. W. B. Riley, who does not agree with my position of withdrawal, but feels that the situation can be corrected from within, is himself the most ready of all to admit the seriousness of this particular phase of the situation. He has said to me often, ''Ketcham, we must disfranchise the salaried servants of the Convention, for they hold the balance of power on any vote taken.'' The inevitable reply to such a statement is that as long as the salaried servants have a right to vote, they would of course have a right to vote on any such resolutions calling for the surrender of their voting power. Since by Dr. Riley's own admission, they now hold the balance of power on any vote, how then can they be disfranchised? One would hardly expect them to vote in favor of disfranchising themselves! That the salaried servant group in the Northern Baptist Convention does hold the balance of power has been proved many times.

At the Northern Baptist Convention held in Chicago, the militant Fundamentalist group presented a complete ballot for all Convention officers and committees. The names on this ballot were taken from the original Convention ballot in every instance where the individual was known to be Fundamental, substitutions being made for only such as were known to be untrue to the historic Baptist faith. Then the entire ballot was printed and distributed on the floor of the Convention along with the Convention ballot. Every delegate in the audience held in his hand two ballots. If he wanted to vote a mixed ticket of Modernists and Fundamentalists, all he had to do was to mark the Convention ballot. If he wanted to vote a straight Fundamental ticket, all he had to do was to mark the other ballot. There was no cause for confusion and neither was there any confusion. We have forgotten the exact figures, but we do recall distinctly that the margin by which the Convention ballot won over the substituted ballot was less than the number of salaried servants of the Conventions (State and National), who were present at the Chicago Convention. In other words, had the salaried servants of the Northern Baptist Convention and its affiliate state conventions, been barred from voting that day, the Fundamentalist ticket would have won. This has happened on many occasions.

One may rest assured that the army of salaried servants, secretaries, under secretaries, clerks, assistants, etc. will pretty much as a whole, vote the machine program. We believe that the disfranchisement of the servants of the Convention is a sound policy, but how it can be done without a vote of the Convention is another matter, and since the army of salaried servants can vote on the issue of disfranchisement, well—there you are!

CONVENTION VERSUS DENOMINATION

Baptists everywhere need to keep in mind that the Convention it not the Denomination. We know full well that the Convention officials make the words synonymous, but that does not make it so. They contend that a church which withdraws from the Northern Baptist Convention has thereby withdrawn from the Denomination. A moment's sober reflection will reveal that this cannot be. If the Northern Baptist Convention is the Baptist Denomination, then we would ask what is the Southern Baptist Convention? The Canadian Baptist Convention? The English Baptist Union, etc.? It ought to be self-evident at once that no Baptist church has to belong to any certain organized group of Baptist churches in order to be "in the Denomination." The Denomination is larger than any or all Conventions. The Denomination was here long, long centuries before the Conventions arrived. Central Baptist Church of Gary, Indiana, and scores of other Baptist churches have withdrawn from the Conventions, but by no means have they withdrawn from the Denomination. If we had done that, we would not be bothering ourselves with the presentation of the evidence in this book.

FACTS FOR BAPTISTS TO FACE

Reproduction of
THE MOST BLASPHEMOUS CARTOON EVER PRINTED
Showing the real spirit of the Bolshevik Movement—Atheistic, Anti-Christian.

Translation of the caption:
"TAKE, EAT, THIS IS MY BODY." (Matt. 26:26)

A front page cartoon, reproduced in original colours, from **The Godless**, illustrated anti-religious weekly PUBLISHED IN MOSCOW BY THE COMMUNIST PARTY OF RUSSIA. A careful study of the detail will disclose a particularly vicious sacrilege, depicted in a style now called "advanced" or "Russian" art.

? Can We ?
Prevent War
Will We Stop Fascism?

These are vital and imminent questions confronting every worker, farmer, professional, and every honest middle-class person.

Professor Robert Morss Lovett, veteran champion of peace and the more abundant life, will discuss these questions.

That preparations for fascism and war are going on with increasing speed is indicated by the newspapers, radio, huge war appropriations, C. C. C. camps, Hearst, Huey Long, Coughlin, N.R.A., terror and double-cross in strikes, inflation (reduction of buying power), etc.

Shall we go through the horrors of another war (compared to which the last war was a children's squabble and in which the civilian population will suffer as much as those at the front) to make again several thousand new war millionaires?

Shall we be lied and fooled into another war by their propaganda of denfense, democracy; (blood) prosperity, yellow or red menace, etc? We must unite regardless of social, religious, or political views to defeat the imperialist war makers and head off fascism. We must fight against being used as cannon fodder and coolie slaves.

The American League Against War and Fascism, a part of the International League Against War and Fascism, is such an organization. The local branch meets in the Brooks House every Friday evening at 8 p.m. and invites you to these meetings.

If you want the proofs of the danger of war and fascism in the U. S. and want to know the program of the American League Against War and Fascism come and bring your friends to listen to

PROFESSOR ROBERT MORSS LOVETT
of Chicago University and vice chairman
of the League, and local speakers.

TUESDAY EVENING, APRIL 23
at 7:30 p. m.

BROOKS HOUSE AUDITORIUM
Corner Conkey Street and Howard Avenue

PART TWO

Communism

I
WHAT IS COMMUNISM

Through the years our heart has been made heavy by the presence of modernism stalking through the corridors of our denominational work, but now we have the added spectacle of Communism joining hands with it and these two monsters are becoming so thoroughly entrenched that we actually despair of recovery. What is Communism? Perhaps this poster which lies before me may give us some idea. This cartoon is reproduced from "The Godless" an illustrated anti-religious weekly, published in Moscow by the Communist party of Russia. Underneath the cartoon are these words, "Take, eat, this is my body. Matthew 26:26." The center figure in this cartoon is a grotesque caricature of the Lord Jesus Christ. Swarming around and over his body is a hoard of men and women. One woman has just pulled a great chunk of flesh from one of the legs of Christ and is gnawing away at it. A man is pictured eating away a foot. Others seem to be tearing an arm from the Savior and greedily running away to eat it. A great hole has been poked in the side of Christ and blood is gushing forth being caught in a big container preparatory to drinking. The most revolting of all is found when we see the abdomen of the Saviour opened and men and women eating the intestines. This is the Communist view of the broken body and shed blood of the Lord Jesus Christ.

Further evidence of their attitude toward Christianity is to be found in such horifying examples as the beheading, almost within the last year, of our two young friends John and Betty Stam on the mission fields in China. A sixteen year old Communist wielded the sword that beheaded Betty.

Much more space could be taken up with the presentation of such evidence. The boast of the Communist leaders of Russia is that they will annihilate God from the face of the earth and likewise from His Heavens. We shall refer later on in this article to the pacifist attitude of the Communist party in the United States.

COMMUNISM IN BAPTIST RANKS
COLGATE-ROCHESTER DIVINITY SCHOOL

The purpose of this article is to show so far as possible in the space permitted, just how Communism has entrenched itself in Baptist ranks. At the very outset let it be understood that I do not charge any Baptist leader with actually being a Communist. So far as I know, no Baptist actually belongs to the Communist party, but what we do contend and shall demonstrate is that on the part of some of the leaders, there is an increasing sympathy with and propagation of some of the Communistic principles which are most deadly.

On December 10, 1933, Professor Charles C. Weber, Industrial Secretary of the World Fellowship of Reconciliation (organized to bring about the recognition of Russia) spoke before the student body of Colgate Rochester Divinity School in Rochester, New York. He announced that the future missionary would have to be a teacher of Communistic and Socialistic principles if he expects to be a success. Quoting from his address, I read:

"The missionary of the future will sustain the workers in their efforts by picketing with strikers and organize protest meetings against police interference. Missionaries should establish birth control clinics. . . . He will point out the contribution of Soviet Russia in her attempt to establish a new social order."

When it is remembered that Dr. Albert W. Beaven, president of this divinity school, at that time was president of the Northern Baptist Convention, and that he is now vice-president of the World's Baptist Alliance, and when it is further known that he condoned the appearance of Mr. Weber before the student body, the implications are not the most reassuring.

ROCHESTER BAPTISTS SOCIALISTIC

In this same city of Rochester, September 28, 1934, the Baptist Union comprised of all the Baptist churches of Rochester and vicinity, passed a resolution which is state Socialism pure and simple. It contained four recommendations, as follows:

1. Society, or people acting through the state, shall assume control of all natural resources of the nation.

2. Society shall control or own all natural monopolies in relation to the necessities of modern living.

3. Society should control or own competitive businesses that control the necessities of life. Competitive profit systems should be restricted to non-essentials of life.

4. Society should take over entire control of money and banking functions conducted as non-profit producing social service.

DR. ALBERT W. BEAVEN

Dr. Beaven, president of Rochester Colgate Divinity School, vice-president of the World's Baptist Alliance, former president of the Northern Baptist Convention, and former president of the Federal Council of Churches of Christ in America, on November 30 signed a letter to the President of the United States, which purported to speak for the ministers in which he says: "You have done far more than any previous administration, but they (the ministers) are convinced that you have not gone far enough." In a later paragraph in the letter which Dr. Beaven signed, he frowns upon the use of police and militia for the quelling of strike riots. The letter urges the President to take "drastic steps" to bring about further improvement. "This improvement," says Dr. Beaven, "involves transferring the distribution of the necessities of life as well as other consumptive goods to co-operatives. It involves the nationalization of the basic industries. . . . . . To the extent that you take steps to make these fundamental changes, we can and will support you."

Dr. Beaven is also a sponsor in Rochester for the League of Industrial Democracy. The League is Communistic to its very foundation and is headed by Robert Morss Lovett, whom even a whitewashing legislative committee could not swallow.

COMMISSION ON CHRISTIAN SOCIAL ACTION

At its convention in Rochester, New York, in 1934, the Northern Baptist Convention appointed a committee of nine known as the Commission on Christian Social Action to bring in a definite report on all matters involved. The Convention ordered that the committee's report should be published in denominational papers at least one month before the 1935 convention in Colorado Springs. The first release of the report of the Committee of nine created such a storm of protest that the committee eliminated some of its most radical recommendations before it made its official report to the Convention.

From page Seven of this report I quote:

"On April 24 and 25, 1935, a committee of the commission met in Chicago immediately in advance of the release of the report for publication after it had been reviewed and approved by all the members of the commission."

Here is the admission that the Social Commission's report in its original form as well as in its final form, was approved by nine men and women who are of sufficient prominence in Baptist circles to be named upon this most important commission. From page eleven of the final report, I quote:

"The course of sanity and safety for America is to assure these liberties (civil liberties) even for those whose ideas are admittedly contrary to our established order and religious faith, and whose political philosophy would deny these liberties to others were they in power."

The last few words of this quotation certainly describes perfectly the Communist party. From page fifteen, I quote:

"We stand for a cooperative commonwealth."

A very familiar term in the parlance of Communists. On page eighteen of the report, the commission frankly endorses and recommends the Consumers Cooperatives. This of course is a blow at all private industry and individual initiative. Quoting from J. B. Warbassee's book, "Cooperative Democracy" Page 258 I read:

"The ultimate aim of the Consumers movement should be to purchase the land from the farmers and employ the latter as agricultural worker."

The Communist Internationale of July, 1928, says: "The Cooperative League of North America contains considerable left wing elements." Quoting from the same magazine I read:

"The United Workers Cooperative Association of New York City is building a series of houses; controls a number of camps for workers and conducts cultural work on a Communistic basis."

THE FAMOUS BROWN ENVELOPE

Last fall every Baptist preacher in the Northern Baptist Convention received a large brown envelope carrying in the upper left hand corner these words, "Pastor's Packet for Social Action" from the Northern Baptist Convention, 152 Madison Avenue, New York. The envelope contained eight pieces of literature including the report of the Commission on Christian Social Action presented at Colorado Springs last June, program suggestions for world peace, etc., etc. There was also a four page folder listing publications which Baptist preachers can secure from the National Council for Prevention of War at Washington, D. C. The National Council for Prevention of War has as its executive secretary, Mr. Frederick J. Libby. The Washington Post of January 23, 1925, states:

"Frederick J. Libby, super-pacifist, executive secretary of the National Council for the Prevention of War, yesterday was denied the right to speak in the public schools of the District of Columbia. This was done by the action of the Board of Education in adopting a report presented at yesterday's meeting of the special committee to investigate Libby."

The report said in part, as follows:

"With the desire to be correct in our conclusions we have sought and have carefully studied and considered the masses of records submitted to us, bearing upon the activities of said Libby; and have been controlled by the broad scope and purposes underlying the patriotic organization of which we are members.

"The perusal of the documentary evidence we have had in hand gives an astounding revelation of the extent and character of the propaganda work throughout the country, originating with the class of revolutionary organizations now operating in this country, whose object and purpose is to undermine and, if possible, to destroy the prosperity now enjoyed by all who live within our borders and who respect our Constitution and laws.

"Through their secret agents and representatives, acting under their orders and instructions, they have become active in their pernicious work; and through organizations pretending to aid the masses, they seek to create discontent, to arouse ill feeling by misrepresenting facts, and so to mislead the misinformed and ignorant classes among our fellow citizens.

"From the evidence submitted to us we have become convinced that Frederick J. Libby is one of the recognized leaders in the movement originated with the avowed enemies of this country."

Seymour Waldman, up until recently was editor of the Bulletins of the National Council for Prevention of War. He is now head of the Washington Bureau of the Communist Daily Worker. With men like this at the head of the National Council for Prevention of War, it would seem a rather strange place to send Baptist preachers for peace material. The famous brown envelope coming from Baptist headquarters contained a 16-page paper called "Peace Action," a great portion of which was written by Frederick J. Libby. The fact that Mr. Libby was barred from the public schools of Washington, D. C., did not bar him from the brown envelope.

MR. LIBBY PROMOTED

Last December, the entire official family of the Northern Baptist Convention and subsidiary State Conventions met in Chicago in the Stevens Hotel for two or three days of conference. According to the official report of that conference, Mr. Frederick J. Libby delivered an address on "How American Baptists Can Help in the Present World Crisis." Was there no one else in all the United States who could tell American Baptists that, without calling in a man who because of his radical statements is barred from the use of public schools and is recorded by the committee of investigation as one of the country's dangerous enemies?

THE FEDERAL COUNCIL OF CHURCHES OF CHRIST IN AMERICA

It would take volumes for us to go into all of the ramifications of the Federal Council of Churches of Christ in America, but we make the assertion and have the proof to back it that the Federal Council is tied up hand and glove with some of the most radical Communistic leaders and organizations in this country.

On April 1, 1935, the Naval Intelligence section presented to Congress, a report dealing with their investigation of subversive activities in the United States. They listed several organizations which were carrying on activities subversive to the best interests of the peace and safety of the United States, among them was the American League Against War and Fascism, National Labor Defense, The National Student League, American Civil Liberties Union, The National Council for the Prevention of War, and THE FEDERAL COUNCIL OF CHURCHES OF CHRIST IN AMERICA.

BROOKS HOUSE IN HAMMOND

The American Baptist Home Mission Society conducts throughout the Northern Baptist Convention territory what they call Christian centers. They are really settlement houses to do work among foreign speaking peoples. Rev. J. M. Hestenes is the director in charge of all these centers numbering around thirty. He is however, personally in charge of the one located in Hammond, Indiana, known as Brooks House.

On the 24th of January, 1935, Mr. Hestenes opened the auditorium of Brooks House to the Communists of the Calumet region for the purpose of conducting a memorial service in honor of the eleventh anniversary of the death of Lenin. Lydia Oken of the Gary Communist Workers' School delivered the address on "What Lenin Did for Russia." According to a poster passed out from door to door in the city of Hammond, the American League Against War and Fascism meets every Friday night in the Brooks House auditorium. The particular handbill which I hold advertises Professor Robert Morss Lovett as the speaker for April 23, 1935.

We understand that Mr. Hestenes is insisting that the American League Against War and Fascism is not a Communist organization and therefore he cannot be charged with opening Brooks House to Communists for more than one meeting. Just why he should open it for one, nobody seems to know. But what about the family tree of this American League Against War and Fascism? I quote from the Communist Internationale of January, 1934, page 78. The editor is giving a report of the various activities of the Communist party. He says:

"We (the Communist party) led a highly successful United States congress against war which brought together 2,616 delegates from all over the country..... The congress from the beginning was led by our party quite openly..... This success was, of course, largely due to the very favorable situation and the position of our party as almost a monopolist of anti-war movement in the United States..... The congress set up a permanent organization on a federative basis called the American League Against War and Fascism."

Please note the open frank statement, that the Communist party considers itself the leader if not the monopolist of anti-war propaganda in the United States. This is exactly the charge we have been making and that scores of these apparently disconnected societies and organizations working for non-preparedness in the United States are but affiliated fingers reaching out from the mighty hand of Communism. Be that as it may, here is the open declaration that the American League Against War and Fascism is a child of the Communist outfit. We understand that the League is not now meeting in Brooks House, but we want the reader to understand that they would have been meeting there had it not been for our exposure.

Robert Morss Lovett, Chicago University professor, was ordered removed from the university staff by the Illinois State Legislature, on account of his Communistic views and connections, but he was nevertheless an acceptable speaker on the platform of Brooks House. We have been told that he did not speak, but if so, the only reason was because we turned the heat on.

It is more than passing strange that while the Communists are amusing themselves drawing pictures of men and women eating Christ's intestines, and clipping the heads off of Christian ministers, that the Rev. J. M. Hestenes opens the doors of the American Baptist Home Mission Society's auditorium to this same crowd. And it is still more than passing strange that while the evidence of all of this has been in the hands of Convention authorities ever since it happened, Mr. Hestenes is still retained, but those of us who produced the evidence have been called "skunks", "traitors", "deserters", "obstructionists", and in fact anything and everything but Christians.

SUNDAY SCHOOL LITERATURE

The infiltration of this God-denying Communism into Baptist circles is further seen in some of our Sunday School publications. The American Baptist Publication Society publishes a paper called "Young People" for distribution among the young people of our Sunday School. Last June a serial story called "New-Altars" ran for four weeks. The stories have to do with life in Russia. In each of the four issues, as a preliminary to the story installment there appeared a few paragraphs of editorial comments. We quote from some of them:

> "American traditions of individual liberty may cause many of us to question the justice of those in power, herding peasants into collective farming against their will, and exiling millions of the more recalcitrant. Nevertheless the program has already justified itself. . . . . But it (life in Russia) daily grows easier. . . . . That the youth of new Russia are less spiritual than their elders is questionable. They have for the time being substituted faith in a new social system for faith in God."

All of this editorial comment is designed to throw a favorable light upon the rule of the Soviet government in Russia.

SOME CONCLUSIONS

The mass of evidence lying here before us would require books to be written to properly present it. We must however, pass all that by. Surely every sane thinking American is against war, but we charge that the Communist at heart is not against war. It is true that almost every organization in this country which has peace as its objective is either Communistically organized or Communistically controlled, but it is also true that the Soviet Communist government of Russia has built up in their home land the most powerful military machine ever known on the face of the earth. At this hour they have more than one million men under arms and have just appropriated multiplied hundreds of 'millions of dollars to be spent this year in the building up of a still greater army. Military training is compulsory in Russia, and yet Communistic influence is tearing American college life into shreds by propaganda against compulsory military training in public institutions of education.

Mr. Hathaway, editor of the Communist Daily Worker in the issue of July 4, declares: "Every day that we can prevent war among the imperialist nations of the earth, gives us time to add one more tank to our great red army." Even a blind man can see that the policy of the Communist government of Russia is to reduce the United States of America to a state of anemic helplessness and then proceed to overthrow the established order and set up the Communist reign in America, and a bunch of pussy-footing, compromising Modernistic pink-tea-drinking preachers seem to have no better sense than to join hands with this Godless outfit.

Every Baptist pastor should have constantly on his desk a copy of Mrs. Elizabeth Dilling's book, "The Red Network." This book gives the pedigree of everyone of these scores of Communistic controlled organizations working in our country, and to this hour not a single, solitary statement in the book of more than 300 pages has been disproved. There is enough in the book to put Mrs. Dilling behind the bars the rest of her life if what she says is not so. The tragedy of it is, not that Mrs. Dilling has told the truth but that there was such truth for her to tell. At any rate, no Baptist pastor or leader needs to be in ignorance as to what kind of a crowd he is working with.

Once more we remind the reader that the facts presented in this book are only a few of the many which could be brought forward, but if the facing of these facts herein presented does not convince one that there is a hopeless situation confronting Baptists, then a book twice the size of this would be useless.

The Growing Menace of the "Social Gospel"

By

J. E. CONANT, D. D.
Bible Teacher and Evangelist

Author of *The Church, the Schools, and Evolution; Divine Dynamite; How to Get Decisions in Personal Work; Why the Pastor Failed; Every Member Evangelism; Is the Devil in Modern Amusements?*; etc.

CHICAGO
THE BIBLE INSTITUTE COLPORTAGE ASS'N
843-845 North Wells Street

Price 30c

Copyright, 1937, by
THE BIBLE INSTITUTE COLPORTAGE ASSOCIATION
OF CHICAGO

CONTENTS

                                                                                              PAGE

   I. *The Growing Ills of the Social Order* 7

  II. *The Perpetual Fight for Human Liberty* . . . 15

 III. *Capital Punishment and Human Rights* . . . 24

 IV. *Our National Government and Religious Freedom* 31

  V. *The Sworn Enemies of Our Constitution* . . . 41

 VI. *The Destructive Power of the "Social Gospel"* . 51

VII. *The Trend Toward Union of Church and State* . 59

Also By Dr. Conant

THE CHURCH, THE SCHOOLS, AND EVOLUTION
96 pages, art stock covers, 35c net

DIVINE DYNAMITE
39 pages, art stock covers, 20c net

WHY THE PASTOR FAILED
48 pages, art stock covers, 25c net

WHY ALL "GOOD PEOPLE" WILL BE LOST
32 pages, self cover, 10c

HOW TO GET DECISIONS IN PERSONAL WORK
39 pages, art stock covers, 20c net

EVERY MEMBER EVANGELISM
225 pages, cloth, $1.50 net

IS THE DEVIL IN MODERN AMUSEMENTS?
44 pages, art stock covers, 20c net

The Bible Institute Colportage Ass'n
843-845 North Wells Street
CHICAGO

Printed in the United States of America

FOREWORD

DISCUSSIONS of the "Social Gospel" are steadily on the increase. Strangely enough, a growing volume of propaganda for it is going out from sources that profess to be mutually antagonistic. Certain aggressive leaders in the professed Church are actually in enthusiastic agreement with atheists in the pushing of a social program which, it is promised, will right the economic wrongs and cure the social ills of humanity.

Such an amazing situation brings confusion to many, while others are deceived into sympathy with the program, because they do not understand the underlying fallacies of this pernicious philosophy.

We are in such perilous days that the minds of God's people are seriously disturbed and their faith sorely tried, as Satan works desperately to deceive, if possible, the very elect. His wiles are most deceptive when he appears as an angel of light, and his ministers most dangerous when they proclaim themselves as ministers of righteousness (2 Corinthians 11:14, 15). And this is precisely the thing he is doing in the "Social Gospel."

Because so many in high places, whom great numbers of God's people trust for spiritual leadership, are but blind leaders heading their followers toward the ditch, this brochure is sent forth with the earnest prayer of the author that God will graciously use it to make clear to its readers the underlying errors of the wholly unscriptural philosophy of the "Social Gospel," and deliver those who are deceived thereby.

J. E. CONANT.

Portland, Oregon.

Chapter I

THE GROWING ILLS OF THE SOCIAL ORDER

CRITICISM of the Social Order is no new thing. Today it is not only widespread but greatly on the increase.

That the social and economic relations of men are all out of order and deeply diseased is too clear to admit of argument.

The whole social fabric is shot through with political evils that permit special privilege and entrenched injustice, with economic wrongs that result in poverty, hunger and wretchedness, and with social cruelties that end in fruitless and ruined lives.

Multitudes suffer tragically, some of them almost to despair, under such wrongs and inequalities, that the cry for relief is heard from many quarters. The call increases for men and nations to become so brotherly that oppression and tyranny will end, injustices will find no more place among men, and wars will cease to the ends of the earth.

The quest for relief, long growing more insistent, is now becoming so feverish that self-announced doctors of the social order are multiplying around us, until the air is being filled with many voices clamoring to be heard, and confusion is steadily on the increase.

The Quest for Power

In the attempt to find the way out of our difficulties, the search is taking the form of a quest for the right kind of *power*, from the right *source*, applied in the right *direction*.

8 The Growing Menace of the "Social Gospel"

Looking into the past, men are noting the time when the place of power in the social order was occupied by kings and emperors who came into power by the accident of birth, and reminding us that the remedy for the ills of society was not found under that order.

Then they note that in more recent days, and even up until now, money has held the place of power. We are shown that wealth, especially as capital, has become so centralized that its power has grown to be all but irresistible, and that now it has waxed so selfish and cruelly irresponsible that man's cry for a social order based on brotherhood is getting only the response of its own echo.

This shows, we are told, that the capitalistic system, equally with that under kings, is a complete social and economic failure, and that its end must be hastened, by violence, if necessary, so as to clear the way for the system that will really cure our tragic ills.

Since both kings and capital have failed to produce a cure, men are loudly insisting that if the *common people,* the "proletariat," are given a chance, they will lead the way to relief. With kings already dethroned, and capitalism, so we are told, soon to be a thing of the past, the common people will lead out into such a realization of the *brotherhood of man* that at last it will be demonstrated that a coöperative social order will bring man to his longed for Utopia. This, it is said, will be the kingdom of God on earth, brought in by the power of human brotherhood.

With such an objective, it is natural that prominent among the agitators in the movement should be outstanding leaders of the modernistic element in the professed Church, with some who are not of that type but who do not see God's program for this Age, blindly following.

It seems never to occur to the increasing number who are listening to these self-appointed analysts of our social ills,

The Growing Ills of the Social Order 9

that the reasoning which seems so faultless and the conclusions which seem so obvious could possibly be leading toward greater confusion and a final chaos. Stung by present suffering under economic inequalities, urged on by a glittering prospect of the future relief promised by these social dreamers, multitudes are trustingly following these blind and blundering leaders toward the ditch.

These leaders cite a sickening list of ills which appear, on the surface, to grow directly out of the capitalistic system. They then proceed to indict the system as the breeder of all the heartless and selfish cruelties which cause these ills. And then they conclude that to destroy the system and change to some sort of coöperative brotherhood will cure our ills. The reasoning seems faultless, but are the conclusions valid? That depends on several things:

1. Has the reasoning started from the right premise when it is assumed that the capitalistic system has caused the greed and cruel selfishness from which our ills arise? Are no men greedy and selfish except capitalists?

2. Are the correct laws of logic followed in reasoning from particular ills to general causes?

3. Assuming that a coöperative brotherhood would really cure our ills, what evidence is there that it can actually be brought into practical operation?

How to Diagnose the Disease

These questions must all have answers that are so obvious that they will appear axiomatic, before people of thoughtful and well-seasoned judgment can even begin to reason toward right conclusions. So the analysis must be pushed back to the *ultimate causes* of our maladies. The *disease* must be diagnosed before the *prescription* can be written. And we can never arrive at a correct diagnosis by such incorrect reasoning as the social doctors seem to be doing, neither can we even guess at a cure from such a superficial diagnosis as their upside-down logic leads them to.

We must therefore isolate and bring into full view the ultimate *general* cause of *all* our ills, before we can hope to make even a start in finding our way to the cause of our present *particular* ills, or to arrive at the cure that will work, if there is such a cure. In other words, we must follow the laws of logic, and reason from the general to the particular, and not the reverse, as our social dreamers are doing.

An illustration of the mischief and confusion caused by this upside-down reasoning is found among believers in so-called divine healing. Here is a person, for illustration, who has experienced what seems to be a genuine, miraculous bodily healing without means, in answer to the prayer of faith. The argument then starts from that *particular* case and reasons to the conclusion that such cases of healing should become *general* among Christians. This compels the further conclusion that those Christians who are not thus healed have something wrong in their lives, or they, too, would experience a similar healing when they go to God for it.

Such a conclusion is wholly invalid, for instead of finding and reasoning from the *general* law or laws of *Scripture* concerning bodily healing, whether with or without means, they reason from a *particular* case in the *experience* of some Christian with whom God has dealt graciously in His own sovereignty, thus reversing and nullifying the laws of logic, and arriving at conclusions that cannot be sustained from Scripture, when rightly understood, and that certainly do not work out in practice.

The reasoning of the social planners is of the same order. They will cite, for example, some *particular* case of successful coöperative or governmental economic action, and then walk straight on to the conclusion that this kind of action should and could be made to work in the *general* field of the whole economic and social structure. But such reasoning is a reversal of the laws of logic, and the conclusions are wholly unreliable.

Getting Back to First Causes

The only safe and reasonable thing to do, therefore, is to get back to *first causes,* and we will then have some reliable premises from which to start, and can arrive at the remedy for our ills, provided we follow the laws of logic to the end.

What, precisely, then, is the ultimate cause of the terrible economic and social wrongs of our time? If it is the particular economic and social order of which we are a part, then why have these same ills kept recurring with deadly repetition in every economic and social order of every civilization the world has ever seen? Why do the denunciations of the prophets of Israel, that nation most favored of God, outline, with amazing accuracy, the social ills of our day? Why does James (5:1-6) denounce the murderous economic wrongs of this very hour, if they did not exist in his day, and why have these same ills persisted through every form of social order from his day until ours?

The simple fact is that these ills have afflicted humanity through every economic order, from the vicious capitalism that permitted 1,800 men in Rome to own practically the whole known world; that allowed one percent of the people in Persia to own all the land; that permitted one percent in Egypt to own 97 percent of all the wealth, to the other extreme of the numerous coöperative and socialistic experiments that have both been tried and have failed at different times and in different places. And yet no economic order, from capitalism to socialism, has ever made the least contribution toward the cure of man's fundamental ills.

It is amazing how any man, in spite of this clear contra-

12 *The Growing Menace of the "Social Gospel"*

diction of history, can persistently claim that if we should scrap our present order and begin to live by a coöperative and communal program, every one could have a fair share of the products of labor, and a fair chance to be freed from what are said to be the wrongs of the present order.

Was It Communism in the Early Church?

If such a program can really be made to work, it certainly should have worked 1,900 years ago, in the case of the early Church, as described in Acts 4:34 to 5:11. For the foundation was there laid for the most perfect communal society that can be conceived of, under the most ideal conditions that can be imagined, and yet it proved to be a dismal failure in a short space of time.

Analysis of the facts in this story will show that if such a program, attempted by such a people, under such favorable conditions, was a failure, no group of people can ever hope to make it work.

Nine facts in this story come to light under analysis that show why such a coöperative or communal program could never be made to work.

1. It was not a new economic system, because only civil government can introduce and maintain such a system, and also because there was no community of ownership, either of natural resources or of the means of production, but of the means of subsistence only.

2. The people who adopted the program were all spiritual, for they had all been born again, and so they were as fully united around one altruistic purpose, and in one bond of fellowship, as human beings on this earth can ever be.

3. Their original motive was entirely unselfish, for private, selfish interests had no place in the program.

4. Their primary purpose was spiritual, not economic, for

The Growing Ills of the Social Order 13

their community of possessions was only incidental to their main purpose, which was coöperative spiritual service.

5. The community of goods was wholly voluntary, for it was not commanded, either by the Holy Spirit or by the apostles.

6. Its principles were the very opposite of those of Communism, for they said: "What is mine is yours"—a thing impossible to any but the saved; while Communism says: "What is yours is mine"—a thing inevitable with all who are lost, for self is first always with them.

7. It was followed with full liberty, for there was not even a hindering example of failure in any other church. It was followed by the church in Jerusalem only.

8. The community soon became the victim of deception and fraud through Ananias and Sapphira, and of selfishness through neglect of the needy, and finally the whole program failed.

9. This failure on such a small scale with such an ideal group proved it to be an impossible economic system for the world at large, for the whole world-system is always in helpless slavery to selfishness and greed, and is forever practicing fraud and deception.

It not only shows extremely superficial thinking, therefore, to blame our ills on the capitalist system, but it is the very upside-down reasoning that selects a particular economic order from the many that have existed, and concludes that because certain terrible ills seem to prosper under it, this system is therefore the cause of all our ills in general. That is, it is reasoning from the particular to the general, and is logic walking backward.

There is but one safe method to pursue, if we are to find the ultimate cause of our ills, which began in principle with what Cain did to Abel, and that is to get back to *God's ulti-*

mate purpose in the creation of man. For when that purpose is brought to light, we must, in all reason, find in it the only safe foundation for any adequate philosophy of characteristic human behavior.

If God's purpose is found to be *benevolent,* and if we find *malevolence* instead existing among men, we then have the presumption established at once that such a spirit arises from man's failure to respond to the benevolent purpose and attitude of God, and we will be on our way, not only toward discovery of the ultimate cause of our ills, but also toward the finding of a remedy, if any can be found. This is therefore where we must begin our analysis.

Chapter II

THE PERPETUAL FIGHT FOR HUMAN LIBERTY

THE most profound statement made anywhere in God's Word concerning His ultimate purpose in the creation of man lies in the simple words: *"God is love."*

That defines and conditions every relationship between God and man. There is no attitude of God, even to that found in His condemnation and judgment of those who refuse His love, that is outside of, or foreign to, that love. For the holiness and righteousness which condemns and executes the penalty on those who *hate* His love is but love in action on behalf of all who *respond* to His love. All who hate God's love are out of all spiritual harmony with those who yield to His love, their feeling toward them tending to become intolerant, even as they are intolerant of God Himself. And so God can do no less than shield those who love Him from those who are intolerant of Him and of them, and this can be done only in the separation of one group from the other.

Starting, then, from the profound fact of God's glorious purpose of love for mankind, we can move on to an understanding of man's attitude toward this purpose. Think of what this wonderful purpose of God involved.

Love is self-giving. Love moves the one it possesses to give himself in every way that will bring happiness to the one he loves. He withholds nothing that will bring joy to the one loved, and bestows everything that will bring true pleasure and satisfaction. Love, therefore, because it is self-giving, demands one who can be loved; for to be able to love, and yet to have no one upon whom to lavish one's love, is torment indeed.

There are three Persons in the Godhead, the Father, the Son and the Holy Spirit, each lavishing eternal and unlimited love on the other Persons of the Trinity, and enjoying the infinite delight of self-giving.

But the Triune God desired also to have objects of divine love outside the Godhead, and so the angels were placed in His universe as the objects of that love. Every angel is a separate and original creation, and God pours out His love on each one in the great angelic host in the form of righteousness and justice, lavishing upon them all that a righteous God could give. And even when a great company of them turned to self-love, which caused them to hate the love of God, He was compelled, still acting in righteousness and justice, to separate them from the rest of the angels, that He might protect those who were willing to receive His love from the disease of sinful self-love, which is the most contagious and fatal disease in the universe.

But there is another side to God's love besides *justice*. So He created and placed on the earth the race of man, foreseeing that there would be a call across the course of human history to reveal to the universe the *mercy* side of His love. Thus, in His governmental dealing with both angels and men, the full-orbed revelation of both the justice and mercy aspects of His love will go out eternally to all the universe.

God's Love Calls for Response

Moving on from the fact of God's love and its nature as self-giving, and from the necessary demand for those in the universe who can receive His love, we arrive at the next

The Perpetual Fight for Human Liberty 17

logical requirement. God's love calls not simply for receivers, but for such receivers as will be able to respond as freely and fully as He gives. For there is nothing that so surely breaks a heart that loves as not be loved in return.

God therefore created both angels and men with the power of choice, and a capacity to respond to Him with an answering love. A moment of thought will make this plain.

Love is *preference*. The one I love I prefer to myself, and defer to him in everything that can make him happy. And preference is *ratherness*. That which I prefer is the thing I had rather have. And ratherness in action is *choice*.

The power to love and the capacity to choose are one and the same thing. God gifted us with this power of choice that we might have the capacity to love Him in return for His love.

Moving on, now, to the next thought, the capacity to choose involves the necessity to make choices, when alternatives are presented. This, in turn, requires the asking of questions in the weighing of evidence, for or against any given choice. All questions that concern our relations with God are, of course, moral questions, and necessarily have a direct bearing on God's purpose of love toward us.

Just as His *heart* purposes our perfect happiness, so His *will* is the realm inside of which those purposes can be made available. That is, those who abide in His will are in the one place where His love operates. It cannot make happy nor even reach those outside of His will, who live in the realm of self-will. In the asking of questions, therefore, in making choices, the final question, sooner or later, is sure to come up for choice.

The Ultimate Moral Question

The final moral question is, of course, the one beyond which it is impossible for thought to go, and outside of which there can be no other moral question, under any circumstances, through all eternity. This question, contrary to what one might suppose, is the simplest question that can be asked. It is just this: *Is God's will or my own will best for me?*

There can be no moral question outside of that, and there is none beyond it. That question involves every other moral question whatsoever, for it takes in everything that relates to God's purpose of love toward us, since it has wholly to do with what His will is set to carry out for our welfare and happiness, none of which can possibly be carried out unless we are wholly in His will.

When once this question arises, it must be answered. There are only two possible ways to answer it: either by the *authority of the Creator,* or the *experiment of the creature.*

There can be no absolute certainty that the answer of God's authority will prove sufficient for every creature through all eternity. There is nothing to prevent some being, somewhere, at some time from asking: "How do I know God's will is best for me, when I have never tried my own?" and then deciding to try the experiment of his own will to find out.

But even though there can be no certainty that the answer of God's authority will be final, the answer of experiment *is* final. When the experiment has once been fully tried, there can be no appeal from that answer. It is final because it is complete.

The child creeping about the floor, attracted by the comfortable feeling from the warmth of the stove, tries to put his hand on it to see if it will not be more comfortable. The authority of the mother keeps him at a safe distance, but his question is not answered. Then he eludes her watchful eye and lays his hand on the stove. His cries of pain tell that he has found out what he wanted to know. His mother's *authority* was not sufficient, but the answer of his own *experiment* is final. "The burnt child dreads the fire."

The Nature of Sin

The question as to whose will was best arose in the universe before man was created. The most wise, capable and beautiful being God ever created came to regard the answer of God's authority as not sufficient, and so he came at last to where he said two words: "I will." It makes no difference what followed those words. When they were spoken without reference to God's will, sin entered the universe. This is the sum and substance, the warp and woof, the fiber and texture of sin. Simply to say, "I will," with no thought of God's will, is the very essence of sin.

These two words, when once they were spoken, shut Lucifer and all his hosts completely off from all the benefits that abiding in God's will had brought them, and would have continued to bring them forever, if they had stayed in that will.

But no! Five times this highest being in God's universe said, "I will," climaxing it with the awful defiance, "I will be like the most High" (Isa. 14:12-14). From that hour *a war of wills* has raged in the universe, without a moment of cessation. The only issue in this war, for time and eternity, is that of dominion. *Who shall sit on the throne of the universe?* Whose will shall be in eternal control? This is the one and only question, the first and final issue, and this war will continue until it is eternally settled that *God's will is best,* and that it shall forever go forth unhindered from His throne.

After the war on God's will was begun by Lucifer and his hosts, man was placed on this earth as a race, all mankind being in Adam in his creation. What happened to Adam, therefore, involved the whole race, because of the laws of nature according to which God created us.

God had happy contact daily with Adam and Eve, and gave them constant experience of the blessedness of being in His will, that they might have abundant evidence that His will was best. Then when He had given them all the knowledge of Himself that they could receive in their negative condition of innocence, He permitted the way to be opened for them to make the choice of wills permanent and have their characters fixed in righteousness by choosing His perfect will in preference to their own.

But though every inducement to choose God's will and every warning against choosing their own wills was set before them, wholly without excuse they chose their own wills, and stepped out of God's will and all it would have brought them. Adam and Eve at once went into *slavery*, and bondage to sin has passed on from them to the whole race. Every one born on this earth has been committed, by birth, to a preference for his own will, and defiance of all who would try to force it into control.

Tell the sweetest natured child that ever lived not to do a thing he never before had the least desire to do, and from that minute he is not satisfied until he gets it done. Even if he is too young to talk, he says in actions as defiantly as grownups can ever say it in words, "I would like to see any one keep me from doing what I want to, or force me to do what I don't want to!" This determination to maintain our wills against all others, including God's, is born in all of us as an inheritance from Adam.

The Fight for Freedom

This is slavery! It is a bondage to sin so real that all men realize in a measure the handicaps we are all under, though many do not realize why and are constantly seeking for

The Perpetual Fight for Human Liberty 21

escape. Even Paul, after he was saved, but before he had learned the secret of victory and freedom, cried out: "For what I would, that do I not; but what I hate, that do I.... For to will is present with me; but how to perform that which is good I find not. For the good that I would I do not: but the evil which I would not, that I do.... O wretched man that I am! who shall deliver me from the body of this death?" (Rom. 7:15, 18, 19, 24).

This is what lies behind man's constant cry for freedom throughout the entire course of human history. Multitudes do not know just what it is that they long to be delivered from, but they sense that they are in bondage and they cry out for liberty.

In the light of what we have been thinking, it is easy to see that it all goes back to that final question of wills. Sin has inclined us to our own wills, and there is no bondage more cruel. But we were created with the craving for freedom, and can be satisfied with nothing else, and so this has been the one all-absorbing quest of the race from the beginning.

One great section of mankind has been fighting for freedom *from* the will of God. But those who know that God's will is best, because they have submitted to it and found out by experiment, have always fought for freedom to submit to His will, with no man to say them nay. The ceaseless fight for freedom has thus divided mankind into two warring camps, each group seeking to eliminate the other. Those who want freedom *from* God's will, want freedom also from those who do His will, and so they say, even as the demons said to Christ: "Let us alone." And many would be glad to have the earth rid of all those who seek to do God's will.

But God's people seek to eliminate the other group by winning them from their own wills into that company where

God's will is accepted, so they cannot let them alone any more than light can let darkness alone. Having found that submission to God's will has delivered them from slavery to their own—"for whom the Son makes free is free indeed"—they cannot keep from seeking, urged on by the unselfish joy of their new-found freedom, to win into the same freedom those who are the helpless slaves to self, sin and Satan; and they desire liberty to herald the good news of deliverance to all men, without exception or distinction, with no hindrance, direct or indirect, from any source. And why not? Nothing could be more in harmony with the infinite and eager yearning of the heart of a loving God who made us for freedom!

A Clue to the Cause of Our Ills

We thus arrive at the clue to the cause of all man's ills which opens the way to find the remedy. For having isolated the ultimate cause of all humanity's troubles, we can understand the reason for characteristic human behavior, and also understand why God offers just the remedy He does and no other. We can see also why man's remedies are not only futile but fatal. To state it in simple fashion, God's purpose in our creation is found to be only *benevolent*, for He is love.

Man's reaction to this divine attitude is seen to run all the way from cold indifference to intolerance and malevolence. The reason for such an attitude is because man has crossed his will with God's will, and not only wants to be let alone by Him, but also by all those whose wills have been submitted to His will.

Such a situation is fully adequate to account for all the economic, social, moral and spiritual ills of humanity, for this is a complete diagnosis of the disease called *sin*, and

The Perpetual Fight for Human Liberty

exactly that, and nothing else, is the sole cause of all man's trouble. He is struggling blindly for freedom from slavery.

From this point on we must set forth the contrasts, as fully as the limited space we have determined on will permit, between God's adequate provision for man's complete freedom to approach and worship Him according to His will, and Satan's ever changing attempts, through those whom he controls, to block man's way to God until he can at last get control of this world himself, for that is what he is fighting for. The fight that Satan is making on God was never more fierce than it is right now, and God's people *must not be ignorant of his schemes,* lest they be found helping him without knowing it.

Chapter III

CAPITAL PUNISHMENT AND HUMAN RIGHTS

IT now becomes as clear as the sunlight what the fundamental motive was in the heart of God when He gave man the gift of *human government.* It was a gift of love.

After man had gone into slavery to his own will, the race was given over 1,600 years of unhindered liberty to find out by experiment whether the following of conscience alone, with no other restraint, but with all the inducements of God's love before them, would bring men back to Himself. But in spite of the testimony of those who walked with God, and a hundred twenty years of the preaching of righteousness by Noah, men went from bad to worse in their attitude toward God, and therefore in *their treatment of each other,* until at last there was such unspeakable corruption, not only moral but physical, and such violence and bloodshed, that there were only eight people left on earth who were morally or even physically fit to propagate the race. God was then compelled, in order to continue the race on earth at all, to sweep all but the eight souls who feared Him off the earth with a flood. Only thus was the race prevented from destroying itself.

Then beginning over again with those eight persons, God established restraints that would preserve to all men their inherent rights, provided those restraints were faithfully maintained, so that the violence and bloodshed that preceded the flood might be prevented. Thus God in mercy threw safeguards around even those who had escaped from the benefits of His love, that they might be free to return to Him when they chose.

This accounts for the form God gave to the foundation law of human government. "Whoso sheddeth man's blood," said He, "by man shall his blood be shed" (Gen. 9:6), which is, of course, the law of capital punishment for the crime of murder. And this law is not only fundamental but perpetual, for it is repeated in the New Testament in Romans 13: 1-7, especially in verse 4.

Thus the intent of that law upon which God established human government is not revenge but measured righteousness, weighed and balanced justice, and faultless and evenhanded disregard of persons, as impartial restraints are put upon anyone, whoever he may be, who would deprive others of the unhindered control of their own lives.

The Foundation for Human Rights

It does not appear at first sight, but with deepening insight it is seen that in this law of capital punishment is safeguarded *every inherent human right*. This should be reason enough why this law should be rigidly enforced. But a reason infinitely above and beyond that of maintaining *human* rights is the safeguarding of the *rights of God Himself*. God's rights in the human race are *property* rights, and they are preëminent. He created us and we are subject to any disposal He sees fit to make of us.

Because He is love, He sees fit to *lavish His love upon us*, and having created us with that in view, and with the capacity to receive and respond to His love, *He has the right to safeguard us from all interference with such a response*. So the law of capital punishment was given primarily to safeguard *God's rights in us,* but our rights are so bound up with His that they also are safeguarded along with His. This is precisely the principle that inheres in the law of capital punishment.

How every natural human right is bound up in this law is easily seen upon a little thoughtful analysis of the principles involved. The purpose of the law is to insure to every human being the *full and unhindered control of his own life,* that he may *possess* and *dispose* of it as he *chooses,* that thus he may be *free* to choose to dispose of it *according to the will of God.*

All who have had the experience know that the moment their wills were surrendered to God's will, they entered at once upon such blessed discoveries of the unspeakable joy and happiness in God's will for them, that they never tire of giving Him praise and adoration, nor of telling others what they have found in His heart of love. His worth to those who have chosen His will is the never-ending theme of song and story, and the unfailing inspiration of the highest and most majestic language that ever fell from tongue or flowed from pen.

The Right to Worship God

All who have yielded to God's will rightly demand unhindered freedom of access to Him at all times and under all proper conditions, both individually and socially, that they may both testify to each other and proclaim to all men everywhere the infinite *worthship* of God's love which they have found in yielding to His will.

This is the right to worship God. The old Anglo-Saxon spelling was "worthship," and we have shortened it to *worship.* God has the right to the worship of all who choose to give it, for it is our response to His love, for which He gave us the capacity.

Man also has the right to worship God when, where, and

how he will, with no man either to hinder his approach, or to enforce the method of approach. We are to be left to God alone. This is the right to *liberty of conscience,* and it is so inherent in our right to approach God, that if it is interfered with to any degree the very right to worship God is itself tampered with.

The right to approach God for ourselves, without the intervention of others, carries with it the right to tell others about the God we approach, not only man to man, but in public assemblage. This is the right to *freedom of assembly* for worship, that we may learn more fully how to experience and enjoy the submission of our wills to God's will, and proclaim its blessedness to all who will listen.

We have the right, therefore, to *freedom of speech,* whether by voice or press, that we may declare God's "worthship" to all who will heed.

This carries with it also the right to *freedom of action* among our fellow men, that we may have unhindered access to them at all proper times to tell them the good news of God's love and His craving for ours. This also includes the right to pass on our knowledge of God to oncoming generations, which therefore gives us the right to *maintain a home,* that our children may be brought up in the fear and admonition of the Lord.

The right to maintain a home and to sustain public worship gives us the right to own and control *private property,* that we may have it to dispose of for such purposes without interference.

The right to private property, therefore, gives us the right to *private profit* from our investment of brawn or brain. The right to private profit and property is, in fact, inherent in the fundamental natural right from which we have been moving forward in our thought. For since everyone has the right to the possession and disposal of his own life, obviously his powers and capacities are also his own personal and private property, since God gave them to him, and he cannot escape from them. Therefore, the knowledge and skill which he acquires and applies in the use of his capacities are also his own private possession, for they cannot be taken away from him. It is thus an axiom that the material and tangible possessions into which any man's personal skill and labor are transmuted are his own personal and private property by the same right by which the capacities that created them are his.

But let three things be noted well: that the one supreme right in which all man's natural rights are bound up is *God's property right in us;* that His right to man's response to His love is therefore man's right to *worship* Him unhindered; and that our right to *private property*, and the *personal profit from labor* with which to acquire it, was given us that we might both maintain a home and sustain public worship, for *only thus* can we safeguard these spiritual rights both to *our own generation and those to come.*

Is the Profit Motive Selfish?

So when anyone proposes the slogan: "Production for use but not for profit," and calls on men to give up the "profit motive" in the interest of a coöperative brotherhood, it is not only an attempt to steal into the back door of our spiritual freedom and drive us out at the front door into slavery, but it is the far more awful offense of *moving upon God Himself,* and trying to rob Him of His property rights in us.

If some one rises to say that the profit motive can never be anything but selfish, he is guilty of ignoring perfectly plain distinctions, and thus creating confusion of thought. He does not make the distinction which must be made, if we are to think clearly, between *selfishness* and *self-interest*.

Capital Punishment and Human Rights

The feeling is instinctive in every normal human being that to take from him without his consent, and for no just cause, the material property into which his own personal skill, strength and capacity have been transmuted, is nothing short of outrage and tyranny. The instinctive sense of injustice under such circumstances comes out in the artless resentments of childhood, when other children try to take from them their own things. It is innate in every one of us. This feeling must include, therefore, and make wholly normal, the profit motive. Since "self-preservation is the first law of nature," the private control of that which makes it possible is ours by inherent right.

It is not the desire for profit, in itself, that is selfish, but our *ultimate purpose in making the profit.* For the profit motive can be under the control either of *selfishness* or of *self-interest.* Dominated by selfishness, this motive is for my own sake alone, *that I may get the better of others.* But dictated by a normal self-interest, which is simply the instinct of self-preservation, it is not for my own sake alone, but in order that *I may be a benefit to others,* and not be a burden to society.

Profit under the first motive is a menace to society, and must be condemned and kept under control, wherever it is found. Right here is where government would step in, if it should function as God commanded, not to lead or force people to abandon the profit motive, but to curb the selfish expression of it in exploiting one's fellow men.

But profit under the motive of normal self-interest is a God-given right, which means, of course, that God intends that its normal expression should *never be interfered with.*

It may seem fantastic to some to say that all these rights, and those that grow out of them, are inherent in the law of capital punishment, but there they are, all growing out of it as the oak grows out of the acorn.

And our full enjoyment of these rights is limited in God's purpose only by restraints on the doing of such things as would interfere with an equal enjoyment of the same rights by others. In fact, in the law of capital punishment it is evident that God intends to safeguard all the natural rights of all men, even to those who hate His love and put it from them, and even though they trample on the rights of God and their fellow men, and bring destruction upon themselves. For this law embodies the political and governmental expression of God's infinite pity and yearning love for all mankind in the slavery of sin.

It is now possible, with all this before us, to take another advance step in our thinking. And as we continue to think in terms of human government, let it be well understood that we are *not* thinking in the terms of such politics as become merely the policies of the politicians who consider only the selfish ambitions of persons or parties. We think rather in the terms of the divinely-given, eternal principles of government, and the various attempts being made by Satan through his servants to prevent their operation, in order that he may block God's purpose of love to man.

The one main line of thought through this whole discussion is God's purpose to reach man with His love, and Satan's devices to prevent man from receiving it, and especially the devices he is using in our day.

Chapter IV

OUR NATIONAL GOVERNMENT AND RELIGIOUS FREEDOM

SINCE the basic political principle which God laid down for human government safeguards those who want freedom to *do* His will from all interference by those who want freedom *from* His will, it is easy to see why the war between these two groups has always been fought out mainly in the *political arena*.

Not only has each group tried to eliminate the other in the ordinary contacts of life, each in its own characteristic way, but one group has always sought, through *political* channels, to limit and even destroy the freedom of men in the worship of God, while the other group has attempted to make every proper effort through these same channels to safeguard that freedom, both for themselves and for those who try to destroy it. But the story has been a sad one in that the enemies of God and His people have limited and hindered freedom of worship so much of the time across the entire period since human government began.

After the foundations of government had been laid by placing the sword of the magistrate in the hand of Noah, God commanded men to scatter abroad over the earth, to be fruitful, to multiply, and replenish the earth with inhabitants. But as soon as the dominant influence came to be against God, men were led into defiance against this instruction, and centralized instead, building themselves a city, and finally starting a tower which became an expression of their rebellion against God's will. Then God came down and broke the race into fragments by confusing their tongues, which compelled them to scatter, in spite of their purpose to the contrary. This was where the nations began, for each fragment of the race which gathered around a given language grew into a separate people.

God Chose Israel

Afterwards God broke off a fragment of the nations by separating Abram from Ur of the Chaldees unto Himself, placed him in a land which He bequeathed to him and his children forever, and gave him the promise: "In thee shall all the nations of the earth be blessed."

To make this promise good, God began a course of direct training of Abraham and his children which was calculated to fit that people to be the first, and doubtless the only world-ruling nation, that thus He might through them be a blessing to all the other nations on earth.

But because of their oft repeated disobedience and rebellion, calling for frequent and sometimes severe chastisement, God's progress with them was slow and tedious, until at last they stepped deliberately and defiantly out of His will for them as a nation, and He was compelled to allow the Gentile nations, to whom they were to be a blessing, to become their rod of chastisement, while He set them aside until the time of their national repentance and restoration.

It was not until Israel had forfeited God's purposed place for her as a nation that the Gentiles were permitted to come into prominence. There had grown up some powerful Gentile nations around Israel, but they were held in balance, with no nation dominant, until at last God allowed Babylonia to carry His people away into captivity. From that hour Israel has been either under the heel of the Gentile nations, or scattered among them throughout the earth.

During Israel's Babylonian captivity, God revealed the

Our National Government and Religious Freedom 33

appointment of certain Gentile nations, then existent and yet to come, which should be located around the rim of the Mediterranean Sea, to the place of world dominance. He committed world rulership to them, that through human government they might do their best, under His overruling control, to safeguard the human rights which He had established in the law of capital punishment. And He foretold the whole course of Gentile dominance in the dream of the Great Image which He gave Nebuchadnezzar, and interpreted through Daniel.

Those nations have played their acts across the stage of history, filling in the picture exactly as it was drawn for Nebuchadnezzar and Daniel, until now only the last act of the drama remains to be played.

The Nations Crowd God Out

Beginning with the absolute monarchy of Babylonia, one form of government succeeded another, through Medo-Persia, Greece, Pagan Rome, and on down to our day through nations that have occupied the territory of Old Rome, until every possible form of government, from absolute monarchy to complete democracy, has been tried.

Because the dominant control under each form of government was held by those who wanted freedom from the will of God, every government has muddled on across the centuries until failure has been written upon the history of each one of them—not because there has been anything inherently defective in any of them, but simply because those in control have been intolerant of the will of God in governmental affairs.

The oft recurring persecution of those who have sought freedom to do the will of God has been the result. Even when those who professed to be doing God's will have had *official* control of government, they have been wholly out of God's will in the forbidden union of Church and State, and the severest persecutions of those who really have wanted to do God's will have followed, not only with the consent but often by the direct act of government. So Christ's warning to His Church, "In the world ye shall have tribulation," has been the history of His people across the whole period of Gentile political dominion.

But something new has come to pass in our day. It seems as though God has desired to use at least one national group of Gentiles, before the final Gentile collapse, to illustrate in some measure to all the world what all the nations might have been like, if they had only acknowledged God sufficiently to establish their government securely on the principles inhering in the basic governmental law He gave to Noah.

God Acknowledged in Our Nation

The group of Gentiles referred to is our own nation—the United States of America. God has never dealt with any other Gentile nation as He has with ours.

Fleeing to these shores for freedom to worship God without persecution or coercion, the Pilgrim Fathers withstood privation, hardship and suffering with eagerness, even risking their lives gladly, for the happy enjoyment of the freedom they had been denied on other shores. Then to make certain that all their inherent rights would be preserved to their posterity undiminished, they declared their independence of all other nations and governments, and their "firm reliance on the protection of Divine Providence." God granted their desire and gave them their independence.

Then they went about to establish a government which would safeguard perpetually, for both friend and foe of God alike, every natural right given by God to man. The Convention which met to set up that kind of State, gathered at

Our National Government and Religious Freedom 35

the seat of Colonial government in Philadelphia to carry out a purpose utterly unheard of by any other nation that had ever existed. But true to the sinful perversity of human nature, they forgot God and left Him out of their deliberations for weeks, until at last they saw they were getting nowhere.

Then one morning, Benjamin Franklin, a man who was not known for his piety, arose before the Convention, when they were about to adjourn in disgust and despair, and said: "Mr. Chairman, we have been groping for four weeks in darkness, searching for the political truth, and have not found it. How is it that we have not invoked the divine guidance of the Father of lights upon our proceedings? The longer I live and the more I know, the more I believe that God governs the affairs of men, and if the sparrow cannot fall without His notice, is it probable that an empire can rise without His assistance? 'Except the Lord build the house, they labor in vain that build it.' I firmly believe this, and I also believe that without His concurring aid, we shall succeed in our political building no better than the builders of the Tower of Babel. I therefore move you that from henceforth we open our daily deliberations with morning prayer."

It was voted, and from that moment they began to make progress in the framing of that document, which makes our nation unique among all the nations that have ever existed.

Then on July 4th, 1776, the Continental Congress passed the following resolution:

"Resolved, that Dr. Franklin, Mr. J. Adams, and Thomas Jefferson be a committee to prepare a design for a seal of the United States of America."

The mind of God was sought in selecting the ideas that were to be woven into the seal. As a result, the great seal is a pyramid, composed of thirteen courses of stone, with the apex stone missing. Instead of the apex stone is the All-Seeing Eye of God above the Pyramid, watching over the destinies of the nation. Above the eye is the motto: "Annuit Coeptis," meaning, "God hath prospered our undertaking."

Not only was God acknowledged and appealed to for guidance and wisdom in laying the foundations of our government, but the sentiment of dependence on Him has been reaffirmed by every President from the beginning.

During the darkest hour of the Civil War, "In God We Trust" was ordered stamped on our silver coinage, and when some years ago there was a move to leave it off, there arose at once, all over the country, such a protest against it that it has not been mentioned since.

In his immortal Gettysburg address, as also in other addresses and State papers, Lincoln expressed the same sentiment.

In our National Anthem we sing, "In God be our trust," and as we sing "America," we say, "Our fathers' God, to Thee, Author of liberty, to Thee we sing," acknowledging that He is the One who gave our fathers the wisdom to found this country on the principles of liberty.

Thanksgiving Day is also an annual acknowledgment by the nation of our dependence upon His bounty and providential care.

A Nation Prospered of God

It is no wonder, therefore, that our nation has enjoyed an advancement and prosperity in every desirable way such as no other nation in all history has ever dreamed of. The reason is not hard to find. Our government is based on the principles found in the law that God gave to Noah, and modeled after the pattern of the only nation whose government was ever prescribed by God—the nation of Israel. This

Our National Government and Religious Freedom 37

was not done purposely, probably not even consciously by the founders, but doubtless because God was appealed to in the forming of the government. He obviously guided those who laid the foundations of our nation to the only form of government the world has ever seen that safeguards all the natural rights of its citizens, and that will continue to do so as long as it stands unchanged.

The similarity between our government and Israel's is most interesting. Israel had thirteen tribes, including the Levites, and this nation began with thirteen states. The fundamental law of Israel was the Ten Commandments, the political aspects of which were based on the principles of liberty inherent in the law God gave to Noah. Our Constitution, including the ten amendments called the "Bill of Rights," provides that the Constitution, and the laws of the various states which shall be made in pursuance thereof, shall be the supreme law of the land. The Constitution insures to every citizen every God-given right of *person* and *property* which lies in principle in the fundamental law of government given to Noah, and includes all the political principles in the Ten Commandments given to Israel.

Israel had complete liberty of conscience to worship God as He directed. Our first amendment safeguards that freedom to us, and will do so as long as the Constitution stands. No other Gentile nation ever had such a safeguard.

According to Josephus, Israel had a Senate and a Constitution, the same as we have. The people of Israel were completely protected in all just methods of acquiring and using private possessions, and therefore in production for private profit and the ownership of personal property; and our Constitution gives us the same protection.

The various tribes were governed from some selected tribal seat of government, corresponding to the capitals of our various states. The boundaries of the tribes were to be kept intact, and in other ways they had tribe rights as we have state rights, and form a union of forty-eight little unions, a "compact of sovereign states."

All of this indicates that while Israel was under judges, no centralized government headed by one man was possible, for it was a Theocracy, with God overruling through the judges in the affairs and events of the nation. In like manner, a centralized government is impossible in America as long as the Constitution stands as it is and remains supreme.

The "Checks and Balances" of Our Government

It was unquestionably under divine guidance that the framers of the Constitution provided for three branches of government: the Legislative (Congress), the Executive (the President), and the Judicial (the Supreme Court), for under that arrangement the checks and balances of the three departments of State, as long as the Constitution is supreme, prevent a centralized government in the hands of any man or group of men, for it is a government by law and not by men. And since the Constitution safeguards every right that inheres in the law that God gave Noah, in that sense, at least, He is overruling in the administration of our government, through the Constitution that was framed under His evident guidance. No Gentile government like it has ever existed before.

W. J. Cameron, on February 2, 1936, in a broadcast on "The Constitution" sponsored by the Ford Motor Company, made some very discerning comments on our fame-crowned document. He said:

"The peculiar glory of the Constitution of the United States is that it is not a charter of rights granted by a government

Our National Government and Religious Freedom 39

to a people, but a *limit of powers*[1] to which a vigilant people restricts its government. It is not a government edict which the *people* must obey, but a people's law which the *government* must obey. 'We, the people of the United States,'—these seven potent words *were* and *remain,* all subsequent upheavals notwithstanding, the most revolutionary words on record."

Farther along in his remarks he looks deeply into the nature of the Constitution and says: "The secret of the Constitution's innate rightness is in its profound harmony with *natural law,* with *moral principle,* with *public conscience,* and with the *political wisdom* won through the age-long travail of our people. These are its bases. Hence nothing is constitutional or unconstitutional merely because of certain words written on a parchment, but because of its agreement or non-agreement with *natural law* and the *moral government of life,* which that parchment has somehow magnificently understood. This is the secret of the Constitution's innate authority."

Finally, Mr. Cameron exclaims: "Defend the Constitution?—it is *defending us* from fallacies that the experience of 3,000 years condemns; from *dictatorship* which is abhorrent to every American concept; from the *totalitarian state* that regiments men's bodies and denatures their minds and *forces their consciences*—from these and like evils so widespread on earth, this Constitution is daily defending us. It stands between us and the great blasphemy that man is the creature of the State."

Yes, the Constitution, thank God, has thus far defended us from those who want freedom from the will of God, and who therefore want to rob us of our freedom to do His will. And it will continue to safeguard our rights to us as long

---

[1] Emphasis supplied, except for the words, *"were* and *remain."*

as the President, the Congress and the Supreme Court bow to its supreme authority, and leave its fundamental principles in the place of power.

It is no wonder that William E. Gladstone, one of England's greatest former statesmen and an outstanding Christian leader, said: "The American Constitution is, so far as I can see, the most wonderful work ever struck off at a given time by the brain and purpose of man."

Chapter V

THE SWORN ENEMIES OF OUR CONSTITUTION

IT IS needless to say that our Constitution has enemies. We all know it. Founded on principles whose Author is God, how could it escape the enmity of those who are His enemies?

Controversies over it have arisen now and again through the years, and it has withstood all assaults until now, but that is no guarantee that it will continue to do so. Its enemies seem to be increasing in number and power, and the most alarming and insidious movements are under way for removing from us the protecting power of our Supreme Law.

Amending the Constitution need alarm no one, as long as the amendment enlarges the scope or makes more effective the carrying out of the fundamental principles that insure to us our rights of *person* and *property*, as they are now safeguarded to us.

But if anything happens to undermine and ultimately remove from us the protection of these principles, either by muffling the voice of the Constitution and weakening its authority through limitations on the Supreme Court; or by skillful but hypocritical evasion, while professing to uphold it; or by some amendment which opens the way to side-step its protecting power; or by any other method whatsoever, we will be on our way toward the complete loss of all our liberties, and the day of dictatorship and tyranny will be at hand.

42 *The Growing Menace of the "Social Gospel"*

The Supreme Court justices, from the beginning of our national life, have done only what they took solemn oath to do in defending the people from laws which, according to their grasp of the principles in the Constitution, threatened the safeguards of the people's rights, to whom the Constitution belongs. Even though they might have made a minor error, now and again, in the interpretation of some of the principles of the Constitution, yet the people's rights have all been preserved to them up to this good hour.

So if men make an outcry against the Supreme Court because they do not dishonestly construe the Constitution to fit laws that would open the way for a centralized government, they thereby advertise to the nation that they are twisted thinkers, who understand neither the principles of the Constitution nor the functions of the Court.

The Constitution and Eternal Principles

The Constitution, especially the "Bill of Rights" in the first ten amendments, is *not* a compilation of *changeable policies* which can and should yield to changing national conditions, but an embodiment of *eternal principles* which can never be *changed* without being *destroyed*.

And the Supreme Court is simply the Constitution using the only voice it has, and speaking up for the rights of the people. Indeed, it is the people themselves speaking out for their own rights in the only way that can effectively stop those who would take them away.

It is thus as clear as the sunlight why the enemies of our Constitution are sure to attack the Supreme Court. They know they *must* either destroy the Court, or place enough men with their philosophy on the Bench to control the Court decisions, before their way would be open to accomplish their destructive purposes. They know also that if such a plan can be carried out, the Constitution will have ceased to speak out for the rights of the people, for it will have become but a perverted tool of the nation's enemies. Amendment of the Constitution would then be as needless as it would be doubtful of success.

Toward Centralization of Government

We are living in a day when the people of some of the world's great nations have either lost or are drifting toward the loss of their rights and liberties. Behind this loss, both that sustained and that impending, is a strong world-trend which has already given Communism to Russia, Facism to Italy, and Naziism to Germany, and which is making visible progress in other great nations, our own included.

The goal of this trend is the centralization of government into the hands of one man, which would mean for America an end of government "of the people, by the people, and for the people," and the coming in of a dictatorship in its place. Those who are fostering this world-trend have as the most advertised object of their enmity the right to own and enjoy private property, but the final goal is the *complete loss of religious liberty* and all that goes with it. For that would follow inevitably with the loss of the right to own property.

These enemies are revolutionaries, bent on banishing God and all knowledge of Him from the earth. They are frankly atheists, and are aggressive, belligerent and determined.

These revolutionaries are in two major camps, and they proceed by two different methods, but both their inspiration and their goal are the same. The leaders are all atheists, and they are out to make the world atheist.

One camp of these revolutionaries goes by the name of *Socialists*. Of their purpose, Leibnecht declares:

"It is our duty as Socialists to root out the faith in God

with all our might. Nor is any one worthy of the name who does not consecrate himself to spread atheism."[1] All Socialistic literature abounds with this sentiment.

The program of the Socialists is to proceed by the peaceful method of securing and enforcing laws that will gradually fasten the chains upon us, until we finally wake up to what has happened, but too late to escape. It is the method of revolution by evolution, if that is not a contradiction in terms.

The other camp is that of the *Communists*. That their ultimate purpose duplicates that of the Socialists is well known. It is the substance of their own testimony.

The All-Russian Communist Party says: "The most important question on the program for the Communist International is the militant demand, the fight, against religion."[2] This is the supreme object of their whole program. Communists proceed to the carrying out of their purposes, when the setting is right, by fostering strikes, uprisings, riots, kidnaping of private property for a ransom, and other such methods, until civil war becomes possible, which is then followed by the seizure of the government itself by revolutionary terrorism.

Property Rights and the Worship of God

Not only is it the ultimate purpose of both Socialists and Communists to blot out faith in God, but they agree that they must destroy the right to private property in order to accomplish their end.

Socialism says: "Let there be no mistake about it, Socialism is an attack on the institution of private property. . . . Definitely and clearly, our purpose is to deprive these people of their present way of living."[3]

Communism says: "The theory of the Communists may

[1] "The Conspiracy Against Religion," Boswell Ptg. and Pub. Co., London.
[2] "The Atheist at His Bench," issue No. 8, 1928.
[3] "The Case of Socialism," by Fred Henderson.

be summed up in a single sentence: Abolition of private property."[1]

And T. D. Woolsey says of both: "The essence of Socialism and Communism lies in the abolition of private property."[2]

Right here is a good place to quote Daniel Webster. A hundred years ago he said on the floor of the Senate: "There are persons who continually clamor. They complain of oppression, speculation and pernicious accumulation of wealth. They cry out loudly against all banks and corporations, and all means by which small capitalists become united in order to produce important and beneficial results. They carry on mad hostility against all established institutions. They would choke the fountain of industry and dry all streams.

"In a country of unbounded liberty, they clamor against oppression. In a country of perfect equality, they would move heaven and earth against privilege and monopoly. In a country where property is more evenly divided than anywhere else, they rend the air shouting agrarian doctrines. In a country where wages of labor are high beyond parallel, they would teach the laborer that he is but an oppressed slave.

"Sir, what can these men want? What do they mean? They want nothing, sir, but to enjoy the fruits of other men's labor. They can mean nothing but disturbance and disorder, the diffusion of corrupt principles, and the destruction of the moral principles and habits of society."

Vandals Loose Among Our Rights

Could any one have described more perfectly the very situation before our eyes today? It is not hard to see what the leaders of this clamor—these vandals with the urge for destruction—really want. They have been seized by the

[1] "Commercial Manifesto," by Carl Marx, Rand School Edition.
[2] "Communism and Socialism."

46 The Growing Menace of the "Social Gospel"

passion for power, and are being borne along by its intoxication.

This passion seems inherent in human nature. Many well-meaning people who try to forward well-intentioned reforms are in the grip of this urge. And many have the innate and passionate desire to persuade or even force others to conform to their ideas and be governed by their theories. Among them are brilliant young intellectuals whose passion is to blueprint the behavior of their fellow men. Being dreamers of schemes that are either visionary or vicious, but that look well on paper, and being eloquent and persuasive with a pen or before a crowd, they find fertile field among the classes who feel themselves downtrodden. So they seize the chance to rally and organize such people in a way that will elevate themselves to the place of power. They make loud and eloquent professions of their love for Labor, but they always forget to tell how much they hate *work*.

Many of those who are thus rallied are honest, thrifty, ambitious and self-respecting, and they are persuaded that they are out to get justice, even as their leaders say. But the great majority, among whom are the greedy, dishonest, lazy, shiftless, dole-minded ne'er-do-wells, are simply urged on by the primitive instinct of the *lure of loot.* So they follow their leaders in the idiotic hope of plundering the capitalists of the very capital that gives them their living.

It is easy to see where the passion for power and the lure of loot will lead their victims when these forces get teamed up together. And just that is what is happening on a world-scale today.

Sir Arthur Clay, of England, says of Socialism: "The force which gives vitality to the Socialist movement is the primitive instinct of predatory self-interest,"[1] which is simply another term for the lure of loot.

---

[1] "Syndicalism and Labour," London.

The Sworn Enemies of Our Constitution 47

And Dr. Arthur Shadwell refers to Communism as "an appeal to the natural appetites and passions,"[1] outstanding among which in this connection are of course the passion for power and the lure of plunder.

But behind these two passions is Satan, using those in their power to further his object of creating such a situation that God's purpose of love may be defeated.

Simple Axioms of Human Government

In view of this world trend, and of the progress already made in our country by these enemies of our liberties, it behooves us to take a good look at what would befall us if our enemies should ever succeed in nullifying our Constitution, or preventing it, through the subversion of the Supreme Court, from speaking its word of authority for our rights. For if we fail to fight for our own rights, we thus step aside and give Satan our permission to rob God of His rights in us. So we must bring before us some of the simple axioms of our form of government, that we may understand why our enemies are proceeding as they are, and how to defend our right to worship God.

A noted educator has outlined the possible forms of government, which he shows are but three. He says: "A people can ground its government on a centralization of power, a decentralization of power, or an organized balance of power. There are these three ways and none other."

He then summons history to show that "the centralization of power has invariably ended in tyranny," because, even though there is profession of benevolent intentions, such a government always seeks to perpetuate itself, and once entrenched, it grows domineering so as to maintain its power, and finally becomes tyrannical.

It is also shown that "the decentralization of power,

[1] "The Communist Movement," London.

48 *The Growing Menace of the "Social Gospel"*

when pushed to its extreme, ends in anarchy," for the more complex the social and economic demands become, the less efficient such a government is sure to be, until chaos finally arrives.

An organized balance of power, it is concluded, "will keep power centralized enough to achieve efficiency without tyranny, and keep power decentralized enough to achieve freedom without anarchy."

And this, in the providence of God, is our form of government. For the supreme governing power is so centralized that it resides wholly in the Constitution, and not at all in one man or any group of men, for it is not a government of men at all but of Law. And, fortunately, it is of such fundamental law, since God is its author, that it never needs to be changed or added to. And yet our governing power is so decentralized that it resides in all the people. For we, the people, are the real sovereigns of the nation, through the Constitution, which defends us from both tyranny and anarchy.

Then the two extremes of centralized and decentralized power are welded into an organized balance of power in the "checks and balances" by which the Constitution, functioning through an impartial and wholly unhampered Supreme Court, prevents the Congress from making or the Executive from enforcing any law that would deprive, or open the way to deprive even the humblest citizen of any of the liberties guaranteed in the "Bill of Rights."

There is also another way of looking at the principles of our government. The people must either be sovereigns over the government or subjects under it. The government must either be sovereign over the people or the servant of the people. In short, the people must either control or be controlled, for governmental control must reside somewhere.

If the people are sovereign, then our liberties are under

The Sworn Enemies of Our Constitution 49

our own control, just as all our inherent rights ought to be. But if the government is sovereign, then our rights will become mere privileges, to be doled out to us under any conditions the government might see fit to impose, or denied to us altogether, whenever the instinctive passion for power forced the leaders to impose a condition of tyranny so as to continue in power. Therefore, a centralized leadership is intolerable in free America.

The Pathway to Serfdom

Mr. Justice Matthews expressed this principle most clearly in a decision handed down from the Supreme Court some years ago. He said: "The very idea that one man may be compelled to hold his life, or the means of living, or any material right essential to the enjoyment of life, at the mere will of another, seems to be intolerable in any country where freedom prevails, as being the essence of slavery itself."

Therefore, if we want to safeguard to ourselves and our children the right to worship God, with all the other rights that go with it, we must fight to keep the Constitution, the Supreme Court and the Congress functioning as they have always done in the past, with no change that would ever permit a centralization of leadership to arise.

After all, what is this fierce struggle that is going on in the life of the nations today but that world-wide and endless fight for freedom from the slavery imposed by sin?

As always since human government was given by God, the fight still rages fiercely in the political arena. And the battle lines are still drawn between those who think that to submit to God's will is slavery, and that other group who know by experience that to be in bondage to one's own will is slavery indeed, and that in God's will alone is there real freedom.

So it is easy to see why such things are happening in our country. God, in His providence, has governmentally safeguarded His own rights in us and our rights under Him, and that is why His enemies have become the enemies of our Constitution. For until that is removed or nullified, God's will is dominant in the nation, through its Supreme Law, and the call to submit to His will cannot be kept from going forth. Satan is behind this whole movement to remove from us our safeguards, and God's people must know it and fight for His rights and their own.

Chapter VI

THE DESTRUCTIVE POWER OF THE SOCIAL GOSPEL

OUR national and international situation is disturbing enough, but the growing Social Gospel propaganda is by far the most serious and menacing aspect of our present national trends. For just at the time of all times when the Church should be fighting for freedom and defending the faith, a movement is gaining momentum which is giving aid and comfort to the enemies of our faith and the forces that would destroy our freedom.

The so-called "Social Gospel" is this movement, and its leaders would have us believe that it is the old gospel given a practical application for the needs of our day. But it is simply Socialism by a name that will make it most attractive to church people, and its most powerful sponsors are certain leaders in the professed Church who are friendly to the Russian system, and who even have words of praise for Communism.

Nearly all the major denominations are under the control of Modernistic leadership. Even if this propaganda was confined to that element in the churches, it would be serious enough, but the most menacing feature of it is that so many who have no sympathy with Modernism are yet following their social doctrines, simply because they are blind to God's program for this Age of Grace. And so without realizing it, they are helping the enemies of the Church toward the destruction of our freedom to worship God unmolested, by

52 The Growing Menace of the "Social Gospel"

socialistic doctrines that not only sanction but even accelerate these trends toward chaos.

Christ came the first time to regenerate the *individual*. He comes the second time to regenerate *society*. So the Social Gospel turns out to be "another gospel," which is no gospel at all, but merely a program for achieving social harmony and material prosperity, as all who know the real "good news" of the Bible recognize.

The proposed regeneration of society is not God's program for this Age, but for the next, when Christ will reign in Person over this earth. So it is foredoomed to failure, even before it starts. The only social regeneration possible in this Age is the direct result of individual regeneration. No one can either set up or maintain the program the social planners propose but Christ Himself, for only He can take and keep control of society. And this He will not do until He reigns on earth in the soon-coming Age that follows this one.

The simple truth is the Social Gospel fits the mental attitude toward God of none but *unbelievers in His Word,* and so it should be left to them alone. As long as men believe God rules in human affairs, and that His administration is just and righteous, as His word teaches and as all true Christians believe, they will bear patiently those wrongs He pledges to right hereafter that are not righted here. But those who no longer depend on Him to deal righteously with them will decide that if they do not right their own wrongs in this life, they will never be righted, and so they will try to get their rights by taking matters into their own hands.

This is not to say that wrongs should not be righted, here and now. Wretched indeed would be the soul who would fail to support a program for human relief that would work, and to oppose such a program would be cruelty personified.

The Destructive Power of the Social Gospel

But it is to say that if wrongs are not righted because of the submission to God and the *personal regeneration of those who commit the wrongs* there is little or no likelihood that they will be righted here and now. The betterment of human conditions has never been accomplished except as a by-product of the gospel of salvation through Christ's shed blood, preached in power and believed in sincerity. Whatever wrongs cannot be righted by following that program, cannot be righted at all during this present Age.

A "Gospel" with No Foundation

The Social Gospel will certainly never accomplish the relief of human ills, for the foundation on which it is built will not even bear its own weight, let alone the weight of the huge burden it seeks to lift.

The *philosophical* background of the movement is a speculative theory, never proved and incapable of proof, and which is completely repudiated, both by the logic of the known facts, and by the most capable and independent thinkers on the subject. The theory referred to is that of *evolution,* for the Social Gospel grows out of this theory as the oak out of the acorn. Remove all traces of this theory from the main objectives and program of the Social Gospel, and there would be nothing left of it.

The essential element in the *doctrinal* background is the growing faith in the universal brotherhood of man, which those who believe in it propose to realize on earth, here and now. This doctrine rests alone on man's deep-seated yearning for such a brotherhood, but there is no foundation for it in Scripture. The teaching of God's Word is the very opposite, but Modernistic believers in universal brotherhood are wholly blind to it.

The doctrine of universal Fatherhood necessarily follows,

54 The Growing Menace of the "Social Gospel"

and this is also wholly anti-scriptural. Those who maintain this doctrine ignorantly confuse *creative* with *generative* Fatherhood. The first is natural, the other spiritual.

There is a scripture which says: "Have we not all one father? Hath not one God *created* us?" (Mal. 2:10). In the meaning of this passage, God is equally the Father of mankind, monkeys and mosquitoes. For it defines *creative* fatherhood, and in that sense He is the Father of everything He has created.

But another scripture reads: "As many as received him, to *them* gave he the right to *become* children of God" (John 1:12). We cannot *become*—come to be— what we already *are*. This verse, therefore, defines *generative* Fatherhood, and says it is only for "as many as received him." No others are the children of God. No universal, spiritual brotherhood is possible, therefore, because there is no universal Fatherhood.

And yet, utterly false as these two doctrines are, they are arbitrarily put into the foundation of the Social Gospel, with a fancied universal brotherhood of man as the goal. And the movement has come to have such momentum that attempts are beginning to be made to force such a brotherhood on unregenerate man.

Is the Church the Kingdom of God?

The *historic* background of the Social Gospel is to be found in a serious misconception of the nature and mission of the Church, growing out of an apparently innocent confusion of terms. Those terms are the "Kingdom of God," the "Kingdom of Heaven," and the "Church."

The kingdom of God embraces all who are subject to His will, including the angels. The kingdom of heaven is heaven's rule over this earth only, and is world-wide. But the Church is an "ekklesia," the Greek for a "called out com-

The Destructive Power of the Social Gospel

pany," and could not be *world-wide* and a company called out *from* the world at the same time.

Both the Church and the kingdom of heaven are *in* the kingdom of God, and yet all three are distinct. Sometimes in Scripture the term "Kingdom of God" refers to the kingdom of heaven and sometimes to the Church, but it is in the sense that the greater includes the less.

A misunderstanding grew up in the early centuries, however, by thinking the Church and the kingdom of heaven were the same thing. Seeing, therefore, that the kingdom was to be world-wide, also supposing the Church was to grow until it was world-wide, and finding that a time was coming when righteousness should cover the earth as the waters cover the sea, this condition was set up as the goal to be reached by the Church. And this notion still largely prevails.

Naturally, therefore, the doctrine of evolution, and the notion that the Church is the kingdom, and is to increase until the whole world is included, have furnished inspiration for the present "Kingdom of God Movement." They fit together as a hand fits a glove.

It is also the natural outgrowth of this misconception that the cry of the oppressed, the wronged, and the unjustly treated should enlist, in the growing demand for social justice and a more abundant material life, those in the professing Church who hold these mistaken views. And it is what might be expected when the call increases for a realized, universal brotherhood as the one great means of reaching this utopian goal, for the natural, unregenerate man can comprehend no other program.

The Social Gospel, resting on such a foundation of mistakes and untruths, has within itself the seeds of total failure, and the coming downfall will be most tragic. For its rapidly-growing momentum is sure to continue, unless God interferes, until the confusion it creates will at last bring the world to such chaos that a super-man will be called for to take world affairs under control and straighten out the tangled mess.

The Kingdom of God Movement

There is probably no concrete example more typical of the Social Gospel program, or more advanced in realization, than the "Kingdom of God Movement" under Dr. Kagawa in Japan. It is said to embrace twenty-five million, or one third of the people of that nation, and it was greatly popularized in America by Kagawa's much publicized and largely attended lectures during his visit here.

The obvious product of Modernism, Kagawa writes from the standpoint of the pantheistic evolutionist, and his "Kingdom of God" program is the perfect embodiment of that philosophy. His use of such evangelical terms as the "blood," "atonement," "redemption," "salvation," "faith" is disarming to the spiritual reader, until he discovers that Kagawa's meaning for these terms grows out of pantheistic and evolutionary conceptions, and is wholly destructive of their meaning as used in Scripture.

Kagawa starts with the conception that "Love is God," thus destroying the truth of Scripture at the beginning. This love rises from the "cosmic will" as the eternal "love of the universe" (a pantheistic conception); has possession of many in varying degrees up to "fully conscious love"; takes form in the spirit of brotherhood; finds expression in coöperation, both in social, economic and spiritual realms, and works out in his "Coöperatives," in the economic field, and in its call for coöperation; and in the spiritual realm, between Fundamentalists, Modernists, Buddhists, Mohammedans,—all faiths, in fact, "for these are not Love's divisions," says he. "Love knows how to embrace, but not to differentiate." Then

The Destructive Power of the Social Gospel 57

he cries, "Classify me not by creed. I belong to nothing but Love."

There are economic Coöperatives in England, Finland, Denmark and other places, and the Church has no word to say concerning those that are *purely economic,* as long as their program does not tend to destroy man's natural and spiritual rights and liberties, or encroach on the Church's mission.

There can be no question raised about collective public enterprise. The extension of public enterprise is *not* Socialism, as long as it does not result in the extinction of *private* enterprise. Any collective *public* activity that results in preserving or enlarging the sphere of *private* enterprise is commendable. But when the community joins hands in doing anything in a way that prohibits or makes it impossible for those same things to be done by *private* enterprise, that is Socialism, and it is destructive of our rights and liberties in the material, and therefore, ultimately, in the spiritual realm. And if Kagawa's Coöperatives are a form of social action which must sooner or later end private enterprise, they would lead to an end of private profit and property, for it is Socialism.

Economic Coöperatives Invade the Church

Moreover, Kagawa does not stop in the economic realm, but actually invades the sphere of the Church with his economic program, for he calls his Coöperatives "true Christianity," and expects the Church to put it first in her program, saying that "Becoming a Christian is organizing a Coöperative."

The Modernistic Federal Council of Churches, in a seminar they sponsored in Indianapolis during the 1935-36 holiday season, adopted a resolution which said: "We are convinced that the Coöperative Movement is one of the major techniques in making possible the kingdom of God on earth. We believe that the churches and religious organizations have an opportunity to supply dynamic and motivation for this most promising movement."

Thus the trends in both Church and State are on the lines of what the Church is calling the Social Gospel, but which, in the State, is nothing but Socialism. And when the Church and the State are united in carrying out such a program, what is that but a union of Church and State.

It is therefore imperative that we get back to the principles which make a successful union of Church and State forever impossible.

Chapter VII

THE TREND TOWARD UNION OF CHURCH AND STATE

CIVIL government was established by God. It was given to maintain righteous relations among men. In order to insure such relations, the State was commissioned to punish those who transgress the human rights God established in principle in the law He gave Noah, even to the judicial execution of the death penalty as a just punishment for the crime of murder.

In other words, the State was not commissioned to show mercy and grant forgiveness to sinners against human rights and liberties, but to safeguard those liberties by the enforcement of just penalties on all who transgress them. Exact justice and civic righteousness are the watchwords of the State.

But when we turn to the Church, we find it wholly diverse from the State in nature, and therefore in mission. The Church is composed of a people called out from every tribe and nation, race and tongue on earth, and is made up only of those who, through acceptance of the "good news" of salvation from sin through the shed blood of Christ, have been born again, and have thus become "partakers of the divine nature." Thus the Church is not composed of nations, but of individuals out of every nation. The real Church is smaller, also, than its enrolled membership, for far too many who have never been saved are on the rolls of the professed Church.

The Church's One Mission

The Church is commissioned to do *one thing only* in the world. In outlining that mission, Christ said: "As my Father hath sent me, even so send I you" (John 20:21). That we might know how He was sent, He said in another place: "The Son of man is come to seek and to save that which was lost" (Luke 19:10). As a means for bringing the lost to salvation, He instructed the Church that "repentance and remission of sins should be preached [told about] in his name among all nations" (Luke 24:47).

Then we find as a background for this that Christ's pre-crucifixion and pre-ascension instructions to His disciples declared the whole mission of the Church to be summed up in the word "witness." Just that; nothing else. And these instructions are all gathered together in what has been called the Great Commission: "Go ye into all the world, and preach [tell out] the gospel [good news] to every creature" (Mark 16:15), which means that the gospel is not "good advice"—it is simply "good news."

Then in His last words before His ascension, after promising the power of the Holy Spirit in which to fulfil His command, Christ said: "And ye shall be witnesses unto me ... unto the uttermost part of the earth" (Acts 1:8).

Finally, to make sure that Christ's instructions would not be misunderstood, the Holy Spirit, when He came on Pentecost, empowered every one of the disciples to *witness informally* concerning the "good news" of salvation, later moving and empowering Peter to climax their testimony by *formal witnessing* on the same theme, and the result was 3,000 individuals, out of "every nation under heaven," were brought to personal salvation through personal faith in a personal Saviour. Thus the Holy Spirit led the disciples to

The Trend Toward Union of Church and State 61

carry out Christ's commands which He had given them, and illustrated how it was to be done by the way He led them on the day of Pentecost.

As time went on the Church did nothing more than this. The result was that even though they had begun at nothing, in a hundred years the whole known world had become evangelized, the gospel penetrating even into Cæsar's household, and if the Church had stuck to this program, the world would have been kept evangelized until this hour.

It is perfectly clear, therefore, that the Church is not commissioned to convert the world, nor to educate it, nor to civilize it, nor to help solve its economic problems, nor to Christianize its social order, and certainly to take no part in governing it. She is simply to "preach the gospel to every creature," nothing else, nothing less, that whosoever is willing to believe the "good news" may experience the power of God unto salvation and transformation.

But this program was too effective to suit Satan. So he finally had a spiritual, witnessing brotherhood divided into "clergy" and "laity," and then he stopped the universal witnessing of the "laity" and confined it to the "clergy." Then came the Dark Ages!

And today our universal testimony is being nullified, though in a different manner. Pastors and people—especially pastors—are turning aside to a work that is calling in thunderous tones to be done, but which is *altogether the work of the State*. Thus the Church is being led not only into wasting time, but into work that is hindering her testimony when she does give it.

Union of Church and State Impossible

Perhaps the chief reason many are being led into work that does not belong to the Church is because they have

62 *The Growing Menace of the "Social Gospel"*

failed to see the distinction God has put between the Church and the State, because of the radically different nature and mission of each.

The State is an agency of *civic righteousness;* the Church a witness to *divine grace*.

The State is built and maintained to fulfil a mission of *justice;* the Church to fulfil a mission of *mercy*.

The State starts out on her mission with a *sword;* the Church goes to her mission with an *olive branch*.

The State is divinely *authorized* to use force to compel obedience to her righteous laws; the Church is divinely *forbidden* to use force in getting her message accepted in the world.

The State is to execute a just *penalty* on sinners against the rights of man; the Church is to proclaim *forgiveness* to sinners against the righteousness of God.

The State is concerned with the *temporal* relations of *citizens* with *each other;* the Church with the *spiritual* relations of *sinners* with *God* and *man*.

As *citizens* we are to render to Cæsar the things that are Cæsar's, and be subject to the "powers that be"; as *Christians* we are to render to God the things that are His, and be subject to Him in all things.

Thus it is perfectly obvious that since their respective natures and missions are mutually exclusive, a successful union between Church and State is wholly impossible. For in any attempted union between them, it would be inevitable that one would *dominate over the other*. So if the Church was dominant, the exercise of force which belongs only to the State would creep into use in the Church. History illustrates this. And if the State ruled the Church, the spiritual rights and liberties of men would soon disappear. History proves this also.

The Trend Toward Union of Church and State 63

Our national history has illustrated to all the world the success that is certain to accompany a complete separation between Church and State, when the Church sticks to her mission and does not grasp after the functions of the State.

But the Social Gospel is leading us afield, and turning the Church aside to official efforts to right the economic wrongs of the oppressed. But those things not only belong wholly to the State, as such, but for the Church to enter officially into that realm of activities would be to close the door in her own face to her divinely-given message.

We must not forget that the Church is not narrow, provincial, national, or even inter-national, but *universal* in nature and mission. The moment she becomes class conscious, therefore, and begins to constitute herself an *attorney* for one class against the wrongs, real or fancied, of another class, she has vacated her commission, denied her Lord, become a judge and a divider among men, and invited the world to throw her universal message into the discard because of her respect of persons.

The one who has a just cause needs the gospel. The one who oppresses and robs men of their rights needs the gospel. The Church was commissioned by Christ to give *each one* of them the gospel. So any minister who sets himself up as a self-appointed attorney for the oppressed against the oppressor, sets class against class, closes the door to one class in his own face, and becomes too narrow to present a universal gospel to the other class. He has no longer any place in the pulpit, and he should recognize it, leave the ministry, hire an office, and put out an attorney's "shingle."

The Social Gospel a Divider

The Social Gospel is a divider between classes. Its very nature makes this unavoidable. Paul said the kingdom of

God is "righteousness and peace and joy in the Holy Spirit." Man's miserable substitute supplied us by the Social Gospel says it is "food and drink"—material welfare—the very thing Paul said the kingdom of God *is not*. But because a more abundant material life is deemed the kingdom of God, the Social Gospel demands of its adherents that they stand for the oppressed against the oppressors, thus dividing class from class, when both of them need the "righteousness of God which is by faith in Jesus Christ," where there is "no difference [no classes]; for *all* have sinned, and come short of the glory of God."

Dr. Kagawa indicates what a divider his "Kingdom of God Movement" is when he says: "In Kobe a young man once came to me and said he wanted to be an evangelist. 'Have you the courage to go to prison?' I asked him. 'Have you the grit to lead a strike?' 'No,' he answered. 'Then give up the idea of becoming an evangelist,' I said."

Imagine an evangelist leading a strike against employers of labor, and then going to those employers with the gospel of Christ! He would be driven from the place, the glory of the gospel would be trailed in the mud, and the employers, if no one else, would be removed far from any willingness to hear the gospel from any source.

The Social Service program of the Federal Council of Churches includes "justice," "equal rights," "proper housing," "education," "recreation," "child labor," "hours of labor," "a living wage," and other like things which are wholly the God-given responsibility of the State, for they are all matters of purely temporal welfare. And it is not the official business of the Church to meddle in these affairs that are not in her commission, as the Federal Council is doing. Her mission in the world lies in a realm and through a service which alone will make any degree of effective social service possible.

The Trend Toward Union of Church and State 65

The Church and Unrighteous Government

But some objector may ask: "Is the Church to take no interest in whether the State administers justice and demands righteousness among her citizens?"

A most vital interest! And it is because of this interest, properly directed, that she is *not* to try to force her social service programs on the State, or take them to the State to get them done; but that she *is* to take the gospel to every person in the nation, including the administrators of the affairs of State.

If we take our social service programs to godless officials, they may listen respectfully to our appeals, but they will then turn away and do as their unregenerate hearts move them to do. But if we take the gospel of salvation through Christ to them and win them to Him, they will need none of our programs, for they will know what to do without our telling them, and they will do it.

A young pastor went to a church in a city of 25,000. Soon, some of his church leaders told him they thought he should attack the city administration, for the mayor, department chiefs and members of the council were so corrupt the city had become notorious.

Asking for time, he prayed about it, decided on his course of action, and secured a ten-minute appointment with the mayor.

When he kept the appointment, after some general remarks, he said to the mayor, "I want to congratulate you on the honor and responsibility that were laid on you when you were chosen mayor of this city. But I want to tell you that there is a greater honor waiting for you—something far bigger than the office of mayor of a city like this."

Thinking this stranger might represent some high-up politician, the mayor listened with evident interest.

"You ought to be a servant of Jesus Christ," said the young minister.

In astonishment the mayor said, "No one ever spoke to me like this before."

The time being up, the minister left, but the next day the agitated voice of the mayor said to him over the telephone, "Won't you come and talk with me? I have thought of what you said ever since you left. I must see you!"

Two weeks later, not only did the mayor come into that pastor's church, but the chief of police, the fire department chief and five aldermen also yielded themselves to Christ.

That city was cleaned up!

This is the kind of interest the Church is to show in the way the affairs of State are administered. And if this method does not work, nothing will.

Dr. P. T. Forsyth, long Principal of Hackney College, said: "In some Welsh counties the judges on the circuit have nothing to do. And it is not due to the police but to the preachers." And he continues, "Christian revival implies revival in public duty, public spirit, the civic temper, the social mind, and the universal conscience.... It is the constant tendency of the greater revivals to become social and national."

The Church and Social Service

"But is the Church to do no social service whatever?" some one may ask.

Most emphatically, *yes!* "The poor always ye have with you," said Christ, and we are told to do good unto all men, especially to those of the household of faith. In many ways great numbers of Christians are giving needed help in a manner that opens the way to give the gospel to those in need. Certainly the Church should do social service in the

The Trend Toward Union of Church and State 67

name of Christ, and just as certainly she should keep from meddling with the functions of the State.

A man stood on a corner in a London slum and looked out upon the cruel poverty and wretchedness of the East End. Moved with the compassion of Christ, he said: "*I cannot relieve them, but if I can bring them into touch with Christ, He will.*" And William Booth, inspired by that purpose, went and preached to them the gospel of the Son of God, and his family, his officers and his Army kept on preaching it around the world, until more real, genuine, practical social service resulted than has been accomplished by all the social service experts and their agencies put together.

The Social Gospel is not being exploited, therefore, because there is no other way to get real, practical social service done. It is because the *same old fight* of those who want *freedom from God's will* is assuming a new and subtle camouflage which, through a union of Church and State, stealthily slipped over on us, will permit them to *rob us of our natural and spiritual liberties.* For when the union to which the Social Gospel is leading takes place, it is the end of all spiritual freedom.

Our concern may well increase, therefore, with the growth of the Social Gospel. It means nothing less than ultimate social and economic revolution, with no possible escape from the political revolution now shaping up, which will at last regiment the nation into a socialistic planned economy. And since our present form of government is a perfect safeguard for our rights and liberties, and the one that is being framed to take its place opens the way to dictatorship and ultimate tyranny, it does not need a prophet to forecast the end to which the Social Gospel will bring this nation, unless God undertakes, through His awakened people, to turn us from the present trend toward ruin.

The Church Meddling in State Functions

Dr. E. Stanley Jones, in a radio message, said that the speakers in the "Preaching Mission" which swept across this country had the boldness to ask "that we as a nation take the kingdom of God on earth as our goal," and that we should seek to know "what its implications are, both to the individual and in the collective life, in the way of *economic* and *social reconstruction*."

A "Commission on Social Action," reporting at their Colorado Springs session to the Northern Baptist Convention which appointed it, suggested that the Church should refuse longer to confine its activity to the religious realm alone, but should seek an official place in economic and governmental affairs. The report said:

"The influence of our (denominational) position was effective in making the separation of Church and State and the establishing of religious liberty a part of the fundamental law of our land."

Then in another part of the report, in speaking of the official attitude which the Church should take toward the State, these inconsistent words occur:

"The Church should not concede to the political State even neutrality, let alone absolute sovereignty in all matters aside from religious worship and exercises."

If the Church should not concede to the State absolute sovereignty, for example, in the realm of material welfare, what else is left but to *share* such sovereignty with the State? And how can the Church share with the State even the slightest degree of sovereignty in that realm or any other, and yet escape a union, to that degree, of Church with State?

A generation ago, in acknowledgment of our debt to the pioneers who fought until the First Amendment was written into our Constitution, and in the renewal of purpose to maintain our priceless liberty of conscience and our right to worship God unmolested, the American Baptist Home Mission Society said in a memorial to Congress:

"It is the unquestionable honor of our religious ancestry that, seeing clearly the imperial dignity of the human conscience, as Christ made it free under His sole and supreme Lordship, it is constantly and consistently contended that the right of the State shall pertain to civil things only."

The hour is fully ripe to present a memorial to the *churches,* clarifying the imperial duty of the State to retain and maintain, without official interference from the Church, those functions designed to safeguard the temporal welfare of her citizens, and contending that the official right of the Church should pertain to spiritual things only.

God had ready His chosen leaders in the fight of those early days for a separation of Church and State, who rose up and compelled the State to take hands off the Church. We should now cry to Him for leaders who will rise up to lead a new crusade for the Church to keep hands off the functions of the State. Any union of Church and State, under whatever camouflage, will never reach our trouble, for the producing cause of every ill that afflicts humanity is *sin.*

The Remedy for Sin the Real Answer

And so the only possible real and lasting relief from our ills lies in the *remedy* for sin. The only remedy the world ever heard of that always works is the "good news" of salvation from sin, through Christ's shed blood alone, proclaimed in the power of the Holy Spirit.

The only effect the Social Gospel can possibly have is simply to repress the outbreak of the disease in one form, which would only force it to break out in another. The disease must be cured before the symptoms will disappear.

Therefore, preach the gospel! For this is the only possible escape from the complete loss of all that makes life worth while, here or hereafter, which the present trend in our nation threatens to bring about. The people of other great nations have already lost, or are now losing, the rights we still enjoy. And it *can* happen here, no matter what the blind and cock-sure optimists may say, for it is already beginning to happen.

"The nations that forget God shall perish," says His Word, and in spite of all our former dependence on Him and His great blessing because of it, if the present trend finally leads us outside the pale of His protection by removing the safeguards of our rights and liberties which He enabled the founders to establish for us, what can await us but the fate of the other nations that are forgetting and defying God?

Of one thing we may all be sure! If the professing Church does not wake up and become once more the "salt of the earth" which has not altogether lost its saltness, the awful corruption about us can only spread until the unspeakable things that are done in secret today will be done in open and God-defying brazenness tomorrow, and our nation, as we have known it, will be headed toward the oblivion of those nations that forget God.

High Time the Church Came Back

When God is compelled to speak to our nation in floods, in droughts and in devastating dust-storms, in order to arrest and rebuke those who try, by their "planned economy," to take the care of the people out of His hands, it is high time the professing Church came back to her first love, that He might once more speak through her the word that would arrest the nation in her trend toward moral chaos and national decadence.

The Trend Toward Union of Church and State 71

Our trouble is in neither the social nor the economic areas of life, but altogether in the moral and spiritual. It is not our circumstances to which we are enslaved, it is our *sin*. The economic welfare of our nation is such that the standards of living and the buying power of the laboring man average on the level with the middle classes of Europe and the rich in Asia. The sole cause of all the discontent and the growing spirit of defiance is wholly internal and not at all external.

It is simply the same old conflict between God's will and man's will, and the same unending intolerance toward those who do God's will which Cain accorded Abel. The present trend is being led secretly by men of the spirit which recently made it possible to stage a "blame-giving" performance on our day of national Thanksgiving, and to sing to the notes of our Christian Doxology:

> "Blame God from whom all cyclones blow;
> Blame him when rivers overflow;
> Blame him who swirls down house and steeple,
> Who sinks the ships and drowns the people."

When men are saying, in a spirit of growing defiance, "Let us break their bands asunder, and cast away their cords from us" (Ps. 2:3); when leaders in the professing Church are joining with atheistic Socialism and Communism in their program of regimenting our lives and destroying our liberties; and when multitudes of true Christians are blindly following these leaders down the road to chaos, it is high time for those who see these things to sound out the warnings and entreaties of God's Word to come out from among those who cause the confusion, lest they be partakers of their sins.

If ever our nation was in need of the prayers of those who know how to pray; if ever the lost multitudes about us were in need of the help of those who know how to lead them out of darkness into light; if ever the truly saved in the apostate churches needed the light of God's Word on what is going on before our eyes, that hour is now!

> "We are living, we are dwelling
>   In a grand and awful time;
> In an age on ages telling;
>   To be living is sublime!
>
> "Hark! the waking up of nations;
>   Gog and Magog to the fray;
> Hark! what soundeth is creation's
>   Groaning for the latter day.
>
> "Will ye play, then? Will ye dally
>   With your music, with your wine?
> Up! it is Jehovah's rally!
>   God's own arm hath need of thine.
>
> "Worlds are charging, heaven beholding;
>   Thou hast but an hour to fight.
> Now! the blazoned cross unfolding,
>   On! right onward for the right.
>
> "Oh, let all the soul within you
>   For the truth's sake go abroad.
> Strike! let every nerve and sinew
>   Tell on ages, tell for God!"

THE CONFLICT OF CHRISTIANITY WITH ITS COUNTERFEITS

By

W. B. Riley, A. M., D. D., LL.D.

———◆———

Author of

*The Bible of the Expositor and the
 Evangelist (40 volumes)*
Is Jesus Coming Again?
Wanted—A World Leader
My Bible, An Apologetic, etc.

COPYRIGHTED BY
W. B. RILEY

Foreword

IN sending this volume to the public by way of the press, we are not unaware that its discussions take us on to battle-ground. It is, by its very nature, calculated to provoke counter-criticism. This criticism, however, will not come from any of the people named in the book, nor even the theological parties whose course and conduct it seeks to uncover. Modernism never gives audience to an opponent's ideas, nor does it deign reply to its capable critics. There is, with its fraternity, a tacit understanding and agreement to close both eyes and ears to all except its own plans, programs, and purposes.

Men, however, who pride themselves on keeping to the middle of the road, on being fair to all concerned, on superior mental and moral balance, will make up the critics of this volume, if past experience constitutes a criterion.

In this instance, as in that of another recent volume, WANTED—A WORLD LEADER, I pledged to take whatever blows come, with calmness; yea, even with content! I count the privilege of speaking the truth valuable above personal standing or mental comfort.

For full fifty years now, I have seen young men, in the hope of promotion, meekly surrender to self-appointed superiors, and men in middle life who have attained only to such mediocre success as to convince them that, if their way was to be satisfactorily continued, they must seek friends in places of ecclesiastical power, and relegate their convictions of truth to the realm of silence, since to voice them further might jeopardize preferment.

For the same length of time I have observed upon strong men, who, before their natural force began to abate, had been willing not only to take blows, but dared to give them; but who, at the first signs of decline on account of age, suddenly soften and cease from all conflicts, seeking safety, also, in the shadows of "The Great."

The very pathos of these observations has compelled in me this prayer, "Oh, Lord, preserve thy servant from seeking popularity or position at the expense of thy truth; and grant, when age threatens with its physical and mental ravages, that he may at least be so Divinely preserved in theological stamina and moral fibre as never to run up the flag of surrender, or even to hint a truce with the enemies of God or His Word."

While not yet conscious of the weight of years, I have already outlived the most of my generation. How marvelous has been His Goodness to give me so long a ministry! But life is not in length of days! True life is in an unswerving loyalty to the God who created us out of the dust, and redeemed us by the precious blood of His own Son.

My prayer is that my faith in Him shall never falter, and that the breath of life may go from this body before I show to the enemies of the truth any sign of weakening.

I count the battles over the Word of God, THE WAR of all twentieth-century wars; and I live in the confident hope that the Allies of Christ will prove victors, and *"the gates of hell shall not prevail against the true church"* — His little flock.

W. B. Riley

I

The Conflict Of Christianity With Its Counterfeits

CHRISTIANITY has lived in conflict and by conquest! As in the case of its Founder, its very life was sought from the first! Judaism, the mother of Christianity, attempted the strangulation of the babe while yet it was in swaddling clothes. The rulers of Roman heathenism and the philosophers of Greek Gnosticism alike opposed its progress at every point. As a religious faith, it has had to fight its way from the hour when first it saw the light. This conflict is well expressed by Uhlhorn as it was waged with "Heathenism," and admirably voiced by Andrews as it was carried on with "Anti-Christianity." In all of these battles, Christianity has come out of the contest a victor.

It must be conceded, however, that warfare has changed in method. When, more than two millenniums ago, ten thousand Greeks, under Miltiades, marched forth against ten times their number, to the battle of Marathon, they met the enemy in an open field, and the clear victory was a tribute to the intelligence and valor of the Grecian conquerors. It told the tale of mind and merit!

Modernism makes such fair fighting impossible. The enemy no longer exposes either his person or his program. By ingenious devices, he falsifies the whole field of fight! In trenches digged under cover of darkness, he hides; by barrages of smoke and flame and gaseous fumes he accomplishes at once the cover of his own forces and the discomfiture of the enemy; and by every conceivable camouflage he seeks to deceive and disconcert, even as in the European War. Taking possession of the territory of his opponent, before intimating that war is on, he wages a conflict as unfair in method as it is foul in morals.

To say that the "New Theologian" has brought his method from Germany, as well as his message, is to state the matter both truthfully and tersely. Christianity has had a comparatively fair fight with heathenism, and in its contest with anti-Christianity the conflict has been waged in an open field; but the battle with Modernism is altogether after another manner. Here the enemy is not in the open, and the warfare is correspondingly difficult. Never in all history has Christianity itself been so menaced as it is by Modernism.

The Use of Camouflage in the Conflict

The use of camouflage in this conflict is the seriousness of the whole situation. Of all enemies, the *counterfeit* is the most difficult to discover and to dislodge. To fight it, is to fight a semblance, not the substance.

The camouflage in criticism is increasingly apparent. Albert Ritschl is held by some to have been the father of New Theology. That may account for the fact that camouflage characterized it from the first, for Ritschl openly defended the clothing of new thoughts and new theories with the well known garments of orthodoxy. Like the passing of a spy beyond the lines of the enemy by equipping him with the password and clothing him in the uniform, so Ritschl sought to invade the field of Christianity with enemy ideas clothed in friendly phrases, and he defended his conduct on the ground that such procedure gave greater promise of success! The result is that skeptical young men, candidates for ordination, "cram" conservative Confessions and pass examinations favorably before fairly critical councils. Pastors of most liberal views deftly conceal the same while corresponding with Committees seeking safe leadership; while certain professors in Colleges and Theological Seminaries, in stating what they teach in their classes, have paved the way for popular approval by quoting from most acceptable orthodox authors — only to show, however, in later words, that they put into the sentences thus employed a meaning such as was never dreamed of in their original delivery!

So far has this camouflage been carried that certain critics have sickened at seeing their co-laborers indulge in the same, and have even dared to protest against the procedure as being non-ethical if not non-moral! Certainly Professor Gerald Birney Smith of the University of Chicago was never suspicioned of conservatism; and yet, that he retained *some* ethical ideals is made perfectly clear when he says: "If there be allowed a spirit of ingenious juggling by which the newer (Theological) Science is made to yield something resembling the older conclusions, the sense of honor is inevitably dulled." He also condemns "new meanings" "smuggled in under familiar labels." He charges the men who attempt this with "time-serving." A Unitarian writer declares that a friend of his who recited with his congregation every Sunday a creed in which he no longer believed thereby "forfeited his self-respect." So far has this camouflage gone that another destructive critic expresses the wish that modern writers would furnish a glossary to attend their books, explaining the meaning of the terms employed! Let us remark in passing that such a glossary would doubtless comport favorably in intellectual and literary value with that provided by Mrs. Mary Baker Eddy!

Thus it falls out that *the critic concedes and in some instances even defends the camouflage.* It does not require a man of exacting moral ideals to realize that such a procedure involves most "elastic consciences." Such, in fact, is exactly what President McGiffert — though himself a liberal — denominated them! Is it any wonder that the men who think themselves out of denominational fellowship and who go with their conclusions to the small hut of Unitarianism look with a certain degree of disdain upon their "Fellows of Unbelief" who abide in the more spacious and comfortable apartments of orthodoxy! How else can my former neighbor, J. Herman Randall, feel toward the Unitarian Baptists that still feed at the full table of that Trinitarian denomination? How else could Dr. Hugh Orr look upon those disloyal Methodists who still drew fat salaries and held Bishoprics, while they repudiated everything for which John Wesley and historic Methodism stood?

Some years ago, "The Zion's Advocate" said, with perfect justice, "When men surrender their faith in the supernatural and in the fundamental doctrines of the Christian Church, and can no longer preach and teach them, why do they not, like honorable gentlemen, resign the responsibilities which they have accepted, and go out and establish a platform of their own? If they have the truth, why do they not show their confidence in their teachings by organizing their own institutions instead of continuing to receive their support from those whose beliefs they have solemnly promised to espouse? I think that common honor and honesty would lead them to such a step."

Will they take it? No! The overwhelming majority of them have decided that since the fare within is good, and, as yet, even special honors are not denied them in that fellowship, they will remain to enjoy both! One seeks to justify this on the ground that the Liberals' departure might leave evangelical denominations to the leadership of "reactionaries," and thereby become "dangerous to intellectual and religious liberty"!

What is the conclusion of the whole matter? Is it

not necessarily this — that *the Critic's use of the camouflage covers conscienceless cowardice?*

In the interest of gentility, this statement were best not made by orthodox men. We can reach it, however, our enemies themselves being witnesses. James Martineau, the famous Unitarian, said: — "I am persuaded that honorable laymen, themselves of broad church sympathies, are more alive than is commonly supposed to the essential immorality of the liberal clerical position."

An editor of Chicago's greatest daily, commenting upon the positions taken by a Baptist Professor in a Theological Seminary, once said: — "Is there no place to assail Christianity but a divinity school? Is there no one to write infidel books except the professors of Christian theology? Is a theological seminary an appropriate place for a general massacre of Christian doctrine? Mr. Mangasarian delivers infidel lectures every Sunday in Orchestra Hall and no one is shocked; but when professional defenders of Christianity jump on it and assassinate it, the public — even the agnostic public — cannot but despise them. If the expression of these infidel sentiments by Christian teaching makes a marked and saddening impression on mature minds, how must it affect the young people in attendance at the University? These young people are not contaminated by the teachers of Spiritualism, Theosophy and Free Thought who abound in Chicago; but when the very men whom they regard as pillars of the faith bend under them like a broken reed, it is inevitable that they will leave the University confirmed infidels. Even so, we are not championing either Christianity or infidelity, but only condemning infidels masquerading as men of God and Christian teachers."

The amazing thing is that liberal ministers generally do not awaken to this outrage; and still more amazing is it that instead of curtailing they are increasing this deception! A professor writes a book entitled, "The New Orthodoxy," and from the first word to the last, it contains not one "orthodox" sentence! Another writes a book on "The Second Advent," and, in spite of his title, his covert intention obviously was to prove the impossibility of such an event! A tract appears entitled "Baptist Fundamentals," the main body of which was devoted to a denial of the faith of the Baptist Fathers! Tacoma, Washington, announced a Bible Conference on "Christian Fundamentals," but lo, every speaker appearing on the program was an *opponent* both of the Fundamentals themselves and of the International Movement which has made twenty years of notable history under that same name! The intent of all this becomes increasingly clear.

The author of "The International Jew," speaking of the Hebrew's ability to break in where he was not wanted and control what he had not created, says that in both Germany and Russia "the social system had encrusted around the Jew, keeping him in a position where, as the nations knew by experience, he would be less harmful. As nature encysts the harmful foreign element in the flesh, building a wall around it, so nations have found it expedient to do with the Jew. In modern times, however, the Jew has found a means of knocking down the walls and throwing the whole national house into confusion, and in the darkness and riot that follow, seize the place he has long coveted.

It is a perfect parallel of what has taken place in Protestantism. Evangelical religion, by a series of clear, strong confessions of faith, had walled against the Unitarian infection; but by massing their forces and making continuous assault upon both the right and content of those Confessions, the Liberals have thrown the theological house into disorder, and under cover of the consequent confusion seized the coveted position in schools of second grade, in colleges, theological seminaries, and universities, and are now struggling, with all the power at their united command, to capture the pulpits of Protestantism and the offices of denominational organizations, and thus make the rout of Orthodoxy complete. This attempt explains the clash of arms on the battlefield of theology and the array of opposing armies!

The Creeds To This Conflict Are Irreconcilable

I have weighed well these words! I know the challenge which they contain, but candid men know also their content of truth.

The creeds of the two parties are now plainly declared.

A few years ago it was difficult to get any definition of "The New Faith." Men indulged themselves in such rhetorical deliverances that it was difficult to separate the sense from the sound; but now the philosophical fogs are clearing away a bit, and the new theories are assuming more definite shape — and in no feature does Orthodoxy discern the face of a friend.

Modernism is a *philosophy* — pure and simple! Orthodoxy is an *experience* based upon a *revelation!* The exponents of the first are devotees of Descartes and Darwin. The disciples of the second are converts to Christ and students of the prophets and apostles.

Modernists, as devotees of Descartes, believe in the divine immanence and are practically *Pantheists.* Christians, as disciples of Christ, believe in the divine transcendence, and are always *Theists*.

Modernists, as devotees of Charles Darwin, look upon the Bible as an "evolution." Christians, as disciples of Jesus, hold with Him that the Bible is a *revelation*.

Modernists, enamored of the evolution theory, seek to develop the natural good in man, and trust to education and environment for redemption. Christians, accepting the speech of Jesus as *ex cathedra,* hope for salvation only through the regeneration of the Holy Spirit and by the merit of the shed blood.

Modernists, clinging to the Descartes philosophy of divine immanence, count themselves divine in nature, and make the inner consciousness the court of last appeal. Christians, believing the Bible to be a divine revelation, reckon themselves human and sinful, and look to the Christ of the Scriptures as their one and only Lord, and to the teachings of Christ, prophet and apostle as constituting the authoritative basis both of creed and of conduct. The result is that Modernists oppose all dogmas, discard all fixed doctrines, and trust the philosophy of the day to fit the fact to fate; while Fundamentalists turn to a Book the teachings of which they believe to be as stable as the North Star, and the light from which will never fail, *"till the day dawn and the shadows flee away."*

To the Christian, *Christ* is the essence of Christianity and the Bible is the encasement of Christian philosophy. To the Modernist, "Christianity has no essence; no real, absolute truth, either as concerns religion or morals."

Herman Randall, once a Baptist minister but now in both theory and fellowship Unitarian, speaks the modern "shibboleth" as follows: — "My own conception is that if all the creeds and dogmas and paraphernalia of the churches in Christendom to-day could be set aside, nothing would be lost"; while the orthodox British theologian P. L. Forsyth grieved the "losing of the creed that can alone produce an experience."

This all leads to a further remark — *the proclama-*

tions of the contending creeds prove them to be poles apart.

It is all very well for a liberal, retaining position in the camp of the conservatists, to seek to allay suspicions by saying, "There is as little danger of undermining religion by new definitions of theology as there is of blasting out the stars of Heaven by new astronomy;" but the fact remains — as A. J. Gordon once suggested — that the same people who fail to blot out the stars or the sun from the heavens "may prick the eye with a pin and thereby as effectually blind it to light, as though the sun ceased to shine." Whether that be the deliberate intent of the Modernists, we will not now debate; but by comparison of their philosophies with our revelation we can incontrovertibly prove that these have less in common than the starless midnight and the shining mid-day!

To illustrate, let us take the great cardinal thoughts of Theology.

What of the GOD of Modernists? Answer — "God is a symbol to designate the universe in its ideal achieving capacity"; or "God is the Spirit animating nature, the universal force which takes the myriad forms of heat, light, gravitation, electricity and the like." Compare these definitions with the Fundamentalists' belief in "one God eternally existing in three Persons — Father, Son and Holy Spirit"!

Take the CHRIST of the Modernists — who is He? Or rather, in the interests of correct speech, *what* is He? The Modernist says He is "no more divine than we are, or than nature is; of natural birth, and so, not deity"! Compare that, if you please, with the evangelical belief that "Jesus Christ was begotten of the Holy Spirit and born of the Virgin Mary and is true God"!

According to the Modernists, the soul of man is just "a flowing form of divine activity"! Compare that, if you please, with the evangelical idea of the soul's distinctive independence and conscious responsibility!

According to Modernists, "sin is a fall upward in the process of Darwinian development"; or, as one put it, "sin is a search after God"! Compare that, if you like, with the evangelical teaching that "sin is the transgression of the law," or, as the great Joseph Parker expressed it, "sin is a brutal blow in the face of God"!

As to THE ATONEMENT, the new teaching is that the atonement was "a negligible quantity in the work of salvation"; and the Bible expression of it as having been accomplished "by the shedding of blood," is the subject of the skeptic's increasing scoff and scorn as "the Gospel of the shambles"! Compare that, if you will, with the evangelical faith that "God made Christ to be sin for us, that we might be made the righteousness of God in Him" and "being now justified by His blood, we shall be saved from the wrath of God through Him"!

Compare — did I say? Is there any point of common ground where comparison can be instituted as between these opposite poles of doctrine? None whatsoever! One might just as well try to reconcile the midday with the midnight, or effect a compromise between truth and falsehood, or establish a desirable affiliation between Heaven and Hell! Modernists have not only attacked God — denying His transcendence — and Christ — denying His essential deity — and the soul — denying its independent responsibility — and the atonement — denying its sacrificial success! They have once and for all repudiated the Scriptures themselves, which to the Christian believer have ever been the only basis of spiritual knowledge, and the last court of appeal in all matters of creed and conduct.

Even this is not the last step taken by Modernists in their assault upon Christianity. Prof. Roy Wood Sellars of the University of Michigan once said, "The very attitude of worship must be relinquished" — and he does not represent an extreme, repudiated by the professed Christian instructors of "liberal" sympathies, since it is practically one and the same thing whether men cease altogether from the worship of God, or decide, as Prof. Gerald Birney Smith of the Chicago University Divinity School said, "that the worship of God, in a democracy, will consist in reverence for those human values which democracy makes supreme"! The late Professor Walter Rauschenbusch and President McGiffert, both Theological teachers, Dr. Henry Fredrich Cope, once General Secretary of the Religious Education Association (so-called), and Frank Crane, the big writer of little editorials, united in the demand that God should surrender His claims of autocracy — if He is to retain "our respect"! Is there aught that infidels of other days urged which is not now adopted — and even *outdone* — by so-called "Christian" Liberals? What thinking man could belittle the infinity of space between Modernism and Orthodoxy, or fail to apprehend the fact that daily they are drawing still farther apart?

Time holds no promise of even a patched up peace.

Thirty years ago, Liberalism was timid, and so far as it was expressed by professed Christians, its ideas were carefully couched, and kept the semblance, at least, of Scriptural suggestion; but within the last ten years, boldness has developed into brazenness, and no bones are made about voicing any unbelief; while taking issue with the Bible has become a popular pastime of certain University and Theological professors. Retaining their respective denominational "labels" as badges of honor; deftly creating "Boards of Control" known to be sympathetically liberal or spiritual indifferent; filling the School treasury by forced drives, out of which the professor's salary grows increasingly fat, they now declare "an independence of all denominational opinion," and boldly assert that they will "teach what they please" without let or hindrance from any quarter!

So long as Germany retained the opinion that she was right in the former World War, so long as the resources she was filching from the occupied fields of others were sufficient for the sustenance of her army, and so long as her aggressive warfare was winning additional ground and bringing added honors, no armistice was given the least consideration; and as for *peace*, she regarded that as desirable only when her conquests were universally complete.

A kindred arrogance pervades the army of "New Theologians," and, strange to say, kindred conditions account for it. Incomprehensible as it is to Conservative men and believing Christians, these Rationalists regard themselves as being in the right! Unjust as it may be to feed one's forces from the larders of the people fought, Modernists believe that "the end justifies the means," while the capture of the schools of the North, their partial victories in the schools of the South, and the prospect of taking over denominational organizations and an ever increasing number of pulpits, give to the infidelity of Modernism an energy such as the skepticism of past centuries has seldom known.

To make peace with such fighters is practically impossible. The tide must first be turned—and turn it *will* if the present dispensation continues. Evangelical churches are tired of this infidel lordship. Evangelical people are sick of the husks of Rationalism and are yearning again for the fruits of the Spirit. They are beginning to realize their losses — in closed schools, in depleted Mission treasuries, in rejected publications, and in seceding churches. There is a growing rebellion against the ruthlessness of "the new religion." Christianity is not easily crushed! The true Church holds her Master's promise of power against the gates of Hell.

Again and again she has been trodden down — only to rise in renewed and unexpected vigor. Again and again she has suffered apparent defeat, only to return to the field with fresh fighting powers.

Modernism may be the apostasy of prophecy; but if so, her victories will be short-lived, and the final conflict will not end in an armistice resting on "fourteen points" only partially thought through and prematurely signed, nor will the peace of the future be contingent upon the formation of an efficient "Federal Council."

On the contrary, "the Lord of Hosts" will bare His arm. Unbelief will be beaten back to the pit whence it emanated. "Truth crushed to earth will rise again" and rise to rule as is Truth's eternal right. Already both parties in the contest of Christianity with Modern Criticism are recognizing — to coin a word —

The Unbridgable Chasm of the Conflict

The evangelical denominations are in twain to-day.

This fact is seen by all careful students, and conceded by the honest among them. The regnant forces now at work upon the problems of faith have no tendency whatever to heal the breach, but rather constantly to widen the same. To announce this is "treason" in the judgment of the faith-traducers.

For calling attention to this cleavage we expect to be charged with having helped to create it, and our responsibility will be identical with that of the flying horseman who warned the dwellers in Conemaugh Valley of the broken dam and coming flood. Let the men who cut the dykes and loose the devastating floods of infidelity know that history will discern clearly between the creators of this iniquitous deluge and the observant announcers of the same! Noah announced but did not produce the flood. The dam is broken; the breach is past repair! The deluge of infidelity rises! It is now a fight to see what salvage is possible to faithful men.

On the one side "The Federal Council of the Churches of Christ in America," "The Religious Education Society," the "Boards of Control," and the increasing leadership of the schools, secular and denominational, tend to an increasing liberalism in thought, to the supplanting of Christianity by rationalistic skepticism, while "The Christian Fundamentals Movement," the multiplied Bible Conferences, the rapidly growing Bible Training Schools, the outstanding pastors and the remaining orthodox Colleges and Theological Seminaries, together with the overwhelming majority of the laymen in the Churches make an ever increasing phalanx of fighting men who believe, beyond debate, that the Lord of Hosts is with them.

It is the clash of these contending forces that is heard in the Annual Conferences of the several denominations, in the two-fold form of "minority" and "majority" opinion. It was the crash of these contending forces that resounded from shore to shore when the subject of "The Inter-Church Movement" was before the Annual Conventions. And let not the Liberals forget that the greatest single endeavor ever attempted by them went down to final if not disgraceful defeat, when the "Inter-Church Movement" came to signal, if not disgraceful, disintegration.

This line of division is theological and not denominational. In the main it is not a question of denominational control, but rather of evangelical or non-evangelical creed. That is why it affects them all alike! In each of the denominations there are men, devotees of Liberalism, who by word of mouth and printed page have sought to create the impression that a few disgruntled fellows of the denominations have stirred up dissension because all did not consent to ride with them on their "doctrinal hobby" or adopt their "peculiar methods of Bible interpretation." But it becomes increasingly evident that this attempted explanation is the cuttlefish act! It is an inking of the waters to hide their own infidelity! They might as well come out into the clear and admit the facts involved. Dr. Henry B. Smith once said: "One thing is certain — infidel science will rout everything except thorough-going Christian orthodoxy. All the flabby theories will go overboard. The fight will be between a stiff, thorough-going orthodoxy and a stiff, thorough-going infidelity." Those words, written in the Princeton Theological Review of 1913, were prophetic and are confirmed by the present lines of conflict. Such are the forces that face one another today. Between them a compromise is impossible and a truce is undesirable!

To part in peace is the only proper and Christian procedure. But how? Who shall go, and what shall be taken and what shall be left? I know perfectly well the protest that will meet this proposition. The Liberals of the world favor continuance in fellowship with the Conservatives. Why shouldn't they? That relationship holds their only hope of continued life! Their position is like that of the drunken man who clung tenaciously to the post, saying partially in the speech of our Revolutionary Fathers, "Together we stand: divided I fall"! When and where has Liberalism ever stood alone? What strength have the confessed Liberal Churches of the world today? How easy to compute their numbers! How quickly can you call the names of their colleges! How many fingers are required to enumerate their Theological Seminaries? What surveyor's task is it to stake out their wee territory? They are like the parasites that grow on the tree; they can only live by drawing sustenance from the larger evangelical bodies. Apart from them, they have ever been without power. But a principle never to be forgotten is this — that retaining them means decline, if not death, for the healthiest body in which they incyst themselves.

Let history teach us! Cerinthus found place in the first century Church, and his followers multiplied. John — instead of calling a prayer-meeting to see if his views of doctrine would not fellowship those of this early "Unitarian" — quit the bath-house when this skeptic entered it, lest God in judgment strike the place, and then wrote an epistle begging true brethren not to receive him or his into their homes! Yet the faith of Cerinthus was far nearer to Christian teaching than is the infidelity of Modernists! The effect of the Gnostics upon the early Church was sore enough. They followed the method of Modernists and captured the schools; but in the course of time the Churches repudiated them and enjoyed a consequent revival.

Let the Presbyterians recall the Socinian result in England in the eighteenth century and save themselves from its repetition in the twentieth! As the "Westminster Confession" then cleared the air and called the denomination back to the Book, so they again rose in 1910 and 1916 to reaffirm their faith and largely turn Unitarian infidelity from their fellowship; but now they need a new anti-Albany affirmation.

Let not the Baptists forget the consequences of the Arian teaching in England, nor the wilting effect which reduced them from a prosperous people to a nonentity, never to be recovered until the "New Connection" purged itself of this leaven and came again into the favor of the Lord!

Let the Congregationalists be not unmindful of the time when the Unitarian parasite so ate into that New England Christian body as to carry away at one time and by the most infamous "legalized plunder" one hundred and twenty-five of their churches and leave them but a single evangelical body in the City of old Boston! Dr. Jefferson of the Broadway Tabernacle, New York — himself a Liberal — referring to these defections from the

Trinitarian faith and the bitter fruits of them, says: — "I can understand how a delusion can maintain its ground for one generation or a half dozen generations, but I cannot believe that a delusion would be mighty over the truth through sixty generations. The two conceptions (Trinitarian and Unitarian) have met again and again, and every time they have met, the lower (Unitarian) conception has been routed and driven from the field. Nineteen of God's centuries have come out of eternity since Jesus died upon the cross, and all of them have put the crown on the head of the higher conception of Jesus and broken the sceptre of the lower conception."

That, perhaps, is the very reason why Edward Everett Hale, in his old age, was compelled to say, "I do not see why so simple and democratic a religion as Unitarianism has not swept the country long ago." The success of falsehood is fitful; its final failure is as certain as the existence of God. Truly, as one said of Unitarianism, it is like the farm which John Randolph of Roanoke described as "sterile by nature and exhausted by cultivation."

There may be some churches in America that prefer Modernist pastors, Modernist associations and Modernist State Conventions. Let them have them! There may be some schools in America founded by the money of Modernists and maintained by funds from the same source, whose Boards of Control and Faculties and Curricula are openly framed in the interest of Modernism — Rockefeller Colleges. There may be some foreign stations so far gone over to rationalism that they prefer Unitarianism to Fundamentalism. Such schools and missions have the right to live and to be defended by the laws of the land in teaching their infidelity; but neither those churches nor those schools and missions have any right to continue as ecclesiastical parasites, feeding upon the rich blood of evangelical bodies and bearing their honored names; and if these bodies have in them the spirit of John, or the life of Jesus, they will say, calmly but firmly, "no further fellowship"! *"He that is not with me is against me. He that gathereth not with me scattereth abroad."*

Maintaining, as our inalienable right, the installation of such pastors only as stand for *"the faith once for all delivered,"* the maintenance of such schools as hold the Bible to be a message from God, the adoption of such literature as exalts Christ as Lord, the commissioning of messengers at home and to foreign fields whose names will not be "anathema" because they bear a message which is "another gospel," we will go on glorifying Christ as very God, and giving to the world His gospel as its one and only hope! However great our loss in numbers, we will be stronger in spirit and for service, on the day that those who have quit our faith are refused our fellowship also!

II

The Conflict Over The Theological Counterfeit

THE Denominations are passing through one of those spasms of doubt to which the Churches have long been subject. It is doubtful if past convulsions — including Socinianism, Arianism, Deism and Unitarianism — have in any case been so hurtful, or even so threatening, as is that fit of Rationalism by which we are now diseased and distracted!

It is a good time to recall our Lord's promise to His Church that *"the gates of hell shall not prevail against it,"* and yet to administer such corrective measures as may give promise of producing normalcy of faith.

Increasingly modern critics have repudiated and flung away the great cardinal doctrines, such as the inerrancy of the Scriptures, the Personality of the Godhead, the sinfulness of man, and the necessity of an atoning Saviour, the deity of Christ and its attendant doctrines of the Ascension and the Return; but many of these same Modernists have majored upon "liberty of conscience" as the single remaining tenet of the new interpretation of Christianity!

The inanity of their arguments against the cardinal doctrines has been shown again and again; and it now seems to be a necessity to uncover their illogical — yea indefensible — theories of "personal liberty" in matters of faith, by showing how that doctrine rapidly degenerates into the license of infidelity.

The Liberties of Faith

That there are certain liberties to be maintained in the matter of belief, is beyond dispute. In this, as in all other points of real progress, Christ Himself is our exemplar. He was not held by the mere "traditions" of men, nor bound by their blundering interpretations of Scripture. More than once He said: — *"Ye have heard that it was said by them of old time * * * but I say unto you * * * "*. — a remark followed by no discarding of Scripture, but by a higher and more meaningful interpretation of the same. Paul, easily His chief apostle, claims a kindred right, and resents the bringing in of false brethren to *"privily spy out our liberty which we have in Christ Jesus."* But it is very important to discover what that "liberty" is, and to what extent "independence" and "freedom of thought" can be defended or even tolerated in its light!

Speaking from the standpoint of the Christian Scriptures, three things seem to be fairly clear.

It is the liberty of believing what is written in the law and the prophets; the liberty of seeing in Christ the significance of symbol and ceremony, and the liberty of accepting and propagating all demonstrated truth. *The liberty of believing what is written in the law and the prophets.*

"The law and the prophets" constituted "the Bible" in our Lord's day; but certain men of that time — like our Modernists — were not content either with the content or the extent of *"the law and the prophets."* There were some things in "the law and the prophets" that they did not like, and they sought to tear them out. There were other things *not* in "the law and the prophets" which they wanted, and at their pleasure they wrote them in, so that by their "traditions" they *"made void the Word."*

From the beginning, Christ believed the Book, and

to the end of His days on earth He taught the same. It was the disciples' failure to believe *"all that was written in the law and the prophets"* that He excoriated as they journeyed to Emmaus (Luke 24:25). It was by an appeal to "the law and the prophets" that He explained *Himself* (vs. 27) and by an appeal to the same that He demonstrated the meaning of His resurrection and the gospel ministry of repentance and remission of sins (Luke 24:44-47).

The Psalmist said, *"I shall walk at liberty for I seek thy precepts."* Paul and his apostolic brethren seem to have found all needful "personal liberties" within the confines of the same. There are few books of the Bible so doctrinal and polemical as Romans, Corinthians and Galatians, and yet a careful study of those three Pauline Epistles will impress one with the fact that the phrase *"It is written"* is repeated thirty-four times.

The battle of the New Testament Church was that of extricating an inspired and recorded Scripture from the heaps of human tradition — established, but uninspired custom. Those who had thus lumbered the Word of God had doubtless done it in the name of "interpretation"; and at this moment Modernism is endangering the true liberty of every believer after a kindred manner.

Every man has a right to independent thought, but he who thinks "above that which is written," apart from that which has been revealed, is using his liberty *"for an occasion to the flesh."* *Again — Christ and His Apostles exercised the liberty of seeing the true significance of symbol and ceremony.*

The Judaized were incapable of interpreting the Sabbath beyond the statement *"in it thou shalt do no work,"* and, consequently, condemned Christ for healing on that day — not seeing that He was Lord of the Sabbath. When His disciples, being hungry, plucked the corn on the Sabbath day, their critics gave demonstration of the same incapacity to distinguish between symbol and substance. Neither Christ nor His apostles abrogated the Sabbath, nor did they essentially disregard it, but, rather, sensibly and spiritually interpreted it. That is a liberty not to be denied to any saint. In this same manner they treated circumcision and other symbols.

Some of us believe "baptism" to be the immersion of a believer in water; but we have no notion that the ordinance is a saving one, or that the act is significant save to those who see its great object-lesson — death to sin, burial with Christ, and resurrection to walk in newness of life with Him (Rom. 6:4 f).

Even greater revelations, divinely right in themselves, are made wrong by misunderstanding, or by mean and paltry interpretation. Literalism may, and sometimes does, stand for littleness; and liberty in interpretation is not littleness in understanding.

I confess frankly that while I believe profoundly in the Baptist view of the ordinances so far as their physical form is concerned, I have no patience whatsoever with those individuals in my denomination who see only damnation for every man disobedient in that outward expression and every woman who mistakenly supposes she is to be utterly loyal to the second ordinance, "the Lord's Supper," but may treat with neglect the first — baptism. Disobedience to God's plain Word is never a minor offence; but it is a thousand times better to change even the form of a ceremony than to lose its significance. The man who practices Biblical baptism, but denies the authority of the Bible or the necessity of regeneration, is far less a Christian than the man who accepts some human substitute for the ceremony, but retains the spiritual intent and significance of the plain command.

Increasingly we are sympathetic with that Denver pastor who said, "In my early life I was terribly worried to know what God would do with the pious unbaptized. In later years I am even more concerned to know what He can do with the impious baptized."

Christ said, *"Ye are my friend if ye do whatsoever I have commanded you,"* and He might have added, "Ye are my intelligent friends and my efficient friends if you see the objective of the performance and move through the symbol to the thing signified."

Once more —

We are to exercise the liberty of accepting and propagating all demonstrated truth.

When Christ said, *"Ye shall know the truth, and the truth shall make you free,"* He was probably thinking of the Bible alone, for it was Christ Who later said of God's Book, *"Thy Word is truth."* To this hour it is doubtful if there is any fundamental or necessary truth which cannot be found within its sacred pages — and found there in more perfect form than human ingenuity will ever phrase it. If one would know the truth of history, let him read the Bible. If he would know the steps of creation and the law of succession, let him read the Bible. If he would make himself acquainted with sound philosophy, let him read the Bible. If he would discover the supreme sociology, let him look into the Scriptures. This remark applies to practically every known science.

But to allay the Modernist's fears that we will become Bibliolaters, making of God's Book a "fetich" for our affections, and finding in it the only writings of interest, let us hasten to remark that we stand for utter "academic freedom," and have unwavering confidence that any truth and all truth is profitable.

Orthodoxy has ever been the patron of learning, the defender of intellectual freedom, and the advocate of progress. Our refusal to "cackle" with every discoverer of dinosaur eggs ten million (?) years old, or to enthuse over *"science falsely so called,"* has led some men to name us ignoramuses," call us "reactionaries," and warn against us as "light-extinguishers," but is it not well to recollect that to this hour the Christ of the "Fundamentalists" is *"the light of the world"*? The Christianity of the Bible is, to this blessed moment, the world's most advanced religion, and loyal devotees of the divinely inspired Book, known as the Bible, remain until now pioneers in truth-seeking and the patron saints of established science. But — mark you — we said *"science"* — *not* "speculation," *not* "theory" nor "guess," *not* "philosophical imaginings" but *demonstrated truth!* Within that realm, we applaud the unlimited privilege of accepting and propagating!

Science is as sacred as Scripture — in fact as sacred as God, since both Scripture and Science are emanations of His Spirit. The *truth* in any realm and in all realms is desirable. It should be sought assiduously, and, when found, be widely proclaimed. Such liberty no sane man will ever seek to restrict; but let us clearly understand

The Limitations of Theology

Nothing could be more unjustifiable than that Modernist definition of the task of theology as the attempt to "think over our religious inheritance in the light of our present problems so as to formulate for today and to transmit to the coming generation an expression of faith vitally related to our present life."

The task of Theology is to tell men the truth about God! If *that* be not true, then language loses its meaning and Greek roots convey no message!

Theology — instead of being under the necessity of adjusting itself to the ever changing experiences of men — is a fixed science far more unchangeable than the science of astronomy. Sometimes a star wanders, but in the truth about God there is no possible variation.

This leads me to make three remarks: — *The Christian believer is limited to a single name as Saviour.*

"There is none other name under heaven given among men whereby we must be saved." (Acts 4:12) To those students who have made themselves familiar with the history of pretended Christs or even of divinely-begotten (?) sons of women, Dr. Harry Emerson Fosdick's declaration of supernatural claims akin to those made for Jesus of Nazareth, is nothing short of sacrilege. The absurdity of his argument was clearly revealed in the rejoinder made by the venerable and scholarly Dr. Bates. He named the father and proved the *human* origin of every one of them, and left our Christ the solitary, non-contested Son of God! Consequently, when any man denies the deity of Jesus Christ, he exceeds the limitations of a sound theology and puts himself outside the pale of the Christian profession — no matter what church-membership he may hold or what braggart claims of evangelical views he may boast.

Theodore Parker, when he remarked, "It is absurd to maintain that Christ entertained no theological errors in matters of importance," treated all Biblical theology with contempt; and when he denied to Christ supernaturalism, he did so deliberately, understanding that thereby he was assaulting the citadel of Christianity itself. When the Modernist tells us that no authority is to be given to the teachings of Jesus Christ "beyond what every man's own mind or heart or conscience can give him," he is not only tearing the crown of deity from the brow of our Lord, but is deliberately doing so to place the same upon himself! And when the same Modernist further says that "in displacing Christ from the eminence given Him by the Church, we see only another idol shattered," he approaches perilously near that blasphemy of the Spirit which is pronounced unpardonable in this life or in the life to come!

It is little wonder indeed that such teaching has finally eventuated in an open break with the infallibility of the Book, and finds voice in sneers and slurs against the very term "theology."

That capable scholar and facile writer Samuel J. Andrews in "Christianity and Anti-Christianity" justly remarks: "That heathen enemies should have said like things in the first days of the Church does not surprise; but that these things should be said in Christendom, after so many centuries, by learned and accomplished scholars, and welcomed by many thousands of all classes, high and low, shows the workings of a spirit of hostility to Christ which like a smouldering fire is getting ready to burst into a fierce flame." But when did such flames of opposition, even though they reached the white heat of persecution, do aught else than drive believers back to Jesus of Nazareth as the solitary Saviour, and result in the centralization of all hope for the soul, for the Church, and even for the world, in and upon Him?

Man may wander at his will in philosophy but *not* in Biblical theology. There his bounds are fixed, *"for ever settled in heaven,"* and in that, Christ Jesus is the one and only sufficient Saviour.

It is the way of grace, *"for by grace are ye saved."* All other ways of "salvation" are but blind alleys for the soul. Paul, the prime Christian theologian of all the centuries, nearly two thousand years ago sought by all the power of an inspired pen to put that fact clearly before us. Writing to the Galatians, he said: — *"I marvel that ye are so soon removed from him who called you into the grace of Christ unto another gospel, which is not another, but there be some who trouble you and would pervert the gospel of Christ; but though we or an angel from heaven preach any other gospel than that we have preached unto you, let him be accursed. As we said before, so say we now again, if any man preach any other gospel unto you than that ye have received, let him be accursed."* (Gal. 1:6-9)

In the light of such a Scripture, what shall we think and what can we say of those Modernists who strike at the heart of grace itself, the vicarious atonement, and who hold the sacrificial idea to scorn, subjecting the same to caricature and vilification? These are the men who would displace the gospel by a Marxian Socialism; who would substitute for inspired Scripture the philosophy of a Kant or the psychology of a Ross or the superficial pratings of a Burch or Patterson.

If the present generation continues to be taught by such superficial and anti-Christian teachers as now so frequently disgrace that noble profession, and by such shallow naturalistic and Bolshevistic text-books as are now in use in State Universities and increasingly imposed on High Schools and even the grades, the *"highway of holiness"* will be blotted out, and the very path to righteousness and heaven will become weed-grown and forgotten! Shall the Christian believer consent to such a procedure? Not unless he too is smitten with a deadly "flu" of unfaith or with the even more destructive "black death" of indifference.

And yet again —

The Christian believer is limited to a single Book as a revelation.

That Book is, of course, the Bible — the Book of which Joseph Parker, author of "The People's Bible," so eloquently wrote under the justified title "None Like It"; the Book which, as compared with all other books, is, like its incarnate expression, Christ, not only without competitor but without kinship; the Book which, like its Master, *"speaks as never man spake,"* and does the works that no other writing has ever wrought.

A Modernist dares to remark, "We must be making our own religion," but logical lengths of "Modernism" are now being reached by those who say, "We must make our own revelation"! It is years since Dean Farrar, Dr. Horton and Professor Marcus Dodds proposed a Bible for children and families founded on the theories and alleged discoveries of the "Higher Criticism." Professor Kent tried his hand at abbreviating God's Word and changing it at the points where he said prophet and apostle had so evidently made mistakes, and leaving out those portions where, according to him, the Master Himself slipped in memory or voiced Judaized impressions! Chicago University cannot afford to be behind Yale at any point — so one of its Professors took the New Testament in hand to train it to modernistic moulds! It is time for the Universalists to speak next, and tell us the content of *their* Bible, and then for the Unitarians to reduce and redact divine revelation a bit farther, and finally for Van Loon and H. G. Wells to complete the job and give to the world an entirely new product, but called by the good, old and greatly honored name, the Bible! So who will say that there are any limitations in theology!

As Dr. Franklin Johnson once wrote: — "Suppose the Bible does teach that the human race once fell from a state of innocency, what of that? The Trinity, what of that? The substitutionary Atonement, what matters it? The Second Coming of Christ in visible, personal form, what of that? Higher critics, recognizing no central or supreme source of authority, smilingly sweep it all aside, and yet, strangely enough, turn about and in the next breath pay glowing tribute to the grand old Book as a most worth while volume!" — all of which gives pith and point to his further comment: "What a fall! In 1869 I saw the Emperor Napoleon III. He was at the summit of his career, a confident, strong and regal figure. Beside him sat Eugenie, fair as a lily and as little concerned for the future. A few months later he was hurled from his lofty station and shut up in captivity. He was still worth while, but the great world had ceased to care for him. That is the change which higher criticism, where it is accepted, makes in the position of the Bible, whose robes of royalty it declares to be full of rents and stains, whose throne it overturns, and whose sceptre it gives to the human soul, leaving it indeed worth while but uncrowned."

Is this the Bible of the believer? In God's name, is this rag of a remnant the only revelation left to believers? We spit defiance in the face of such a suggestion, and remind our auditors that — as true today as when the poet wrote it —

> "A glory gilds the sacred page
> Majestic like the sun.
> It gives a light to every age;
> It gives but borrows none.
>
> The hand that gave it still supplies
> The gracious light and heat.
> Its truths upon the nations rise,
> They rise but never set."

That is the Book which every true Christian believes and every true evangelical stands ready to declare: "We hold it truth without any admixture of error, the only complete and final revelation of the will of God to man: the true centre of Christian union, and the supreme standard by which all human conduct, creeds and opinions should be tried."

It is this ignoring of the limitations of theology which has resulted in the

License of Infidelity

It is that degeneracy from the liberty of believing what was written in the law and in the prophets to the license of infidelity concerning the same which has rent the present camp, dividing her membership into hostile cliques and bringing on a war that for bitterness, suffering and far-reaching destruction will greatly exceed that which swept the world from 1914 to 1918. Every good student knows the multiplied forms in which that license has found expression.

It is the license of infidelity to substitute reason for revelation.

Before the rise of Romanism, the recognition of Bible authority made for unanimity, power and conquest for the true Church of God; and when at last Romish errors forced a revolution on the matter of where authority lay, every Protestant body that ever came to power put itself on record as believing that that authority was in, and with, the Book divine!

The French Confession said: — "We believe that the word contained in these books has proceeded from God. It is not lawful for men nor even for angels to add to it, to take away from it, nor even to change it."

The Belgic Confession declared: "We believe that the Holy Scriptures fully contain the will of God, and that whatsoever men ought to believe unto salvation is sufficiently contained therein."

The Westminster Confession asserted: "The whole counsel of God concerning all things necessary for His own glory, man's salvation, faith and life, is either expressly set down in Scripture or by good and necessary consequence may be deduced therefrom, unto which nothing at any time is to be added."

The Church of England said: "The Holy Scripture containeth all things necessary to salvation so that whatsoever is not read therein, nor may be proved thereby, is not to be required of any man."

The Congregationalists said: "Like our Pilgrim Fathers, we acknowledge no rule of faith but the Word of God, and declare our adherence to the faith and order of the apostolic and primitive churches."

The Baptists have never (save at Indianapolis) stood elsewhere than on this ground: "We believe that the Holy Bible was written by men divinely inspired and is a perfect treasure of heavenly instruction; that it has God for its Author, salvation for its end, and truth without any admixture of error for its matter."

Even the Modernists, if you please (all their present unbelieving bishops to the contrary notwithstanding) lack the temerity to attempt even to change their declaration that "The Holy Scriptures contain all the things necessary to salvation, so that whatsoever is not read therein, nor may be proved thereby is not to be required of any man."

Tell me that men can depart from these teachings and yet remain in the denominations named! Tell me that foreign mission universities looking to believers for support can tear this position to tatters and yet be defended as evangelical! Tell me that men who hold in no respect whatever this uniform judgment of revelation may, nevertheless, sit in the council halls of rulership and pass out to independent churches decrees which must be adopted on pain of preacher decapitation if they fail, and practically Church-exclusion should they not be cordially received — and I will answer: "It is not only taking the license of infidelity so to do, but it is a license which heads for an atheism of which the destiny is denominational death and even denominational damnation!"

France once followed Reason, refusing Revelation and the history of that movement was written in rivers of human blood!

Russia has for the last twenty years listened for the most part to apostles of Reason who are the bitterest conceivable opponents of Revelation and her wreck is the result!

Germany sat at the feet of these apostles from the days of Wellhausen and his school until those of Nietsche — and his educational program paid, as the price of that privilege, a ruined monarchy which in its fall nearly wrecked the world!

I think of the great Baptist men of yesterday — men like Carroll of Texas, Broadus of Kentucky, Strong and Pattison of New York, Wilkinson and Franklin Johnson of Illinois, and men like Weston, Goodspeed and Royce — and thank God my young life overlapped their mature and even ripened years — and then I look at their pygmied sons and successors and listen to their prattle about "reason" and "science," and am compelled to say, *"As a man thinketh in his heart, so is he,"* and that the license of infidelity can never make such spirits as were developed by love for God's revelation!

Once more —

This license of infidelity seeks to substitute civilization for evangelization.

The Northern Baptist Convention held in Denver, Colorado, will go down in human history famed for one act, namely, that by a deliberate declaration it shifted the motive and objective of missions from the basis of evangelization to that of civilization, and started the Baptist denomination on a program of education versus salvation. How rapidly we have driven under the full sail of skeptical winds out of God's well marked and charted course of "discipling nations" towards the world-reefs of "improving civilization" — the same as those on which Greece and Rome and Babylon went down (at the very time when their success seemed most complete), who can compute?

One of our greatest and most dependable foreign

missionaries fifteen years ago wrote home telling us that in a few years we had increased our educational forces in foreign lands 750 per cent and our evangelical forces but 51 per cent. That was an utter reversal of the convictions and the policies of those great pioneers in mission work, Carey, Boardman, Judson, Clough and others; an utter reversal of the convictions of every mature and masterly mind later on a foreign field, such as Levering, Boggs, Young, Clark and others of kindred age and competent experience.

The Baptist Denomination was re-born and entered upon a period of its history the like of which the world has seldom or never seen when William Carey heard the call of God to go to the foreign field. That glorious history closed when the Denver Convention just mentioned, decided in favor of "civilization" versus "evangelization"; and although the advocates of that deadly policy cannot be expected to confess their mistake, the future historian will clearly record the sure and deadly results thereof. We are told that these things are being righted; but down hill is easy going — to regain ground is difficult.

It is the license of infidelity to substitute Unitarianism for Trinitarianism.

For fully two thousand years these doctrines have stood in the arena of conflict, eternal antagonists. For nearly sixty generations the truth of Trinitarianism has triumphed — yet never once in that time has Unitarianism quit the contest. Why should it be expected so to do? Satan still lives, and his millions of experiences have taught him the value of his trump card. Has he not temporarily triumphed with it again and again? Why, then, should he not in the twentieth century fling it upon the world's table afresh?

Trace, if you please, the history of this camouflage of Christianity, this emasculated faith, this counterfeit of the truth. Our Presbyterian brethren once set their great Annual Assembly rife with debate. Over what? Over the very same subjects that once, in Socinian form more than a hundred years ago in England, came near to sending that denomination to its doom. The only thing that saved them was their Westminster Confession — which clarified the air and called them back to the Book, the only basis of Christian faith and life.

How dare Congregationalists forget the time — only a hundred years removed — when the Unitarian blight came upon that New England body, or the Baptists forget the consequences of the Arian teaching in England and the wilting effect thereof that reduced our forefathers from a prosperous people to a nonentity, sending paralysis into every part of the denomination until "the New Connection" purged itself of that leaven of error and came back to the Book as its basis of belief, and, under the blessing of the Lord, enjoyed more than a revival — truly a resurrection!

Look down yonder Eastern sea-board and mark the havoc which Unitarianism has wrought. Time was when Harvard University belonged by right of birth and breeding to the evangelicals; when Princeton was a mighty power, and when Rochester University was loyal to the revelation of God's Word. Time was when Union Theological Seminary enthroned Christ as the Son of God, and exalted the Bible as the eternal and adequate revelation of the divine will, and emphasized every cardinal doctrine of the Christian faith, making of men mighty ministers of the Word. Time was when even Andover was thronged with men coming from both sides of the sea to sit at the feet of the great souls who steeped these students in a knowledge of the Book and sent them out as flaming evangels to all parts of the world.

But today, when you call the roll of these schools, you name the captains of the hosts who marshal their

The Theological Counterfeits

forces to fight the authority of the Book, the deity of Christ, the blood atonement, and every other Christian fundamental! In full line behind them stand those other schools, Theological Seminaries made possible by the sacrifices of believing men, genuine Baptists of the old order, and as we believe of the divine order, viz. Crozier, Rochester, Newton Center, Brown, Colgate, Chicago University — in fact the only objection to naming others is the lack of limitation in number!

The majority of our schools are lost to God and the Gospel, and today they are seats of unsound teachings and the prolific mothers of Modernist preachers — all because Satan, having succeeded with his trump card, Unitarianism, so often in the past, and knowing as he must know that the end of the age draws nigh, is working it now as he never worked it before.

Is it not shockingly suggestive that every Unitarian paper and ever outstanding Unitarian pulpit is just now eloquent with the praises of our leading Modernist ministers and laymen? "Birds of a feather!"

Brethren of the Baptist Denomination — a people made by loyalty to the Book — I conclude this address by begging you — Back to God, the Creator of the heavens and the earth; Back to Christ, the atoning Saviour of sinful men; and Back to the Bible, the only rule of Baptist faith and practice!

III

The Counterfeit In The Attempted "Inter-Church"

"*FROM the days of John the Baptist until now, the kingdom of heaven suffereth violence, and the violent take it by force.*" (Matt. 11:12)

This text has uniformly surprised, and even astonished, the Bible student. On its face it seems to contain contradictions. The verses immediately preceding it hold evident compliment for John, the forerunner of Jesus. He was the messenger sent to prepare the way for the Son, and of him Jesus said, "*Verily I say unto you, among them that are born of women there hath not risen a greater than John the Baptist.*" So far, the speech is plain, and as easy of interpretation as of understanding: but when He adds, "*he that is least in the kingdom of heaven is greater than he,*" we are puzzled: and when He continues, "*The kingdom of heaven suffereth violence, and the violent take it by force,*" we are positively perplexed.

Consulting commentaries will not relieve this mental disturbance, but rather increase the same, as the majority of them fail to make any distinction whatever between the church of God and the kingdom of heaven, and by that failure give a false interpretation to the text — an interpretation which unnaturally strains the text, an interpretation which takes words from the text itself and puts upon them meanings not found in any dictionary, and an interpretation which will not fit in with either Old or New Testament teaching concerning the Kingdom. Weiss, that clear thinker and marvellous writer, holds both a sane and Scriptural view of this verse, namely, that it was a political endeavor to force the Messianic kingdom and crown the uncrucified Christ.

That view of it explains what is meant by saying that John was *"less than the least in the kingdom of heaven."* He was a mortal man — *they* will be immortal and incorruptible. This view of it harmonizes perfectly with the Bible usage of the word "violent" and the singular employment of the word "suffereth." That view also explains the course of Church history, and the false conceptions of the kingdom that have finally resulted in the world movement known as the "Inter-Church Movement."

In the light of that fact, we call your attention to three phrases in the use of which the text takes on suggestive meaning — the Promised Kingdom, the Proposed Kingdom and the Kingdom of Prophecy.

The Promised Kingdom

Israel's prophets had abounded with promises of the coming kingdom. From the time of David, those promises had multiplied in number and increased in interest. To him God had said, *"The house and thy kingdom shall be established for ever before thee."* As he dwelt upon this promise, David later said of his coming Son, *"He shall have dominion also from sea to sea, and from the river unto the ends of the earth. All kings shall fall down before him; all nations shall serve him."* Through the minor prophet Zechariah, God spake again — *"The Lord shall be King over all the earth."* In the book of Daniel it is recorded: — *"And in the days of these kings shall the God of heaven set up a kingdom, which shall never be destroyed, and the kingdom shall not be left to other people, but it shall break in pieces and consume all these kingdoms, and it shall stand for ever."* (Dan. 2:44)

These are only a few of the multitudinous references to the coming Kingdom — with which all Israel was familiar. In expectation of that Kingdom, they lived; for the hastening of that Kingdom, they prayed; and for its appearance, they watched. It could hardly have been a personal experience of regeneration for which the Psalmist yearned. It must have been, rather, the coming of that which was the Utopian dream of every Old Testament prophet, of which he said, *"I have longed for thy consolation, O Lord."*

The spirit of Israel wearied while awaiting its appearance. There is something little less than pathetic in the query put to the risen Christ — *"Lord, wilt thou at this time restore again the kingdom to Israel?"* We can feel the weariness of the waiting in the choice of the words. It is exactly as if they had said — "Lord, we thought when You first came that the Kingdom was at hand. John announced it, and You confirmed his proclamation, but events did not terminate in a crown of authority, but, rather, in a cross and a crown of thorns. Our hopes were destroyed and our expectations well nigh dead. But now that You are alive again — now that You have conquered death and the grave — now that You have outwitted Your foes, dare we hope? Is the day about to break? Is our Kingdom about to come? Is our triumph over Rome and our supremacy over the whole world to be realized now?"

In the very question itself, there was practically a request to this effect — "Do not disappoint us; do not delay us; be not unmindful of how long we have waited, and how ardently we have watched, of how soberly we have prayed, of how eagerly we have hoped! Strain not our patience further!"

This eager interest had been excited by John's an-

The Attempted "Inter-Church" 45

nouncement:

"The kingdom of heaven is at hand" — this announcement had stirred every ember of hope into a flame of expectation. Thousands had thronged about Him; thousands had turned to Him. In his "Commentaries," John Calvin writes about "the zeal kindled in the minds of men" as they heard John; of there having "flocked to Him" a vast assembly of men, collected by the voice of one. They came in crowds and received not only with greediness but with "vehement impetuosity" the announcement that *"the kingdom of heaven is at hand."* Farrar writes of how "with holy and happy violence" they pressed about Him. They wanted to join the Kingdom forces at once, and some of them even got ready for office and sent their mother to speak to the King about their appointments!

Had all of this a parallel in the Inter-Church World Movement? Certainly! Even the destructive critics of our day who have not wholly lost their veneration for the Bible entertain the feeling that the kingdom promised in these sacred pages is at least possible. Reason — their special guide — suggests that such a kingdom *ought* to come. The social, economic, moral and spiritual condition of the world rather demands it. The pressure of sin and sorrow is so great that sober thought asserts "it ought to come *now*"! The utterances of inspired prophets, for whom they have a little veneration, and of the uninspired — for whom they have much more! — have made certain men feel that the very crisis of the world ought to give birth to "a new Kingdom." Playing the role of prophets, they have begun to proclaim it "at hand," and at the sound of their voices, the people have flocked to them in great numbers. It is doubtful if there is any single theme today that strikes people so favorably as that of "world-betterment."

All this makes it of interest to ask wherein the

people of our text were right, and to learn if possible to what mistakes the people of our day are tempted. The Biblical record is quite full enough for our following it to see what the situation was in John's day.

The Proposed Kingdom

We mean, of course, not the Kingdom proposed by John, but the Kingdom proposed by the people who heard John; the Kingdom proposed by the people who heard Jesus; yea, even by the people who had accepted the announcement of John with joy and the declaration of Jesus with hope.

On the subject of that proposed kingdom there has been little debate. Students of Scripture and of history have easily understood the meaning of the men to whom Jesus here refers. They thought to make the kingdom a political one. They imagined that Christ had already come in His kingly capacity. They firmly believed that the hour had struck for the establishment of the Kingdom. In each and every one of these respects they were as clearly wrong as they were deeply convinced; and in each and every one of them the recent Inter-Church World Movement tracked over again the mistakes of two millenniums ago!

They thought to make the Kingdom a political one. They wanted Christ to be crowned then and there. They wanted to rebuild David's throne and straightway set Christ upon it. They wanted every king of earth to capitulate in His behalf, and every crown to be cast at His feet. They wanted their Kinsman to rule, solitary and alone, and their people to come at once into the rich inheritance of the multitudinous promises. Surely they were not to be blamed for this, as the world in their day was in a bad way and needed both a new Kingdom and another King.

Such was the exact objective of the recent Inter-

Church World Movement! The proposition of Modernism is clearly set forth by Andrews in his "Christianity and anti-Christianity," and is to the effect that "the Church has given too little attention to the practical side of world interests; has looked too much to the future life and too little to this life; has given too great a place to abstract doctrine, to creeds and confessions of faith, and too little to the application of Christian ethics to the social and political evils around us. We have drawn too broad a line between the secular and the sacred things of life, between the church and the world. We must now change our mode of action. We must not ignore any question that affects human well-being. All science, arts, inventions, everything that aids in the culture of man or the improvement of society, comes properly within the Christian sphere." In other words, they imagine it to be the business of the Church to make the Kingdom of God commensurate with the world, and in order to do that, unity of endeavor, if not of organization, is the *sine qua non* of success!

The Northern Baptist Convention, in its alliance with the Inter-Church World Movement, voiced that conception as clearly as the language of competent men could express it. It is not at all to be supposed that any unweighed words have escaped the lips of the leaders, and it is the most unlikely of all things that they failed to say what they meant. The first paragraph of their declaration reads as follows: — "We record our acceptance of the conception that the mission of the Christian Church is to establish a civilization, Christian in spirit and passion, throughout the world," and the animating motive is voiced by our at-one-time official organ, "The Baptist," in these words: — "The world is at the crossroads! The peril to our Christian civilization is greater now than in any hour of the war. The whole world seems staggering toward chaos. Forces are in action and winning victories which, if not met and overthrown, will turn our world into hell." "The world's only hope is Jesus Christ brought into human affairs, and it is ours to say whether or not this shall be done." The "World Outlook," the official organ of the Inter-Church Movement, boasted of having "launched the definite policy of making Christianity appeal to everybody in this period of unrest, even to the most skeptical."

Personally I cannot find in my Bible a passage that even remotely hints a civilization of any sort as the objective of the Church of God! Historically, I find that wherever that conception has obtained it has resulted in such a combination of Church and State as uniformly compromised the testimony of the former and abridged the liberties of the latter. In that combination the Christian's creed has ever been compromised, his walk and conversation scandalized, and his church subsidized!

The name of "Constantine" sums up this entire conception of a politico-spiritual institution, world-wide in its sweep and world-energized in its endeavor.

Christ's early disciples imagined that He had already come in kingly capacity. They believed He was then ready to begin His reign. That was the meaning of the palm-branches and garments strewn in His way when on the foal of an ass He rode into Jerusalem. They were hailing Him as their King; they were ready to fight that the crown might be on His brow. In fact, so violent were they in their endeavor that they laid hands upon Him "and were determined to make Him a king," so that He must needs escape, and for the time being elude their mistaken interpretations of Scripture and their violent endeavor at kingdom-making.

They made no distinction between the first and the second coming of the Christ. They did not understand that His first appearance was "with sin upon Him," as man's Substitute, His destiny the cross, whereas His second appearance was to be *"without sin unto salvation"* and His destiny the crown.

The leaders of the Inter-Church World Movement made exactly the same mistake!

They believed that Christ had come as King already, making no distinction in time between His successive offices — Prophet, Priest and King. They had Him to be a world Ruler in this age. They also believed His crown to be in their hands and that the day of His coronation would be determined by their endeavor. Here again they fell into the error of the people who would bring the kingdom by force, and were following perfectly the Constantine conception even to the point of force. With them, however, it was not the force of arms, but rather that of educated intellect, sacrificial energy and consecrated gold. One of their greatest advertisements carried a quotation credited to Bushnell — "One more revival, only one, is needed; the consecration of the money power to God. When that revival comes, the kingdom of God will come in a day." An opinion of that sort paved the way perfectly for them to fall into the third error entertained by certain believers of Christ's time, viz: —

They thought the hour had struck to set up the kingdom. Their disappointment in Christ's tardiness is voiced in Acts 1:6, *"Wilt thou at this time restore again the kingdom to Israel?"* For forty days following His resurrection He had talked to them of "the Kingdom," but had said not a word as to the *time* of its establishment, for the very simple reason that the time of it was then, is now, and until the kingdom comes will be an unrevealed truth; but they believed it was at hand. The Inter-Church World Movement leaders held exactly that conception, and certain Baptist leaders mistakenly shared it.

If I were not in possession of the document to prove

my words, I should seriously doubt whether my auditors or my readers would believe me when I say that the Baptist official organ did not fail to see nor hesitate to voice approvingly the parallelism between this entire conception and the Constantine endeavor. Here is the language used in that magazine, March 27th, 1920, and employed as an incentive toward raising its proposed millions to be used in the Inter-Church World Movement — "We have an intrepid and gifted leadership; we have an advantageous position in the Inter-Church World Movement; we have a literature of high quality; we have an organization which each day becomes more extensive and more effective. Yet with all these we may fail; indeed we shall certainly fail unless the 10,000 Baptist ministers in the Northern Baptist Convention enlist for the most strenuous service of which they are capable; unless the 11,000 churches embrace the New World Movement as Constantine embraced the cross in the heavens, and devote all their personnel and their material resources to the cause of our Lord Jesus Christ; unless the New World Movement becomes in the consciousness of our 1,500,000 members a spiritual enterprise so compelling, so inevitable, so absolutely indispensable to the peace of Christ's Church and to the salvation of the race that we shall enlist in it, give to it, suffer for it, as we did through two memorable years to win the World War."

The parallelism to the Constantine procedure is perfect. "An intrepid and gifted leadership," an "advantageous position," an "effective organization," the cause of Christ as its objective, an absolute appeal to and dependence upon *human* agencies to establish a world-wide kingdom in the name of Christ! There was not a reference to the Holy Ghost or to prayer in the above impassioned appeal, and there wasn't the remotest suggestion that the coming of the kingdom was dependent "neither upon might, nor upon power, but upon His Spirit," nor is there any reference to the utter necessity of revealed truth as a saving force or a kingdom condition!

The Inter-Church Bulletin of Saturday, April 3rd, 1920, had in big letters across the top of its front page, "Over the goal to make the world safe for the future!" Shades of President Wilson! Have we forgotten how, when the Western Goths begged of the Romans the privilege of crossing the river and settling in Thrace in order to escape the hostile bands that made life in their own country longer impossible, Valens consented to grant their petitions on condition that they should surrender their arms, give up their children as hostages, *and all be baptized in the Christian faith!* Thus the entire nation, numbering 1,000,000 souls, men, women and children, were received at the same time into Thrace and into the Church!

Since "New Theology," most conspicuous in the leadership of that defunct movement, no longer holds *the new birth* as a *sine qua non* of Church membership, the question naturally arises, Would the Movement, had it lived, have favored the step taken by Valens in Christianizing the Goths, and count any kind of a baptism, in the name of Christ, Christianization, and so force the fulfillment of the evolutionary expectation — civilization improved in the name of Christ, nations saved in a day? Doubtless!

Christian Socialism, the dominant element in its offshoot the Federal Council endeavor, is thoroughly committed to the notion that poverty, with its attendant evils, all forms of oppression and injustice, and war and its pestilential consequences, will be swept from the earth only by the introduction of a new social organization and the development of an improved civilization. Their program of a perfected society by the application of ethical principles is their one promise of a reign of righteousness which they designate "the kingdom of God." It doesn't even strike them as strange that they are making this promise in the midst of conditions most unpromising! Twenty centuries of Christian activity are back of us, and the expenditure of men and means beyond measure under the leadership of such intellects as we can scarce hope to exceed, and yet the world today is in such condition that fear takes hold of the hearts of its most thoughtful men, and the very sight of the boisterous waves leads trembling disciples of Jesus to put a new passion into their plea, *"Carest Thou not that we perish?"* The apostates, however, are saying to the sea of humanity, "This is the last storm that will ever sweep over your face and beat your waters into billows," and the sad part of it is that they are not looking so much to the "standing in the midst" of "the Master," nor waiting to hear again His voice, *"Peace, be still!"* as they are stressing the necessity for the Church to socialize the world, and the need of higher education to humanize it, and of science — now a synonym of civilization — to Christianize it! In other words, their whole conception of the kingdom is utterly remote from

The Kingdom of Prophecy

When I speak of the kingdom of prophecy, I am speaking of the only kingdom of God that will ever come to this earth and of the only kingdom that has any claims upon church endeavor; in fact, of the only true kingdom that relates itself at all to the teaching of either the Old or the New Testament. *It is a kingdom* — in plain contra-distinction to *the Church.*

The Church of God is an *"ecclesia,"* a "called out" company. It belongs to this age distinctively; its membership is made up of flesh and blood men; its territory is only so much as it can conquer; its task is evangelism.

The "Kingdom of God," on the contrary, is a *"basileia"* — a universal reign with our King, Christ Jesus, on the throne; the citizens of privilege, those to whom He said, *"Fear not, little flock, it is your Father's good pleasure to give you the kingdom"* — those incorruptible and immortal saints coming to it alike from the grave out of which He is to call them, and from the bodies of mortal men out of which mortality He shall release them: their territory will be all the earth: the limits of their reign with Him *"from sea to sea and from the rivers to the ends of the earth";* the time of their supremacy *"one thousand years":* the extent of their supremacy — *"every knee bowing, every tongue confessing, to the glory of God"!*

Instead of the rich bringing in the kingdom, they will do well if they get into it at all! According to the plainest teaching of the Word, it is the inheritance of *"the poor in spirit,"* of *"the meek"* in station, of *"the merciful"* in conduct, of *"the peace-loving"* in practice, of *"the pure in heart,"* of the martyrly in spirit.

Evangelism alone can hasten its coming.

The great commission — *"Go ye, therefore, and teach all nations, baptizing them in the name of the Father, and of the Son, and of the Holy Ghost, teaching them to observe all things whatsoever I have commanded you"* indicates that the gathering of a people out of the Gentiles is the mission of the Church, while the proclamation of *"this Gospel of the Kingdom in all the world for a witness to all the nations"* is the pledge of the appearance of the end, the consummation in the coming kingdom.

Here again men have missed the way, and none more so than the leaders of the New World Movements! Their program majors on education — *not* on evangelism. One-third of the $100,000,000 once sought to be raised by Baptists was to have gone into secondary schools, colleges, theological seminaries and universities. Almost without exception these schools, through their presidents most prominent professors and principals, were committed to the New Theology — which is only another name for German Rationalism! The deity of Christ was and is in dispute by some of them, and has been decided against by others. The authority of the Bible as a whole is denied, only such portions of it meeting the approval of these professors as make appeal to their personal convictions of the truth. What were we asked to do, therefore? To poison our profession of faith at its fountainhead; to give millions for the education of men who in America, in China, in India, in Japan, would in splendid English or in acquired native tongue deny the fundamentals of our holy faith, and preach *"another Gospel"* (which is not another), while our additional millions provided resources for their support! The "Reverend" George Ashmore Fitch was not the only graduate who in one day denied the virgin birth of Christ, the historical identity of Adam and Eve, the raising of Lazarus from the dead and the resurrection of the body of Christ, and on the same day received the laying on of ordaining hands and was dismissed to China to engage in missionary work at Shanghai! In fact, the Baptist University at Shanghai was at that time so badly tinctured with kindred teachings that its continued support by the Northern Baptist Convention without a judicial trial of the truth-traducers was our denominational sin, and was destined to become our denominational debacle!

To imagine that the multiplication of truth-denying institutions and their more firm establishment by greater financial endowments has to do with the bringing of the kingdom of God to the world is not only to miss the meaning of Scripture, but is to set aside its testimony altogether! With perfect veracity, the Great Commission Prayer League circular stated: — "The world today is politically, socially and industrially in turmoil,. because the Church of the Son of God has practically ceased evangelizing in the power of its 'first love.' It has cut loose its moorings, and is being *'carried about with every wind of doctrine, by the sleight of men'* who *'lie in wait to deceive'* by steathily substituting social service panaceas for 'personal salvation from sin'."

The crisis of this hour has one clear call! For *that*, men ought to be willing to give their millions, yea, more, to give *themselves* — Evangelization, and that with no uncertain speech, in no skeptical tongue, but with power and in the plain Word of God which calls to repentance, requires regeneration, promises salvation from through the substitutionary sacrifice of the Son of God, and sanctification by the indwelling of the Holy Ghost. Such a procedure will hasten a kingdom of righteousness to be established in God's own way and in God's own time.

Finally, *the Kingdom of Prophecy is only promised on and by the reappearance of the King!* The Word of the Lord could not be made any plainer on this subject. It is not the business of *men* to bring in the kingdom! It is the province of *the Son*, Who has gone to receive it and at Whose return it will be set up. To talk of the *kingdom* in *the absence of the King* is to adopt the speech of Christian Socialism versus the plain text of sacred Scripture! To imagine that money in any amount, men in any numbers, institutions in any strength — or all of these combined — can bring in the kingdom, is to provide an explanation of why millions in the professed Church pass their days and months and years and never utter so much as one word about "the bringing back of the King"! In fact, many of them do not seem to remember that it is only upon His return that He is to *"build again the tabernacle of David, which has fallen down, and set up the kingdom that the residue of men might seek after the Lord."* So far have some gone in their apostasy from the faith that many well-meaning men do not believe in the coming and kingdom of the

Antichrist, and entertain no fears whatsoever lest by their corporate schemes in religion and their attempted confederations they pave the way perfectly for his appearance, and even — in sincerity of motive but in ignorance of Scripture — accept a godless kingdom as the Kingdom of God, and Antichrist in lieu of their Lord, only to learn, by the pandemonium that will follow, the difference between *it* and the "millennium" of God's promise!

The hour to which we have come is justly named a crisis time. The days about to be born are probably to appear with veiled faces, and the nights of the future are to know increasing mourning; but the student of the Word of God will be comforted by the Bible's "blessed hope" of the coming of the King and the kingdom that shall be established in righteousness.

Jonathan Edwards tells of having been taken ill at New Haven, where for a quarter of a year he lay in sore affliction, but adds — "I observed that those who watched with me would often be looking out for the morning, and were delighted with its approach, and it brought to my own mind the words of the Psalmist, which my spirit with sweetness made its own language, *'My soul waiteth for the Lord, more than they that watch for the morning'.*"

While the night lingers, the "Great Commission" — *evangelization* — is the marching order of the Churches; consecration of self and means is the individual obligation; and *"to watch for His Son from heaven"* is the believer's blessed privilege!

IV

The Counterfeit Of The Baptist "Committee Of Nine"

IN something above twenty years, the Northern Baptist Convention, in four of its Annual Meetings, has made history. The first of these was held at Denver, Colorado, when the Convention itself fully supplanted the Society Anniversaries that had existed for almost a century.

The second was at Buffalo, N. Y., when the Convention repudiated the "Inter-Church Movement," and appointed a Committee to investigate the false teaching in its Colleges and Universities.

The third was at Indianapolis, Ind., when its theological decline manifested itself in the repudiation of the Old Testament Scriptures and in a meaningless compliment to the New.

The fourth was at Colorado Springs, when the pastors refused to adopt a standardized and centralized scheme for the ministry, but when the Convention received the "bloodless but Red" Report of the Committee of Nine on Social Action.

The relationship between the Indianapolis and the Colorado Springs Convention was direct and logical. The Convention, having once refused to adopt a Biblical creed, was logically certain to drift to *"another gospel,"* which, as Paul declares, *"is not another"* — but is a perversion, rather, of *"the Gospel of Christ."*

When, two nights before the time set for the consideration of this Report, in order to secure some definite program and at the same time have representative speakers, I suggested that a steering Committee of seven be created and that the Fundamentalist group commit itself to their following, I sealed my own lips so far as verbal arguments before the Convention were concerned.

This is not to criticize the creation of the Committee, nor yet the Committee's decision, for in the final showdown it was not even assembled for consultation. The compromise agreed upon by individuals, some of whom were members of the Committee, was, in my judgment, thoroughly conscientious on the part of the two or three involved; but as the Watchman-Examiner of July 4th following, sagely remarked, "a unity which is achieved by the compromise of principles is mere good-natured indolence, which, frequently, is real hypocrisy."

By voting against the Committee's continuation, I at once kept my own conscience clear, and by silence, refused openly to break with my truly beloved brethren. In this chapter I give to the public my reasons for believing that this whole communication on Social Action was both remote from the teachings of Jesus Christ and, consequently, remote from that Christianity which was created by His lips and His life.

There are three statements which I wish to set in order: (1) The Report constitutes a creed; (2) The Report was totally inept; and (3) The Report was "bloodless but Red."

The Report Constitutes A Creed

In other words, the very thing that the Modernists have inveighed against as "unbaptistic," they finally brought to pass, namely, the adoption of a Creed — and they themselves so understand! A youthful representative of Modernism, after the action was taken, remarked to a minister friend, "Now, that at last we have our track laid, watch us go"!

The Baptist "Committee of Nine" 59

Permit a few remarks on this "track-laying."

First of all, *it was the product of a self-created Committee.*

Do not misunderstand me! I am not saying that the Presidents of the 1934 and 1935 Conventions did not unite in naming a Committee; but I *am* saying that the Committee was made up after the manner anticipated when on May 28th of the previous year, at Rochester, a motion made possible its creation. There were nine members named on this Committee.

If there is one of the nine who has ever been suspected of conservatism, the suspicion has not been reported!

In order to render their work easy of accomplishment, the executive Committee recommended the Finance Committee to designate a sum, not in excess of $4,500.00 for the expenses.

It has been the custom of years for the defenders of "special legislation," to pay high compliment to the Committee — designedly created — "for its arduous, painstaking and sacrificial service."

Men who create for themselves positions that look to making for their personal prejudices an audience and a possible adoption, do not thereby place the public under serious obligation. *"Verily I say unto you, they have their reward"!*

This Report was the corollary of the Indianapolis act.

At that time the Convention refused to adopt the creed which had characterized our fathers in the faith. At that time the Convention repudiated the Confession which had been basal in American Baptist history. At that time, by a majority vote, the teachings of the Old Testament were relegated to the mythological scrap-heap, and the plain teachings of the New Testament were laid on the table, to be taken up for interpretation in 1935!

Dr. Shailer Matthews, probably intending to oppose the Indianapolis movement which looked to the adoption of a Confession of Faith in line with Baptist history, declared that "the movement was never planned for this sort of thing and by its very structure is not adapted to exercise its authority." He further remarked, "If we choose to remain Baptists, we must not let the Convention become other than what it was planned to be and what it has always been, namely, an advisory body intended to increase our efficiency in common denominational undertakings."

We turn about now to ask his fellows in "the new faith" to practise their own philosophy, and also to raise the question — if the New Testament teachings were sufficient at Indianapolis without any elaboration whatever, what had happened to those same teachings to make them so obscure in 1935 as to require a 15,000-word exploitation of their content?

This Report was a distortion of the Convention's design.

Justice Hughes of the United States Supreme Court is a great authority with Modernists when he speaks in keeping with their plans and purposes. In this very document you will find him gladly quoted from on the Douglas McIntosh matter! But when his judgment does *not* aid or abet the desired plans, it is conveniently ignored!

When this Committee was first broached, our Baptist Chief Justice wrote a letter to those who were known to be advocates of this anticipated social action, and in it, Chief Justice Hughes said: —

"There is no lack of social and political agencies to deal with these questions, which inevitably give rise to serious controversies between different schools of political and economic thought. I see no advantage to the church in entering into the domain of these controversies. The church has a far higher mission and cannot afford to impair its supremely important function of nourishing the spiritual forces of our people."

But since this piece of advice was not calculated to aid the Committee's objective, it was consigned to the waste basket. Seven ministers and two ministers' wives were set to the task of teaching statesmen!

Some of us regarded it as a very significant thing that when the Report was about to be considered, Porter Beck of Pennsylvania moved to amend by "increasing the Commission to not less than 12, and that one-third of the Commission should consist of business men, inasmuch as the Report deals with economic matters."

In speaking to this, the Committee chairman said: "We sought to secure some business men for the original Committee, but failed to find them" — all of which suggests the possibility that there are not four intelligent business men in the Baptist denomination that could be brought to sign their names to this preachers' Report on social action!

The Hartford "Courant," commenting on the document, had this to say, after having quoted from Dr. Edward V. Dargin, Catholic Canonist, a comment on Father Charles E. Coughlin's activities, to this effect: —

"The unity and the solidity of the Roman Catholic Church, which has survived centuries of agitation and unrest, are not endangered by the activities of Father Coughlin; but the growing impatience of others of his faith with his undertakings is symptomatic of the discord and the loss of goodwill resulting from political activity on the part of clerics."

Then the "Courant" adds: "Baptists of Colorado Springs may well ponder what Father Dargin has to say before they vote to give their pastors license to rush into the political arena as spokesmen for their church."

There is a possibility that somebody might feel toward the Church as the Irishman did about the influence that was back of and round about and above the President! It is reported that a democratic orator, addressing a large crowd, was saying: —

"Who is the man whose wise counsels have guided this Government through a period of such depression as the United States never before saw? Who; other than Franklin D. Roosevelt?"

To which the Irishman, slightly under the influence of Roosevelt repeal of the 18th Amendment, responded:

"I don't like him"!

The orator continued: "Who but Franklin D. Roosevelt has shown such interest in the poor, devised such help for the unemployed, conceived such favor for the aged and the infirm?"

Again the Irishman said:

"I don't like him"!

The orator further continued: "Ladies and gentlemen, as I have studied the acts and course of our President, I have been profoundly convinced that there is back of him, and overshadowing him day and night, a higher power, dictating and determining his career" —

To which the Irishman responded, more vociferously than before:

"I don't like HER either"!

There is a multitude of people who candidly believe that our national confusion would have been less confounded, had her domination been less felt.

When we read from this Report: "The Church should not concede to the political state even neutrality, let alone absolute sovereignty, in all matters aside from religious work and exercises" — we are deeply concerned lest the Church's unwarranted interference in affairs of State should affect her public standing, as have Mrs. Roosevelt's multiplied speeches influenced her own.

The Church is none too popular now. Its administration of its own affairs has not profoundly impressed the world with its exalted wisdom; and when it gives less attention to the administration of Christianity and more attention to the management of the political State, its popularity may easily be still further pauperized.

But we pass to our second statement: —

The Report Was Totally Inept

When thinking upon this subject, the word "INEPT" flashed into my mind, and I wondered if it was the exact one which I needed to express my thought; but when I turned to my Standard Dictionary and found the following definition, I adopted it: —

"Inept means, first, not fit or suitable; unapt;

"Second, not consistent with reason or sound sense, absurd;

"Third, inappropriate, unbecoming"!

Keeping the dictionary definitions in mind, we are justified in some very definite assertions.

This social action Committee's Report was non-suitable.

For the creation of such a Committee, there existed no occasion, and for the rendition of such a Report, there could be found no defense. Religious liberty has been enjoyed by the citizens of this country to the fullest extent. The separation of Church and State has been complete, and, in consequence, their fellowship has suffered no strain.

Not only has freedom of speech been accorded to our citizens, but it has been exercized with an abandon unknown to any other century or country. Our international relations have been strangely salutary, while our economic and industrial problems have been the product of uniform prosperity rather than the result of oppression: and at each and every one of those points, the Baptist contribution has been neither lacking nor lackadaisical.

To a man familiar alike with American history and with the history of our Baptist Churches, this 15,000-word document reads like "MUCH ADO ABOUT NOTHING"! Personally, in my extended years and wide observation, I have yet to meet a single Baptist preacher or to know a single Baptist Church that did not seek the social uplift of the community or that failed to stand for higher moral and economic ideals. From the days of our fathers until now, our ministry and our churches have proved themselves worthy of the compliment the 15,000-word document paid to pioneer missionaries.

They stood for educational institutions, and they have created them almost out of number. They have built a multitude of hospitals; they have opened many dispensaries. They fought the institution of slavery; they denounced the drink evil; they defended women and children against debilitating conditions of labor; they pled for the proper compensation of services; they have preferred peace to war.

In fact, the very things of which this strange document so much complains have been their determined objectives; and the "threatened complacency," which the Committee fears may prevent the "new day" of economic justice, inter-racial harmony and international brotherhood, exists only in de-gospelized imaginations!

It was the substitution of this so-called "Social Gospel," which led B. S. Ding, the brilliant Chinese student of Louisville Theological Seminary, to complain that certain of our missionaries sent to his land, had sought to displace Christianity with mere education and political democracy. Ding said: "They never teach the deep doctrinal teachings, such as the atonement by His blood. They reduce our Lord Christ to a mere man, and it would be better for China if these missionaries were recalled."

Who questions that Modernism in China has aided the Communism which has kidnapped and murdered 375 missionaries in recent years?

The authors of this document would doubtless concede that the thing wrong with the world is SIN, and that the discovery of its antidote is the sorest need both of the individual and of the State. And yet, strange to say, the antidote prescribed by Christ Himself is never so much as mentioned! *The blood of Jesus Christ, as an atonement for sin*, found no place in this communication!

Paul's declaration, *"without shedding of blood, there is no remission"* (Heb. 9:22) and John's statement, *"the blood of Jesus Christ his* (God's) *Son, cleanseth us from all sin"* were alike ignored!

While repeated compliments are paid to New Testament teaching, its most central truth is silenced! Being void of the cleansing blood, it has lost the sole dynamic of salvation, and the extent to which the document was finally adopted by the denomination, meant *"reckoning the blood of the covenant wherewithal we are sanctified an unholy thing."*

The ineptness of this Report further appears in the unworkableness of its philosophy.

Here we shall permit those, with whom it has unquestionably found favor, to attest the truth of our statement by calling four witnesses from the side of the "prosecution" to testify for the "defense." Dr. Harry Emerson Fosdick is entitled to the first place. He says:—

"We need to be very sure that we will never win in

our cause by the rationality of our theology or any theoretical hypothesis. Unless we can produce the same evangelical zeal, the same consuming, passionate devotion to the Kingdom of our Lord, the same sacrificial energy which flowed forth from those so faithful to the 'old' theology, we shall never come to any worthy place among those who follow our Lord Jesus Christ."

On another occasion, Dr. Fosdick admitted that, to date, that zeal and sacrificial energy were lacking.

Professor Meeser of Crozer Seminary also admitted that "it remains to be proved whether the newer theology offers a real Gospel and 'power of God unto salvation'."

Professor George Jackson made a kindred admission, when he said: "It is for the Christian scholar to make manifest that the word of the Cross is still, in this generation, 'the power of God unto salvation'," and the Church waits to see the man that he calls "a Christian scholar" do what Sister Eddy calls "demonstrate"!

Dr. C. C. Morrison, editor of "The Christian Century," insists that "if liberalism does not do better than the old theology, it is without occasion."

For more than a quarter of a century now these theories have been tested, and the churches served by their advocates we challenge to comparison, church for church and member for member, with those who have believed in a verbally inspired Bible, in a Saviour Who was "God manifested in the flesh," and in the atonement accomplished on Calvary's Cross.

There still remains, however, a third definition of "inept."

This Report is "unbecoming" to the Northern Baptist Convention.

Its proper place would have been in an Annual Assembly of the Unitarians! That body of people has always laid emphasis upon the exact points therein con-

The Baptist "Committee of Nine"

tained; and notwithstanding all that they have said on the subject, a spiritual and social and economic sterility has characterized their experience.

They have founded a few schools — and have stolen a small additional number. They have established few missions and have failed in each endeavor. They have built few hospitals, and poorly supported the ones they have constructed. They have played an inconspicuous part in the battles against sin and in the great moral contentions which have shaken America since her "Declaration of Independence."

I sometimes think that the whole Unitarian teaching is, as a noted minister once said, much "like the tail of Halley's Comet, which it is declared contained not in ten million cubic miles a thimbleful of real substance"!

My repeated perusals of this Report have impressed me that it was not the product of research, nor, indeed, did it reveal careful assemblage. Passage after passage is in contradiction to other statements contained in it. It is useless to recite them all, as even a casual reader will catch them; but let me demonstrate by a few illustrations.

On the same page it advocates the separation of Church and State, and at the same time insists that the Church is duty-bound to bring the State into accordance with its own ideas.

At one point it says: "We must not permit such groups as Communists and Fascists to win because of our indifference," and in another it advises that we ally ourselves with the small Socialistic groups!

At one place it advocates a "co-operative commonwealth," and in the same sentence pleads for "the infinite worth of personality"!

At one point it demands free speech to the point of red revolution — and at another condemns those who practise the same! And so on to the end.

But all I have said thus far simply lays a firm basis on which to rest my final claim, namely: —

The Report Was Bloodless But Red!

Its "bloodlessness" we have already shown. Its scarlet color we now bring to exhibition.

It voices an unpatriotic pacifism.

It encourages our youth to refuse service to their country in case of war. It condemns our Supreme Court for not giving citizenship to Douglas McIntosh, an alien whose preferred place in a great American University was not sufficient, but whose path to that station should (in the judgment of this Committee) have been cleared, by kicking the Constitution of the United States into the Atlantic Ocean!

As if it were not enough thus to condemn the Constitution and degrade this flag, members of this Committee seek to corral Christ Himself as a confederate, and quote the words which fell from His lips, *"Put up again thy sword into his place: for all they that take the sword shall perish with the sword"* (Matt. 26:52) — strangely ignoring the essential fact that on a previous occasion, Peter had tried to keep Christ from the Cross and been denounced as "Satan" for so doing; and now this mild rebuke for a second endeavor was never dreamed of as a "pacifist" doctrine until Christ's speech was so strained and distorted!

The same advocates of pacifism forget the word of the Lord Jesus, *"when a strong man, armed keepeth his palace, his goods are in peace."* (Luke 11:21)

They also strangely forget the word to His disciples on their second missionary tour: *"He that hath no sword, let him sell his garment and buy one."* (Luke 22:36)

They likewise forget His declaration: *"Think not that I am come to send peace on the earth. I came not to send peace, but a sword."*

We had at that time in the United States only 160,000 soldiers (officers included). They could all be seated in the Stadium of Chicago; and we had 400,000 criminals, their company daily increasing — men who live by the use of the pistol, sawed-off shot-gun and machine-gun! Before such a menace, should our Army be reduced? Then why not go the full length of pacifism and "fire" the police force of America and leave us to the tender mercies of the crowd that awaits the day of "protocol" clean up?

There are some of us who were not deceived by the Moscow cry — *"Peace, peace"* when we knew that, for the future, their movements portended *"No peace"!* Twenty-two million Russians were even then drilling for war, now, they battle to force Communism on the world!

Still further, *this document actually opposes personal initiative and proposes a "paternal" government!*

If any one does not believe that, let him read what it has to say upon the subject. I quote the very words:—

"We stand for a co-operative commonwealth."

"Concentrated wealth should be devoted to social well-being."

"Competition is rivalry and covetousness and is socially injurious. The service motive should be the incentive to production"; etc.

High-sounding theories, which, however, in every single attempt at practice, have proved dismal failures, wrecking the societies and the States that have adopted them!

I personally have no background that could make me an advocate of the aristocracy of wealth. I was born in poverty, and bred in hardship. I have done the heaviest work and the hardest at 50 cents a day; and yet my estate and my prospects, even then, were a thousand-fold better than is the condition of any of the 130 million

Communistically controlled Russians! I was in a government where individuality was respected, in a government that rewards initiative, in a government that left the body and intellect free to follow the path of the latter's choosing, and unhampered in the attempt to rise to higher station, larger income, improved circumstances and widened vision!

Let those who will, exchange American freedom for Russian slavery; but in so doing, let them not fasten the latter upon free-born Americans, but prove the sincerity of their wild theories by accepting, at Bolsheviki hands, their philosophy full-fledged, and transferring their citizenship from the land of plenty to the land of starvation and brutal murder!

Finally, this document stands for Communistic sedition!

Here I speak advisedly and "according to the book." I shall give you the page and the actual language. You will find it on page 5 of the Committee's Report, and it read as follows: — "We further recommend the denomination actively champion 'the civil liberties' of all groups and individuals."

Note the suggestion of fellowship with "The Civil Liberties Union" — one of the most dangerous and godless of all organizations known to our land; and while the word "Union" is not used, it is surreptitiously suggested by the very language employed.

I quote further:

"The course of sanity and safety for America is to assure these liberties even for those whose ideas are admittedly contrary to our established order and our religious faith, and whose political philosophy would deny these liberties to others were they in power."

If language means anything, this means that when men want to run up the "Red" flag instead of the Amer-

The Baptist "Committee of Nine" 71

ican "Stars and Stripes," they are not to be hindered; and when they want to curse our Constitution and condemn our form of government, and advise their fellows to organize for its destruction, no steps are to be taken by the State to suppress such speech!

There is not a true Baptist living who does not believe in freedom of speech; but there is not a sane Baptist living who does not also hold that such freedom *has its limitations!*

When, in the same Convention, we adopted a Resolution in the following terms: — "RESOLVED that we actively support anti-lynching legislation," by that action we said, "We do not believe that any excited orator has the right to incite a mob for the lynching of the blackest criminal that walks the earth."

But, while we are willing to protect the criminal (— even such a man as came into Minneapolis one day, solicited the services of one of my godly women as his housekeeper, lured her to a shack on an untravelled road, assaulted her, and then brutally murdered her, and buried her with a dead dog in his side yard —) against mob violence — when the Constitution of the United States is involved, when the country's entire good is at stake, when the continuation of all law and order, even Government itself, is in the balance, and when even human interest is pivoted on the action — we are not to restrain even the spokesmen who would overthrow the Government and (Bolsheviki-like) enslave millions of our fellows, and murder other millions at will, eh?

My Minneapolis does not need such advice. A few summers ago, when her streets ran red with blood, shed by Communist agitators, an orator addressed 6000 in our City Auditorium and advised the howling mob: "Kill every damned policeman on the force, and if these citizen-rats accept deputyship, exterminate them!" it seemed to some of us that free speech had changed to sedition!

72 *The Counterfeit of*

The advocacy of such sedition is a source of delight to every Red-flagged and red-handed Communist in the land!

Furthermore, the document specifically commended such pink organizations as "The Liberty League," and "The League of Industrial Democracy."

For my beloved Denomination even to have permitted such recommendations without an exclamation of righteous indignation and with so few voices raised in resentment, is the amazement of all amazements! A few more such sops to the anarchistic crowd, and Christianity in America, like Christianity in Russia, if it live at all, will be found only in dark cellars where two or three dare to assemble for prayer, or in the single Churchhouse, left in our Capitol as a false exhibit for foolish professors and preachers, who, after five days in the hands of the secret police, can return to their respective lands to makes speeches about the "noble experiment"!

When first I read that document, I said: "If three sections could be stricken out of it, it might pass."

When next I read it, I said: "If twenty-one paragraphs could be taken out of it, it might not work evil."

But when I read it a third time, I said: "It is not the content of these 15,000 words that should excite the wrath and indignation of every Christian on earth; it is, rather, its color!"

It is RED — but the "red" in this Committee's Report is the crimson of Communism — without one touch of the blood of Christ!

When the "Bolsheviki" reign that Premier Joseph established in Egypt, subjecting every native to slavery, produced its natural revolt and revolution, causing the Jewish rulers to themselves become slaves, driven daily to brick-making without straw, Judgment against the land was God's decision; but, anticipating the shedding of the blood of the Lamb to take away the sins of the world, He ordered the slaughter of the "paschal lamb" and the use of its innocent blood to stain the two side posts of the doors of the houses saying: *"When I see the blood, I will pass over you, and the plague shall not be upon you to destroy you."* If that God has changed the insignia of salvation for the individual or the nation since that time, the Scriptures have failed to record the fact. On the contrary, however, throughout the Gospels, The Acts of the Apostles, the Pauline and the Petrine Epistles, and even on to the Revelation, it "blundered" on, teaching *redemption by the blood of Christ* AND NEVER ONCE HINTED AT THE SUBSTITUTION OF ANOTHER PLAN!

When the Emperor Yang-Lo of China wanted to secure a larger degree of loyalty to himself, he conceived the idea of the creation of a bell to be hung in the great tower and to be rung daily to call the people to pledge loyalty! The Mandarin ordered to make this bell went to the utmost trouble in gathering the finest of materials to make it a thing of beauty, but it proved a failure. A second attempt ended after the same manner.

Then the Emperor commanded Kuan-Yu to create a third, and said, "If it fails, the penalty will be your death"! Ko-ai, the beautiful daughter of the Mandarin, sought advice of an astronomer.

He said: "Only by mingling the blood of a maiden with the molten mass will it be perfect." Ko-ai watched and waited till the metal was in a molten state, and then she ran forward and leaped into the midst of the same without a moment's hesitation, mingling her blood and yielding her body. The bell was perfect; the Mandarin was saved; the loyalty to the Emperor was secured.

It is a parable! When God sought such loyalty to Himself as would mean the salvation of the individual and of society, He saw that it could be accomplished in no other way than by the shedding of the blood of His blessed Son.

The preaching of the blood atonement has not only characterized the Baptist Denomination from its beginning, but has accounted for its existence. When it suffers that doctrine to be denied, the Denomination is doomed!

The world without that doctrine is helpless and hopeless!

V

The Kagawa-Counterfeit -- The Consumer's Cooperatives

IN the forty years of my residence in Minneapolis, no minister has promised the "Twin Cities" a three-day engagement who was so much advertised as Kagawa. The newspapers announced that 500 preachers from the Northwest would assemble at the Conference of which he was to be the central attraction. For weeks beforehand my desk was flooded with letters from the Ministers' Federation of Minneapolis seeking my aid in this advertisement.

All my predilections were in his favor until a question was raised in my mind by an article published in the Sunday School Times of November 16, 1935. That article led to the purchase and reading of his books, with the result that I am fully convinced that Kagawa's Christ is not at all the Christ of the New Testament, and that his "Consumer's Cooperatives" is a remote remove from the New Testament "Kingdom of God."

But to our Scripture study!

A True Pastor's Obligation

Paul was zealous for the good of the Church at Corinth.

He says so. *"I am jealous over you with godly jealousy"* (II Cor. 11:2).

The man who does not love his people to the extent of a godly jealousy over them is unfit to be their pastor. As the true husband cannot endure that another should steal his wife's affections, so the true pastor will not brook the winning of his people to false doctrines. Their soul interests are his deepest concern.

Theodore Cuyler in "How to be a Pastor" tells of having met in Dundee, Scotland, a gray-headed member of St. Peter's Presbyterian Church who in his youth had sat at the feet of Robert Murray McCheyne. He spoke of him with the deepest reverence and love, and when asked what he remembered most clearly about him, replied, "Just before his death he met me in the street, and laying his hand on my shoulder he said kindly, 'Jimmie, I hope all is well with your soul'."

Forty years had passed, but Jimmie had never forgotten that pastoral interest: and that, in fact, is the true interest.

A pastor may desire for his people comfort of body: he may crave clarity of mind for them, but above all things else he will, if worthy of his office, seek their soul welfare. *Paul also held Christ to be their one and only Saviour.*

He continued: *"I have espoused you to one husband, that I may present you as a chaste virgin to Christ"* (II Cor. 11:2).

Who was the Christ to Whom Paul had espoused the Corinthian Christians? Kagawa's Christ? No! In his first letter to the Corinthians, Paul had for ever defined his Christ as the Christ Who *"died for our sins according to the Scriptures; And was buried, and rose again the third day, according to the Scriptures"* (I Cor. 15:3-4).

Does Kagawa believe in *that* Christ? Not at all! We will prove it by his own words! He does not believe that Christ died for our sins; that He stood in our stead and *"bare our sins in his own body on the tree"* (I Peter 2:24).

He believes, instead, that Christ was a sinner, and says, "Jesus experienced God as the Forgiver of sins"!

He does not believe that Christ was buried and rose again from the dead! In his volume "The Religion of Jesus" — this is his unequivocal statement: "We do not know in what form the resurrection did come, whether it was in the flesh, as the Gospels teach, or in the spiritual body, as Paul tells us" (see page 103) thus attempting to pit Paul against his Master, in spite of Paul's clear statement and elaborate argument in I Corinthians 15 for the bodily resurrection of Christ!

He does not hold that Jesus is the only Saviour from sin, but that every saved man becomes a saviour, and even that society is awaiting their multiplication for its redemption!

In his "Meditations on the Cross," (p. 95) he says, "The human race cannot produce a fitting social order without the appearance of perfect personalities like that of Christ."

Impossible prospect!

He does not believe in the Virgin Birth, or that Christ came down from heaven at all, but calls Christ "the Son of a carpenter," saying "Christ is the summit of Evolution"! (See "Meditations on the Cross," p. 88)

He does not believe that Christ will ever return to the earth, and denounces those of us who hold that "blessed hope." This is his statement on that subject: "There are folks who talk continually about Christ's Second Coming. It will not do to believe them; their emphasis is a mistaken one." (See "Meditations on the Cross" p. 30)

The only Christ known to our Bible is the Christ

Who *"was conceived in Mary of the Holy Ghost"* (Matt. 1:20); Who was *not* a carpenter's Son, and Who was *not* a product of "Evolution" but was *"God manifest in the flesh"* (II John 7); the Christ Who *"was in all points tempted like as we are, yet without sin"* (Heb. 4:15; John 8:46); the Christ Who *"bare our sins in his own body on the tree"* (I Peter 2:24); the Christ Who *"was buried"* and Who *"rose again the third day, according to the scriptures"* (I Cor. 15:4); the Christ Who *"ascended into heaven"* (Acts 1:9); and the Christ Who will *"come again"* (Acts 1:11 and John 14:3).

Since the "Christ" of Kagawa's book is NOT this New Testament CHRIST, but a creature of modern philosophy — a product of the unproven hypothesis of Evolution, little wonder that he ends with the worship of himself, declaring that the terms "Evolution" and "God" point to the same entity! (see "Love the Law of Life," p. 302) And also, "God is evolution itself at work within the ego"! (page 305). Humanism!

If you ask me, then, "Is Kagawa a *Christian?*" I am compelled to reply, "He is not a worshipper of the New Testament Christ."

Paul sought to strengthen the Corinthians against anti-Christian teachers.

Perhaps you ask, "Do you mean to imply that Kagawa is an apostle of the Antichrist?" I answer unhesitatingly, "Yes!" Doubtless unwillingly so!

His teachings are in line with the anti-Christian movements which characterize this century. He denies the inspiration of the Bible, speaking of the Genesis account of creation as "the myth of a Creator making something out of nothing"! Mark the word "myth"! And, to assure yourself that he means to contrast Darwin's teachings with those of Moses, read the rest of his sentence: "Belief in evolution is faith in the progressive entrance into an ever-expanding freedom — from seed to shoot, bud to flower, from anthropoid to human, from man to Son of God"! Then he exclaims, "What a courageous faith! The belief that there is a direct line of evolution from amoeba to man is a more daring and romantic faith than the belief in the myth of a Creator making something out of nothing." (See "Love the Law of Life," p. 298)

Mark his words, "the myth of a Creator making something out of nothing"! Goodbye to Moses in Genesis chapter one, and to Paul in Hebrews 11:3!

Kagawa, then, in common with the Communists of the world, holds the Evolutionary Hypothesis. He also holds in common with them the right of the "proletariat" to govern. With them likewise he holds that Parliaments and Congresses will pass, and that "groups, bound together industrially, will have their representation fixed"; "representatives will express the will of the group" — just as the Bolsheviki now contend — and he says: "Those who govern will be experts in social science" — in perfect keeping with the "Protocol Plan"!

Also in common with the Communists, he believes in Internationalism. That vein runs through all his books; and equally in common with them he holds to the abolition of all distinctive faiths, saying: "No sects there are in Love. Buddhist, Mohammedan, Christian — these are not Love's divisions. Love knows how to embrace, not to differentiate." (See "Love, the Law of Life," p. 312). Then indeed "LOVE" — his God — "is blind"!

Some may resent the intimation even that Kagawa is not a Christian, but he demands it! His exact language is: "Classify me not by creed" ("The Law of Life," p. 312).

There are too many people who imagine that when the anti-Christ arises he will appear — a horrid creature, almost as repellant as the old-time pictures of Satan. The Bible, on the contrary, presents another person altogether — smooth, flattering, philosophical, attractive! *"The world will wonder after him."* And let it not be forgotten that he will appear as Christ Himself, and set himself up in the temple to be worshipped as God (II Thess. 2:4).

Dr. J. Wilbur Chapman, in his volume "And Peter," recites what many others have experienced, — how a friend of his at the base of Matterhorn was besieged by men who tried to argue him into permitting them to guide him up the mountain and bring him down again. Finally, Chapman's friend said: "Show me your papers!" Instantly they all fell back but one. He stepped forward and showed a paper signed by a multitude of people who stated that they had climbed the Matterhorn under his care, and that he had proven a perfect guide, and they commended him to other friends.

The same question would end all the false prophets of the land! Let them show *one man* whom their philosophies have saved, or *one country* improved by adopting the same, and that will at least command respect; but until that time, the testimony of millions of individuals and of many countries to the Name of CHRIST as the one and only Saviour, should be at least sufficient to silence the entire company of claimants!

But I pass to a second point:

The Characteristics of the False Prophet

The first mark of a false prophet is self-glorification.

That mark is most evident in the case of Kagawa. We are frequently reminded by him of his own sacrificial spirit, and his admirers play that up as proof of his Christianity. His secretary, in the introduction to "Love, the Law of Life," depicts him as going "into one of the worst slums" conceivable, and "notwithstanding his tendency to tuberculosis," deliberately investing his life there for four and one-half years. She tells us that after his experience at Princeton, he astonished his friends by returning to slum districts to live. We are told that he even took into his own bed the filthy, and from one of them contracted a disease, trachoma, which came near preventing his entrance into America; and all this is held up to us, not only as a demonstration of his religion, but, as a condemnation of the ordinary profession—and with most people, the argument is instantly effective! However, a few reflections upon these glorified facts can hardly detract from them if they be genuine and justified.

First, when did Christ ever elect to live in the slums? As *we* read Christ, we believe that He sought to lift men to a higher level rather than settle with them on their low grounds. Again, when did Christ ever share His bed with the diseased and loathsome? Would it not be better to provide a bath and a clean bed? The nearest that one can come to making the precepts of Jesus a basis for Kagawa's conduct is recorded in Matthew 25th chapter, where Jesus said: *"For I was an hungered, and ye gave me meat: I was thirsty, and ye gave me drink: I was a stranger, and ye took me in: naked and ye clothed me: I was sick, and ye visited me; I was in prison, and ye came unto me. Then shall the righteous answer him, saying, Lord, when saw we thee an hungered, and fed thee? or thirsty, and gave thee drink? When saw we thee a stranger, and took thee in? or naked and clothed thee? Or when saw we thee sick, or in prison, and came unto thee? And the King shall answer and say unto them, Verily I say unto you, inasmuch as ye have done it unto one of the least of these my brethren, ye have done it unto me"* — a service in which true Christians constantly engage.

However, if one is going to accept life in the slums of his country, and sleep with the filthy, a procedure that some of us fail to approve, let him not forget that when Christ wrought works of mercy, He sought no publicity in consequence; and certainly He did not go the length that Kagawa has gone, of condemning as futile the far more sacrificial conduct.

Take, for instance, Kagawa's attitude toward the great missionaries of the past. We will let him speak for himself in this matter. Axling's "Kagawa," (page 124), reports him as saying: "The old traditional missions whose major goal is the building of denominations must pass out of the picture."

How any one can read this who ever loved the Christ Who commanded them or those great missionary souls who were obedient to His command — such, for instance, as Judson, Livingstone, Morrison and others too numerous to mention — without resentment, is past my comprehension!

Kagawa went among the low of his own people — people to whom he was bound by the ties of blood. Judson and Livingstone and Morrison went among strange and uncivilized peoples — head-choppers, cannibals and so forth—and dwelt there, *not* to "build up a denomination," but to bring sinful men to God! Kagawa slept for nights with filthy bed-fellows to show his love for the individual. Judson, in the filthy prison at Ava, for nine months slept with his shoulders resting in the mud, his feet tied up in the air bound by three pairs of fetters! When he wrote home, later, about it, he said: "The scenes that we witnessed, and the sufferings we underwent during that period, I would fain consign to oblivion."

Set that over against this modernist boast! Tell me *who* proved his love to God and to low men! Kagawa boasts a love that is willing to die for the Lord; but Livingstone exercised that love, dying on his knees in the heart of Africa without so much as reckoning his conduct worthy of compliment! So did John and Betty Stam — murdered by those Kagawa encourages — and yet modernists would have you believe that the objective of Judson and Livingstone and the Stams was just the upbuilding of a narrow, denominational sect!

Since reading these books, it is vastly easier to interpret "RE-THINKING MISSIONS," and also to realize that its philosophy of missions is far more oriental than occidental, more Darwinian than Biblical, more Communistic than Christian! There are some of us who believe that the men and women who a hundred years ago — and even fifty — set sail for foreign shores, with Bible in hand, not only endured more hardship than Kagawa has been able to inflict upon himself, but preached a Gospel as superior to his as the wisdom of Christ is above the economic speculations of man!

The second characteristic of a false prophet is *the use of Christianity as a "sugar coating."* (2 Cor. 11:3).

It is claimed in one of the volumes that John Mott suggested to Kagawa the change of name from "Consumer's Cooperatives" to "The Kingdom of God Movement." The likelihood of that statement is great. John Mott has long been a power in deflecting his fellows from *"the faith once delivered."* The time was when John Mott led enthusiastically those of us of his own age, under the slogan: "Evangelization of the world in this generation"; but he, like other Modernists, shifted from "Evangelization" to "socialization" — practically turning his back upon the "Great Commission" of Christ, to *"disciple" men,* and creating for himself a new objective — to *"right nations"!*

The extent to which he has been able to execute his substitute plan is proved by present world-conditions. Instead of having improved, under the manipulation of these international doctors and brilliant programs, the "black death" of *sin* increases its havoc; and the men and women who, like Noah of old, are busily engaged in inviting individuals to come with them into the Ark of

Safety in Christ, are looked upon by these wiseacres as being little better than nit-wits — as was Noah in his day by the antediluvians! But the record still stands, *"The flood came and took them all away,"* and it is still written, *"as it was in the days of Noah, so shall it be in the days of the coming of the Son of Man."* This is the time for the preaching of the Gospel of God — and *not* for the propagation of false economic philosophies, under the Kingdom name!

Some years ago the Mountain at San Pierre began to smoke. Seeing these great clouds issuing from its top, the citizens became nervous and many of them started to make their escape; but the Governor of the Island selected some scientists and set them up the mountain-side to make a "scientific" investigation and a "scientific" report. Their report was — "No Danger"! Thereupon Governor Moutett threw a cordon around the City and refused to let any men or women pass out who did not carry a permit showing the necessity of their going. Two days went by, and the side of the Mountain blew out, and 32,517 persons (including the Governor himself and the "scientific" commission) lay dead! Better not trust too fully the "scientific" expert!

If there ever was a time when intelligent men should be deaf to the views of professional specialists and alert to the warnings of God's unbreakable Word — to the "smoking" of God's coming judgment — that time is *now!*

Philosopher's *schemes* have ever been *satanic substitutes* for *the Saviour!* (v. 4)

It was so when Christ was on earth. The Devil did his utmost to get Him to adopt a short-cut to success! That fact is evident in each of the three "temptations."

How meaningful the replies of Jesus become in view of the twentieth century craze to settle all questions on a *material* basis, the basis of bread!

Kagawa has already originated at least a dozen schemes for saving the world! His slum-living — hoping by the power of example to lift the low — was but a beginning. To that he has added organization after organization. We are told by Robert Speer that some of his experiments failed, such as his "cheap eating-house," his "box factory," and his "brush factory," but as a labor leader he has loomed large. The very thing that Speer said would never come to pass, namely, that he should swing off from evangelical into purely social and political activity, has taken place! He was not here in America as a soul-winner, nor has there been in his wake any revival in this country that brought men to Jesus. On the contrary, his presence is extremely acceptable to the Jew, to the Labor Unions, to the "liberal" ministry, to "the Socialist Party," and is not in the least opposed even by the "Communists" themselves!

"Consumer's Cooperatives" — sugar-coated by the phrase "The Kingdom of God" — sounds like the philosophy of a public benefactor, and possibly the plea of a real prophet. There are a few of us who have long believed that too many people were profiting between the "producer" and the "consumer"; that meat selling at from 1 cent to 4 cents a pound on foot should not reach the table only at a cost ten times as great; that milk bringing the Minnesota farmer 2½ cents a quart should not cost the poor man's baby 11 cents, etc., etc. The injustice seems to be at least a dual one — an outrage against the producer and a robbery of the consumer; but while that realm provides an opportunity for proper legislation against men and women who profit too greatly at the expense of hunger and cold on the part of their less fortunate fellows, still the "Consumer's Cooperatives" Movement threatens as much the honest and needful retailers of America as it does the dishonest and needless ones!

If this movement should prove successful, instead of solving our problem of unemployment, it would vastly increase the same! There are 1,549,160 retail stores in this country, employing four and one-half million people whose wages exceed five billion dollars per annum.

Are we ready to put this additional number on the "Relief" list? God forbid! Are we ready to dispense with the convenience of the retailer, and either ourselves go to the great Government storages to secure what we want — where no deficiencies will be made up, no wrongs rectified and no adjustments permitted — or else pay the Government as big an amount (if not bigger) for delivery as would be required by the "middle-man"? The individual consumer, so long as he purchases from the retailer, can hold him to strict account for all goods delivered — but who can successfully fight *a government?*

There are some of us who prefer matters as they are, in the United States, to the chaos that curses Russia — where these philosophies have been adopted on a national scale, and where they have murdered 15 to 20 millions of people who dared to express discontent, and brought into the most brutal slavery that the world has ever known 150 million more who endure slave life rather than brave the danger of free speech!

How strange are the workings of the human mind! Forty years ago, I was fighting for my professional life, because I dared to oppose the monied powers of my church and city, and objected to our war of conquest in the Philippines. Patronizing pastors were my enemies, every one! Today, those same pastors are enjoying their fat salaries while propagating a philosophy which, if it obtains, will wreck the very people that pay them! But stranger still is the fact that these endangered laymen, whose personal estates are more and more threatened with confiscation by Communistic theories, rest supinely in cushioned pews, while their own pastors incite a "class" strife which now curses America and gladdens the Communists of the world!

These Modernists *talk* one way, but *live* another! There is no preacher so fat and so well dressed and so little burdened as the present preacher-advocate of "Social" Christianity! The *poor* are not even welcomed in many of their pew-rented Churches!

It is all a mental madness that finds but one explanation, namely, that God is letting the unwisdom of man run its course, prophecy find its fulfillment, and the shadows deepen until the cup of indignation be filled, when the final judgment of sinful man will have the approval of angels, and be admitted as just by devils.

Think, will you, of a man who says "God is love," as Kagawa does, and then, on being visited by a young man who tells him that he is going to be an evangelist, asks him two questions: First; "Have you the courage to go to prison?" Second; "Have you the grit to lead a strike?" (See "Meditations on the Cross," page 37)! And on being answered in the negative, replying: "Then give up the idea of becoming an evangelist"!

That definition of "love" is one with that of Lenin, who said, "We Bolsheviks are going to bring the Social Revolution as much to America as to Europe. It is coming systematically, step by step. The struggle will be long, cruel and sanguinary. . . . What matters the loss of 90% by executions if 10% of Communists remain to carry on the Revolution? . . . Bolshevism is not a seminary for young ladies. All children should be present at the executions and rejoice at the death of the enemies of the proletariat." Evolution — Kagawa's LOVE-God — has never paled at the sight of human blood!

During the last few years we have witnessed the "peaceful picketing" (?) of Minneapolis. We have also;

through the medium of a timid press, heard the faint cries of the dying, and have gotten a glimpse of the blood that runs in streets and alleys; but since the law of "Evolution" and "God" are the same (as Kagawa declares), this is not regrettable! Eh?

This "Evolution" Gospel Kagawa says "just as clearly teaches the authenticity of salvation as does the Father of Jesus Christ"!

But the apostle Paul has not yet finished.

Philosophies Are Tested By Time

"** * * Satan himself is transformed into an angel of light. Therefore it is no great thing if his ministers also be transformed as the ministers of righteousness; whose end shall be according to their works*" (2 Cor. 11: 14-15).

A sincere motive never justifies a mistake.

I am inclined to think that Kagawa is sincere enough. That he believes in himself, it would be hard to question; that he believes in the doctrine of Evolution, he has put beyond dispute; that he expects to see a desirable revolution in economics as a result of his "Consumer's Cooperatives" seems clear; and he even dreams of a day when, without the return of Christ, "every sin will be forgiven; so every error and every failure. The imperfect will become the perfect, ugliness will be changed to beauty, error to truth, and darkness to light." (See "Love, the Law of Life," page 301)

And all of this, mark you, not because Christ is coming to establish His kingdom in the earth, as promised, nor yet because He has declared His intention of gathering out of it *"all things that offend and them which do iniquity"* (Matt. 13:41), nor yet because He Who has pledged Himself to be a *"Prince of Peace"* has guaranteed prosperity and has Himself become the subject of universal worship (Micah 4:1-6) — but through the

"Consumer's Cooperatives" and kindred movements! Hence his statement: "Personally I am pouring my prayers and the reddest blood of my life into the work of carrying forward this quiet, undramatic, economic reformation."

Now what becomes of Speer's statement?

How many, many men have had kindred Utopian dreams!

They have left the Gospel, and by new "schemes" have sought to materialize those dreams!

When I was a boy, my father joined the Granger Movement and invested his money and held offices in the same, and many a night around the farm-house hearthstone he recited to us children the "certain" solution of problems through that organization. Since that time I have witnessed the rise of Union Labor organizations, and have heard the prophecies of *their* leaders that *they* would solve the economic problems of the world!

For the past year or two the air has been vocal with the prophecies of Father Coughlin who is equally certain that *he* has in his own brain the solution of every problem that pesters the people of the North American Continent; and since the arrival of Franklin D. Roosevelt at Washington on March 4, 1933, a whole school of prophets has assembled, and programs of "Relief" have multiplied almost as rapidly as minnows hatch on a late spring day!

But still poverty remains! Unemployment continues! Battles between Labor and Capital increase; human suffering survives, and the prescriptions of all economic "doctors" have, up to the present moment, proved to be but the nostrums of "quacks" whose very failures glorify the success of "the Great Physician," and lead one to recite with new enthusiasm the poem: —

"Hushed be the noise and strife of the schools
  Volume and sermon, pamphlet and speech;
The lips of the wise and the prattle of fools
  Let the Son of Man teach!

"Who has the key of the future but He?
  Who can unravel the knots of the skein?
We have travailed and struggled and sought to be free;
  We have travailed in vain!

"Bewildered, dejected, and prone to despair,
  To Him, as at first, do we turn and beseech;
Our ears are all open, give heed to our prayer;
  O Son of Man, teach!"

That man or that woman who follows any world-figure after he has denied the Christ of the New Testament is destined to a bitter experience, for when *"the blind lead the blind they both go into the ditch together"!*

The deceived are commonly the greatest sufferers.

Look at bleeding Russia today! Twenty-five years ago there were millions of people who wanted a Revolution, and in many respects they needed one; but in their great anxiety to improve conditions they accepted flattering but false leadership, and fell under a slavery a thousandfold worse than ever was experienced under the meanest of Czars!

The reign of the capitalists in America has been a cruel reign! It has been the reign of "racketeers"; it has been the reign of selfishness; it has been the reign of unjustified and unjustifiable oppression. The enormous wealth produced in the 160 years of our national history has not been properly distributed. Gormands and gamblers have appeared among us, and some of them, with pistol in hand, have swept great portions of the wealth of the board into their own pockets! Speculators have taken advantage of human greed; have dangled false baits before hungry eyes; and have hooked the gills of thousands, to their own personal profit!

Great corporations have combined the talents, the inventiveness and the avarice of mighty men, and the public has been milked of millions and even billions! Professed "statesmen" sent to Washington to represent the interests of the people have joined the worshippers of gold, and have fleeced those for whom they professed the deepest interest and most unselfish friendship!

But when we react to all of this so far as to tie in with the present-day Socialist whose Utopian pledges have no more likelihood of redemption than had the Democratic Platform of 1932, or the gilded promises of a Foshay, or an Insull, we simply prove afresh the truth of the indictment of the great showman Barnum, who said, "The American people *love* to be humbugged"!

What, then, is my conclusion? CHRIST — and CHRIST ALONE! CHRISTIANITY — which is *Christ in the heart* — is the Hope of the individual and the Hope of the world!

When I see economic reformers of this day seizing upon some one feature of Christ's teaching — such, for instance, as "the social implications of the Gospel" — and attempting to make of that a talisman with which to work the wonder of world-redemption, I am reminded afresh of an Old Testament story. When the child of a certain Shunammite woman — given to her in answer to the prayer of Elisha — lay dead, and she came to the man of God at Mount Carmel to ask that he come and bring her boy back to life, Elisha turned to Gehazi, his servant, and said, *"Gird up thy loins, and take my staff in thine hand, and lay my staff upon the face of the child"* (II Kings 4:29). Gehazi obeyed, and laid the staff upon the face of the dead child, but *"there was neither voice nor hearing."* He therefore returned to the prophet saying, *"The child is not awakened,"* and Elisha himself came, *"and behold, the child was dead, and laid upon his bed. He went in, therefore, and shut the door upon them twain, and prayed unto the Lord. And he went up and lay upon the child, and put his mouth upon his mouth, and his eyes upon his eyes, and his hands upon his hands; and he stretched himself upon the child; and the flesh of the child waxed warm"* (II Kings 4:32-35).

Finally, the child opened his eyes, and Elisha said to his servant, *"Call this Shunammite."* When she came, he said to her, *"Take up thy son."*

You will not bring dead men back to life by the "staff" of detached Biblical sentences or by philosophic schemes! You will not *save* society with "the staff of life" — mere *bread!*

There was and is but One known to human history Who has power to breathe into the individual the breath of life, and ability to cause the more-festering-than-Lazarus world-corpse to stand on its feet again, and that is "the Prophet of prophets"—Jesus of Nazareth, the Christ of God.

"There is none other name under heaven given among men whereby we must be saved."

VI
The Stanley Jones' "Kingdom Of God" Counterfeit

"AND *this gospel of the kingdom shall be preached in all the world for a witness unto all nations; and then shall the end come*" (Matt. 24:14).

Nearly 3000 years ago Solomon wrote, "*Of making many books there is no end*" (Eccles. 12:12). The significance of that sentence has increased with the race of the centuries, and the statement was never so true as now. Men have attempted to compute the stars, and confess their inability, but as yet we have failed to find any mathematician or statistician who dared to undertake the computation of the world's library!

Naturally where so many minds are involved, many opinions result, and many philosophies are exploited; and of all the subjects upon which men write, none is more fertile of varied philosophies than religion; and of the religions of the world, by far the most book-prolific is Christianity.

Strange, since the Bible, Christianity's text-book, is a clear, consistent and complete presentation of spiritual truth.

However, truth — like the diamond it is — has many facets of light; and by fixing the eye upon one of these small surfaces, and mistaking a part for the whole, it may be grossly misjudged, and that is the very mistake abundantly illustrated in the late books of E. Stanley Jones!

Unfortunately for clear thinking, the general public commonly accepts as sound, if not even sacred, the speech of the man who strikes a popular vein, who is going with the crowd.

The wide advertising, therefore, of E. Stanley Jones, the consequent crowds that have been called about his platform, and the extensive sale of his books, are no more a demonstration of his sanity in economics and soundness in theology than was the popular vote for Franklin D. Roosevelt a proof of his patriotism, or the crowds that used to hear Ingersoll a demonstration of the virtues of infidelity!

Years ago President King of Oberlin University told us that an educated man could so present *any* philosophy as to make it appear desirable. Dr. Jones' books illustrate King's contention. "The Kingdom of God" is their special subject.

In treating this theme, we propose to analyze to some degree the Jones emanations, and we have selected to treat same under three heads: The Kingdom Emphasis; The Kingdom Nemesis; and The Kingdom Genesis.

The Kingdom Emphasis

The Kingdom of God is the Central Theme of the Gospels.

We refer to the New Testament, not because this word "Kingdom" is unknown to the Old, but because there is a distinction and a difference.

In the hundreds of instances where "kingdom" appears in the Old Testament, the word is almost uniformly used with reference either to Judah, Israel or one of the nations. The only exceptions are the prophetic utterances that anticipate New Testament and millennial times.

But when you pass out of the Old Testament into the New, you have the atmosphere of another meaning altogether. "The Kingdom of God," "The Kingdom of Heaven" are not at all limited by the "metes and bounds" of a nation. As God Himself was never a tribal God, so His Kingdom, as outlined in the New Testament, is never confined to one people or limited to one continent.

That the teaching of Jesus, so comparatively full in the four Gospels, had signally failed to cure the Jewish mind of this limited conception, was proved when the Jewish converts gathered about the risen Lord saying, *"Lord, wilt thou at this time restore again the kingdom to Israel?"* (Acts 1:6)

They still expected a Jewish State, with Jerusalem for its capital, and a descendant of David for its King.

Apparently the divine endeavor of Jesus Himself to correct their narrow views, remove their racial prejudices, and enlarge their vision, had signally failed — but *not* from lack of teaching, clear and complete. His parables of the Kingdom *should* have sufficed, but they did not. His statement, *"The kingdom of God cometh not with observation"* (Luke 17:20) went over their heads. His story of the nobleman who went into a far country to receive unto himself a kingdom and to return, must have been meaningless to them; while His affirmations, *"My kingdom is not of this world,"* and again *"but now is my kingdom not from hence"* (John 18:36) were to them words without meaning!

But in view of the history already made, the events that are today transpiring, and the complete agreement of fulfilling prophecy, it is high time that professed Christian teachers should begin, at least, to get Christ's view of *"the kingdom of God"!*

In this century, it has become a subject of supreme interest.

With the arrival of the 19th century, Modernism, having adopted the philosophy of Charles Darwin and seeing the rapid strides that were being made by Christianity in heathen lands, concluded that it had in the church an illustration of its philosophy; and that by the law of "Evolution" the millennium, or "the kingdom of God," was at hand. It reasoned —

"A few years, and the last national barrier to the Gospel of the Son of God would be broken down, heathen religions would be discredited, Satan would be defeated, and the Kingdom of God, in all its fullness, would have come."

No lesser a personage than John R. Mott, then looked upon as the most outstanding of young missionary enthusiasts, thrilled the Church with his slogan — "The Evangelization of the World in this Generation."

But the Darwin philosophy applied to religion has proven as false to facts as it always was in the realm of science. The generation to which young Mott belonged has few veterans left, and the Kingdom has not yet come, nor has the world been evangelized.

Those of us who were "listening in" to the farewell address of Dr. Jones on Wednesday night last (Feb. 17, 1937) heard from the lips of his laudators the sad confession that the world was never in a worse way, and from Dr. Jones' lips a somewhat severe arraignment of the Church of God for its failures. They were all in the condition so accurately described by the apostle James; and when it is remembered that Mr. John D. Rockefeller Jr. was a conspicuous speaker on this occasion, the language of inspiration becomes more significant still:

"Go to now, ye rich men, weep and howl for your miseries that shall come upon you.

"Your riches are corrupted, and your garments are moth-eaten.

"Your gold and silver is cankered; and the rust of them shall be a witness against you, and shall eat your flesh as it were fire. Ye have heaped treasure to-

gether for the last days.

"*Behold, the hire of the labourers who have reaped down your fields, which is of you kept back by fraud, crieth; and the cries of them which have reaped are entered into the ears of the Lord of Sabaoth.*

"*Ye have lived in pleasure on the earth, and been wanton; ye have nourished your hearts, as in a day of slaughter.*

"*Ye have condemned and killed the just; and he doth not resist you.*" (James 5:1-6)

And then follows a significant statement — now needed as never before —

"*Be patient therefore, brethren, unto the coming of the Lord. Behold the husbandman waiteth for the precious fruit of the earth, and hath long patience for it, until he receive the early and latter rain.*

"*Be ye also patient; stablish your hearts; for the coming of the Lord draweth nigh.*" (James 5:7,8)

When one thinks of the almost desperate efforts in the forty years of this twentieth century "to make the world over" by attempting to replace drunkenness with sobriety, injustice with righteousness, lust with love, crime with righteous conduct, sin with holiness, the kingdoms of men with the Kingdom of God, he is reminded afresh of the Master's words:

"*And from the days of John the Baptist until now the kingdom of heaven suffereth violence, and the violent take it by force*" (Matt. 11:12).

In these 40 years I have seen the rise of the Mott Movement to "evangelize the world in this generation" — and witnessed its failure; the passing of the "Brotherhood Movement" — to note a very small spiritual deposit; the birth of the "Inter-Church World Movement" and also its burial—when one of its ardent advocates in delivering the "funeral oration," described it as "an orgy of expenditures." I have also been an ardent advocate of the Eighteenth Amendment, but we have seen *that* buried in the deep grave of adverse public sentiment. I have also heard from the lips of the most outstanding educators the confident declaration that the increase of knowledge would convert the world; have even hoped in the slogan so popular in 1917-18 — "The World War to end All War"; and have not been unconscious of the promising efforts of The Hague, The World Court, The League of Nations in their endeavors at world-redemption.

But seeing that these have all signally failed, I am now no more impressed by the E. Stanley Jones panacea of obliterating all race distinctions, uniting all denominations, reducing all individuals to an economic level, and naming the result "The Kingdom of God," than I am by the statement quoted from Schinkiki, the Japanese statesman, in one of the issues of "Collier's" in 1937 — "The salvation of the entire race is the mission of our Empire."

Patience is a rare virtue; but whether we exercise it or not, the Kingdom of God will not come at our call!

Within this century the Humanists, vocal in our Universities throughout the length and breadth of the land, have been endeavoring to do exactly what E. Stanley Jones is working at, namely, to make *man* the conquering hero. Of them Dr. Jones writes:

"They are sincere and desperately in earnest, but most of them grow tired. There is nothing more obvious on the horizon than the tired Humanist."

We predict, however, that Jones will yet join their company!

John Dewey, James Truslow Adams, Theodore Dreiser, Bertrand Russell and Irving Babbitt are among the self-styled "advanced" thinkers. A few years ago they had, each and every one, his philosophy of world-redemption; but today Dr. Jones admitted that they floundered together in the morass of pessimism. Such is the fate of false philosophers!

One hesitates to speak a word that detracts from the enthuisasm of the optimist; but to date even optimism has not proved a panacea for world-ills; and when Dr. Jones thinks that "the Kingdom of God on earth — a kingdom in which there will be no poverty, no classes, no sickness and no sin" — as "a goal," "can be made in one generation," and never so much as mentions the coming of *the King* to that task, he makes an appeal which is not only contrary to divine revelation, but which is also an insult to reason, since it is evident even to dull observers that the world-drift today is in the other direction!

The meaning of this phrase will be clarified and increased with fulfilling prophecy.

One reason why the Kingdom of God is in the ascendant just now is the circumstance that true Bible expositors have been preaching *"the Gospel of the Kingdom"* in recent years as never before since the days of the apostles. When they read the book of Daniel, they know that *"the end of this age"* is near. When they read the Pauline Epistles and see men *"departing from the faith; giving heed to seducing spirits and doctrines of devils,"* they know that we are in *"the latter times."* When they consent with the apostles that men have become *"lovers of their own selves, covetous, boasters, proud; blasphemers, disobedient to parents, unthankful, unholy, without natural affection, truce-breakers, false accusers, incontinent,"* etc. They know that we are in *"the last days,"* and that the *"perilous times"* have come.

According to the united testimony of prophecy, the Kingdom of God lies just beyond; for, as the darkest hour is just before the daybreak, so likewise we, when we *"see these things come to pass, know that the kingdom of God is nigh at hand."* (Luke 21:31)

The Kingdom Nemesis

The Standard Dictionary defines "Nemesis" as "the Grecian goddess who presided over the moral and proper order of things and visited with retribution any violation of the natural equilibrium."

Beyond all question there have been many violations of God's will for the world, and the judgment following has been Kingdom-delay. We all know that *"the Kingdom was at hand"* with the first coming of Jesus Christ, and that it was offered to Israel, but was rejected and its KING crucified. Hence the words of the Lord Jesus — *"Therefore I say unto you, the Kingdom of God shall be taken from you and be given to a nation bringing forth the fruits thereof"* (Matt. 21:43).

But this is so familiar to Bible students that it needs no further emphasis, and we pass to the annoying delays to which this Kingdom has been subjected.

Several times in the history of the Church it looked favorable for the arrival of the Kingdom. On each of these occasions Satan has shown his astuteness by effecting a combination of truth and error intended to retard instead of to hasten it. Prominent among these have been the unholy alliance of Church and State, the fatalistic indifference to the Commission of the Church, and false conceptions of the Kingdom itself.

We have said *"an unholy alliance of Church and State"!*

For three centuries after our Lord's ascension the onward march of the Church of God was marvellous, even amazing. The Encyclopaedia Britannica, in its ninth edition, said: —

"The history of the world presents no phenomenon

so striking as the rise and early progress of Christianity. * * * It spread so rapidly that in an incredibly short period of time it had been diffused throughout the whole civilized world, and in the fourth century of its existence, became the recognized and established religion of the Roman Empire. When it is remembered that this result was achieved not only without the aid of any worldly influence but in the face of the keenest opposition on the part of all the learning, wealth, wit and power of the most enlightened and mightiest nations of the earth, the conclusion is strongly forced upon us that a power beyond that of man was concerned in its success, and that its early and unexampled triumphs afford an incontestable proof of its inherent truth and its divine origin."

It was at that very point that Constantine reached the identical conclusion of E. Stanley Jones and decided that he would "put the Christian program into operation through the State." The result was a spiritual paralysis — yea even a gangrenous godlessness from which a thousand years did not suffice to recover the Church to her fourth-century health and hopes!

It would seem that *one* such experience would, in the light of Scripture *"love not the world, neither the things that are in the world,"* be sufficient for the instruction of man. But not so, when a widely publicized and eloquent orator appears in our midst!

When the War of 1914-18 was ended, the world was war-sick, and its leaders were, to a man, loudly affirming the folly of that experience, and declaring that they would never be parties to its recurrence; but as Lloyd George said, "there is a new generation now that, not having endured the danger, darkness and death of those days, are keen for another controversy, and are allured by conceivable chivalry, dash and the glories of a new war."

James Stalker in "The Christology of Jesus" tells

us how constantly men return to the thought "only get your State right, with perfect laws and a perfect administration, and everything else will be right. Even sin will disappear; for all injustice will be smitten to the ground, and righteousness will flourish under the protection of authority."

Dr. Jones seems clearly to apprehend this difficulty, and has escaped putting his faith in princes by placing it in that far less stable and more uniformly weak and sinful thing known as "all the people"!

I find it interesting to pit philosopher against philosopher: so I take from R. F. Horton's volume, "The Teaching of Jesus," the following sane statement — modernists sometimes make such — and set it side by side with E. Stanley Jones' plea for a social State, and find the result both interesting and convincing. Horton says:—

"If some wise teacher were to arise among us today, when the air is thick with schemes of social reconstruction, and were to address Socialists possessed with impossible dreams, pressing crude and external reforms, with the words, 'Socialism is at hand; I have come to establish it on earth'; and were then to explain that Socialism would be realized by every one becoming unselfish, unmercenary, and filled with the spirit of love, such a teacher would be howled down by Socialist leaders today. The preacher of the Kingdom of God, in the right sense of the word, was crucified by those who professed to belong to the kingdom of God in His day."

There are many of us who believe He is no less crucified by those apostles of Christianity who preach a kingdom to be established by "the sons of men" rather than by "the Son of God"!

In saying all this, I do *not* mean for one moment to bring a charge of insincerity or non-Christianity against E. Stanley Jones. I believe him to be both sincere and

Christian; but if my study of the Bible for fifty-six consecutive years means anything, he is a sadly mistaken man, and time will demonstrate his kingdom "dementia." When the Kingdom of God comes, the State will pass under its control; but *never* will the State become the instrument or medium of its arrival.

Beyond question this Kingdom has been further delayed by fatalism and indifference.

At one time, "Predestination," a Biblical doctrine, was so misinterpreted by men as to become an enemy of the Master's "Great Commission." At all times the natural selfishness of man has operated to slow down the missionary endeavors of even the Church. E. Stanley Jones will for ever have this strong point in his favor — that he was not disobedient to the heavenly voice, *"Go ye, therefore, and teach all nations."* At the point where he will hear his Master's plaudit, *"Well done!"* many of us will hang our heads for shame.

The sin of the Church is at this point. Her membership has frequently been too well content in disobedience. Her profession of allegiance, even on the part of the majority, has been either hypocritical or self-deceived. Comfortably ensconced in the warmer atmosphere of Christian civilization, thousands upon thousands have been unconcerned, having no disturbing dreams of untaught heathen, and oppressed by no deep sympathy with the needy in the home land.

When it comes to loyalty to the will of the Spirit and the "Great Commission," our hats are off to both Kagawa and E. Stanley Jones!

However, no extent of personal surrender and no measure of service can either justify or atone for teaching which finds no Biblical basis.

Two things there are in the Church of God today which hamper her endeavors and even hamstring her strength — a deadly indifference on the part of the multitude of her membership regarding the interests of the Church, and false interpretations by those who have been carried away by the trends of Modernism.

Candidly, I believe that the latter are more dangerous than the former, for, as Jones himself admits, "Strangled as it has been by its own devotees, crippled by its perversions, and nearly paralyzed by overlaid superstitions, nevertheless Christianity, in spite of all, has filled the world with schools, orphan asylums, hospitals, leper asylums and other institutions of various kinds for the uplifting of humanity, until there is not an island of the sea, nor a place anywhere where this has not happened. The Christian Church, with all its faults, is the best serving institution on earth. It has many critics, but no rivals in the work of human redemption. In the early days, when it was fresh and living, the Christians did so much for prisoners that Licinius passed a law that 'no one was to show kindness to sufferers in prison by supplying them with food,' and that 'no one was to show mercy to those who are starving in prison.' In the same way, the Communists forbid any social work to the churches, instinctively fearing that dynamic of love in Christianity which lies hidden, ready to burst into world-manifestation and world-redemption."

While all of this is true, and much more in its favor might be said, nevertheless it is a fact that the Church has experienced another arrested development within the past twenty-five years.

That brings me to my third opportunity for Nemesis to judge and condemn.

Beyond question, false definitions of the Kingdom have devitalized the Church.

Just about twenty-five years ago, the flood-tide of new philosophies set in. Professors in colleges and seminaries got enamored of the evolutionary hypothesis, and produced books out of number applying evolution to the Christian religion.

In this process they disputed the authority of the Old Testament and the inspiration of the New, filling both with interrogation points. They questioned the deity of Christ! They questioned the necessity of redemption! They questioned the divine origin of the Church! They questioned the personality of the Holy Spirit! They questioned the power of the Gospel unto salvation! They "defined" sin out of existence! They sought to *substitute* for Scripture — teaching "social" theories; and they have been leaders in the world-crisis causing Communism to challenge Christianity itself!

It is one of the misfortunes of Christian history to have so outstanding a personality, so sacrificial a spirit, as either Kagawa or E. Stanley Jones cast in his lot with them. But such is the case, and at every vital point both of these men have linked their labors with the endeavors of destructive critics.

Jones is more anomalous in this company than is Kagawa. He does not espouse Darwinism. He does not deny the deity of Jesus or dispute the virgin birth. He does not hold that Christ was a sinner; nor will he be content to feel that a mere "apology to God" on Jesus' part would suffice to put away sin. So far as we have seen, we believe that he stands for the blood atonement. Many times in his books he clearly indicates his faith in the personality of the Holy Spirit, and urges the necessity of individual regeneration.

But — notwithstanding all of this — he links hands with the critics of the Bible and of Christ, in his conclusions — which we believe to be flatly false. Jesus Christ was not a "Collectivist" — He was an "Individualist"! Never during His life on earth did He seek to set renters against owners or servants against masters; and not once during all His preaching did He body forth the philosophy that "every man was to have according to his need — irrespective of merit."

In discussing this very subject — the Kingdom of Heaven — He used the parable of the talents. *"To one he gave five talents; to another two, and to another one; to every man according to his several ability."*

That is the only *sane* basis for society — and Christ was not only sane, but His sanity was superbly divine! True, the Bible *does* teach that *"God hath made of one blood all nations of men for to dwell on the face of the earth"*; but why forget the rest of the text *"and hath determined the times before appointed, and the bounds of their habitation"?*

I can find no Biblical demand that racial differences be obliterated. Nature's ways, which must be God-ordained, are the opposite! Geese and ducks belong to the same family, but they flock apart. Yellow birds and blue birds, while never mingling, have no sense of social superiority or of racial antagonism, so far as we know.

Stanley Jones' suggestion that we wipe out "color" distinctions by having "colored" people join "white" churches and white people join colored churches, ignores the history which the races themselves have voluntarily made. When the Civil War ended, every colored man in the South was a member of a white Church, but he was not so comfortable with another race as he was with his own, and voluntarily departed.

His white brother aided him to carry out his preference for fellowship with his own; and — God be praised! — that matchless negro Booker T. Washington saw the wisdom of it, and understood perfectly the advantages, personal and social, resulting, and commended the course, instead of seeking to excite strained relations by the suggestion that somebody had sought to "high-hat" his brother!

Still further, one might easily imagine from the farewell address delivered by E. Stanley Jones that he had never heard of "The Inter-Church World Movement" — an endeavor to have one Church of all professed Christians, even though we had to provide denominational departments.

It is possible that Dr. Jones, living in far away India, never heard of the collapse of his Christian idealism, and never knew that the Church of God received a set-back rather than an advance by the experiment.

The simple fact is that the Moscow propaganda has gotten E. Stanley Jones! Everything for which Russia is standing (save its infidelity) he would saddle upon Christianity! But, of course, the view of Russia that Jones has experienced is the tourist vision, the beauty spots provided for passing visitors. Should he find time to do what Carveth Wells did, or to listen to the testimony of hundreds of Russians now freed from that accursed land and daring to bear witness, he would come to entirely different conclusions from those which he has written into his books!

His disposition to reduce all men to the economic level of "necessity" is a Moscow theory which has resulted in the enslavement of the hundred and fifty millions of people to a few thousand overfed and murderous tyrants; and when Communism comes to America we will have a kindred condition!

His insistence upon what he calls "color blindness" or "the destruction of distinction between the races" — so ardently illustrated by the fact that "it is a criminal offense to speak against a Jew in Russia" — blandly ignores the fact that the Russian rulers are Jews, and their own people are the only ones thus protected against criticism, or even promised a privilege of any sort other than slavery!

His proposed "Cooperatives" as against "competition" would result for the world, as it has done for Russia, in the destruction of initiative and interest in life.

His combination of all religious denominations into one collective so-called "Christian" body in America, with denominational departments, might easily have been suggested by the "collective" home of Russia where all dwell together and eat from a common table; but some of us prefer our little country house on a hill, with a breathing space about us — an individuality instead of a Government number!

Above all, his "Christian Internationale" is none other than the "Fourth Internationale" of Moscow; and there are many of us who if we should have to choose between a citizenship in our own country and a world-fate, wound into a revolving maelstrom of two billions, would prefer the former to the latter!

Three things account for the false conclusions to which Stanley Jones has come;

First: Arménianism — which has always glorified man and looks to *him* to right the world rather than to the unmerited grace and power of God.

Second: His Methodism — which at the present moment (with great and blessed exceptions) is steadily adrift and in decline.

Third: The influence of Modernist writers whose wild and Utopian dreams have been accepted as possibilities of easy realization.

It is little wonder that the Church of God is arrested in its growth. It is little wonder that the Kingdom of God seems more remote now than it did fifty years ago. It is little wonder that Jones himself sounds a pessimistic note, saying: "The foundations of society are crumbling before our very eyes. Many of the old securities are gone or going. As I go about the world, I find men with the feelings which the Germans must have had when the Hindenburg line began to crumble."

How pathetic for the very man who sees these things to lend a further push to the approaching collapse!

But, blessed be God, there is a fairer outlook, a *"blessed hope,"* and this we prefer to present under

The Kingdom Genesis

This study is essential to a correct understanding of the phrase "the Kingdom of God."

That Kingdom was adumbrated in the Old Testament Scriptures and more fully revealed in the New.

It would be difficult to state the matter better than was done years ago by John Watson in his book, "The Mind of the Master."

"The Kingdom of God owed its origin to the Theocracy, its inspiration to Isaiah, its form to Daniel, and its popularity to John the Baptist."

The Theocracy was God's attempt to rule the world *in absentia!* Sin thwarted that endeavor! Isaiah, however, from the mountain top of inspiration, saw the day of a second and successful attempt in the Person and Presence of God's Son. Daniel indicated the history that would lead to that glorious time and outlined the events that would prepare the way for its appearance; while John the Baptist, finding Jesus, God's Son, personally present in the world, announced the *"Kingdom at hand,"* and called upon the people to *"repent."*

Jesus, realizing the ready errors into which the eager and egotistical Israelites were falling, deliberately sets Himself to the task of correcting the impression that it was to appear at once, and preparing believers for the long delay that should end in His Second Coming, in power and glory. His apostles — Jude, Peter and Paul — placed that Kingdom not *"in the last days"* but at *"the end of this age,"* and John named the Kingdom "The Millennium."

However, such are its winsome and divine features that the prophetic picture of it has rendered uneasy the thinkers of the age.

John H. Hutton once quoted a most influential journalist as having said, "We have seen the Christ and we are all uneasy."

That is the exact explanation of the present cry — "Thy kingdom come"! The "pattern shown us in the Mount" of revelation is such as to stir the souls of men; and the longer this world is dominated by its present god, and this age is subjected to the will of "the prince of the power of the air," the more loudly will the sick, suffering and oppressed among men call for a change and believers in Christ yearn for His coming — knowing full well that His arrival, and that alone, will accomplish the restoration of all things.

Those who pray, "Thy kingdom come!" and stop there, may imagine that the world could be made over by the decapitation of capitalism and the enthronement of the servant class; but those who complete the sentence, saying, *"Thy will be done on earth as it is done in heaven!"* know full well that such a kingdom is inconceivable so long as man remains the selfish, sinful, greedy and cruel individual that he is.

To those who would give attention to sane teaching we commend Dan Gilbert's book "Our Retreat from Modernism," and endorse without qualification his keen distinction between the Socialist program and the program of the Son of God.

He says: —

"Socialism, as Dr. W. W. Moore has said, attributes what is evil in man to the evil system, and proposes to change the system that it may change the man. Christianity, on the other hand, attributes what is evil in the system to the evil spirit in man, and proposes to change the *man* in order to change the *system.*"

That is why we charge that E. Stanley Jones is far more Communistic than Christian. His books are a combination of commendation and criticism of both Communism and the Church; but his philosophy betrays this professee Christian into more repeated compliments for Communism than he pays the Church!

To use the words of Dan Gilbert: —

"Such is the perverse thinking to which man sinks when he presumes to build with human hands the divine Kingdom."

The Kingdom of God as set forth in the booklet of E. Stanley Jones is remote from that found in the Bible.

On his repeated confession, the chief characteristic of his conception of "The Kingdom of God" is an abundance of "meat and drink"! Over and over again in his books he returns to this plaintive plea: —

"Why in a world of abundance should we have some men overfed and others suffering from hunger?"

And in his farewell address on the air the night he left America he bemoaned the fact that "half of America was stuffed and the other half starved." Had his remark been made in India, it might have been true; in America it is far from fact. Starved men among us are practically unknown, and would never occur should the knowledge of hunger reach the public in time.

The fact is that Jones' philosophies are largely the product of his long Eastern residence, where capitalism is not one half so much in clash with labor as caste is in clash with Christ.

If Jesus ever made aught clear by the Bible, He made it plain that His Kingdom was *not* a matter of *"meat and drink"* (Rom. 14:17).

The "Kingdom" set forth in Jones' books is a Kingdom which if it came at all would come with loud acclaim. Not so with the Biblical Kingdom of God, which *"cometh not with observation"* (Luke 17:20).

The Kingdom of Jones' books is a Kingdom that might arrive with this generation; but the Kingdom of God is one that does not belong to this world, or, as the Greek word indicates, "this age."

The Kingdom of Stanley Jones is one that would be produced from world sources by the united endeavors of men; but the Kingdom of God is *"not from hence"* (John 18:36).

Let me conclude with the only possible remark that could be made consonant with the sacred Scriptures — *God's Kingdom on earth will be realized in the return of God's Son to earth to reign for a thousand years.*

In the language of Dr. Jones himself — "Christ is the one Hope for a world floundering in its own follies." It is in His reign that *"angels shall gather out of His Kingdom all that cause stumbling or offend,"* and it is under His supremacy that *"the righteous shall shine forth as the sun in the Kingdom of the Father."*

The strangest of all mental processes is that false presentation of the Kingdom of God on earth *without* the presence in it and over it of *the King Himself*, concerning Whom Paul wrote to the Corinthians: —

" * * * when he shall have put down all rule, and all authority and power. For he must reign, till he hath put all enemies under his feet" (I Cor. 15:24,25).

The part that man may play in preparing for His appearance is not necessarily inconspicuous. Fundamentalism stands for a fruitful life, and has produced practically all the desired results accomplished in His holy name to date.

But, as John Watson in "The Mind of the Master" declares: —

"When the Kingdom comes, the glory will not belong to Hampden, or Howard, or Wilberforce, or Shaftesbury, or Lincoln, or Gordon, or any present-day ecclesiastical light, Kagawa and Jones included. It will belong to Jesus!"

He alone will have chained the Dragon and cast him into the Pit. He alone will have brought the dead to live again. He alone will sit on David's resurrected throne and sway the sceptre from sea to sea. At His Word, justice will become uniform, peace world-wide, and prosperity the portion of all.

In the language of R. F. Horton again: —

"Some faint aroma of mercy and justice and truth is in our throne-rooms and State Departments because the Son of Man has passed through them; but the blessed actual reign of the Son of Man, where willing subjects love Him and express His will, stands in contrast to all earthly government, and will be the only government that will ultimately survive."

There was one and only one glorious feature to the occasion of E. Stanley Jones' farewell service in New York, Wednesday night, Feb. 17th, 1937, and that was the sentiment of the hymn which concluded the service on the air: —

"Oh for a thousand tongues to sing
My dear Redeemer's praise,
The glories of my God and King,
The triumphs of His grace!"

VII

The Counterfeit Discoverable In The Oxford Movement

Read Galatians 1:6-12

SOLOMON, in Ecclesiastes 12:12, says: *"Of making many books there is no end."*

The time has come when that statement is such a truism that it excites no surprise and seldom a comment. Were Solomon alive now, he would have a kindred remark to make concerning religious movements — "Of making many such, there is no end."

John Watson, in "The Mind of the Master," writes as follows: —

"Nothing is easier than to create a religion; one only needs self-confidence and foolscap paper. An able Frenchman sat down in his study and produced Positivism, which some one pleasantly described as 'Catholicism minus Christianity.' It stimulated conversation in superior circles for years; and only yesterday Mr. Frederick Harrison was explaining to Professor Huxley that this ingenious invention of M. Comte ought to be taken seriously.

An extremely clever woman disappeared into Asia, and returned with another religion, which has distinctly added to the innocent gaiety of the English nation.

One never knows when a new religion may not be advertised. Various interesting societies are understood to be working at something, and each novelty receives a good-natured welcome. No person with any sense of humor resents one of these efforts to stimulate the jaded palate of society, unless it be paraded a season too long, and threatens to become a bore."

Possibly that is the only reason why I should address myself to the subject of the Oxford Movement. We had a slight inoculation of it in Minneapolis a few months ago, and I supposed that the epidemic would thereby be averted: but evidently the doctors of O.M. (Oxford Movement) felt that there were other patients in danger of true Christianity, and thus they have returned to prevent, if possible, that more serious type!

The wonder is that newspapers, existing in a society wherein no small portion of their support comes from real Christians, could yet count the continuous and effective work of the Church a matter of no news moment, while faddists are "front-paged," and played up as if they carried in their satchels and handbags a panacea which would correct all public ills and right all private wrongs!

This week it is not Krishnamurti; it is not Behai. Mrs. Besant is dead, and sister Eddy's agents receive a little less attention than the papers gave to their principal.

It is little wonder, therefore, that the Oxford Movement should have attention. The newspapers are short of stuff! Garbled Christianity is far more novel than the simple gospel of the saving Christ — hence the public excitement.

Paul seems to have anticipated not only this movement but many others of kindred sort, and in the Epistle to the Galatians he prophesied its character before it came upon the scene!

It is "another gospel."

One such is born every month!

We have had the Laymen's Movement, the Brotherhood Movement, the Forward Men and Religion Movement, the Interchurch World Movement, the Youth Movement, the Federal Council movement, the Laymen's Missionary Commission, the Preaching Mission, and others too numerous to mention. They have followed one another in rapid succession; and yet when one takes account of the impetus they have given to the church of God and to the cause of true Christianity, he finds that instead of having put either of them forward, they have positively retarded both! For instance, the "Laymen's Commission" was a deadly stroke against evangelical missions!

To some people, newspaper publicity and parlor meetings in elegant mansions, "all parties in full dress," is a sure sign of progress for the cause represented! But it should not be forgotten that Tertius van Dyke, leaving the Park Avenue Presbyterian Church of New York to accept a country parish, gave as one reason for his resignation the following:

"The people of New York want religion with a jazz tempo. If I were to announce some Sunday morning that I was going to do a flying trapeze act, the church would be crowded! Circus stuff, however, does not make for Christianity!"

Who will dispute Van Dyke?

We have repeatedly resented the charge that the churches were practically the property of the rich; and we have even deeply regretted the circumstance that the rich were too much ignored by the proponents of the Christian faith. We have even voiced our hope that some day missions to the godless rich would become as common as missions to the godless poor; but we had no notion whatever that "another gospel" would be needed for the upper classes; and Buchmanism is "another gospel."

Rev. C. M. Chevasse, Master of St. Peter's Hall,

Oxford, says that "all the religious leaders and responsible persons in the University have grave misgivings after having closely watched the movement for the past several years." He declares: "The worst error is that it lacks an essentially Christian basis."

That is the exact charge which we make against it — that it is Bible-less.

Each new movement finds an easy constituency.

To have named this movement "The Oxford Movement" was unquestionably a politic stroke. Oxford University is world-famed. The "Oxford" edition of the Bible has carried that name into the uttermost parts of the earth, and to the darkest regions of heathenism itself. The "University" is supposed to be a place of mental illumination. The output of the Oxford Press has unquestionably carried spiritual light to the ends of creation. How worldly-wise, then, was the use of this prefix to the name of the Movement!

It arises, also, at a time when its popularity is practically assured! Just as the Atheists of the world were feeling out in every direction to find something upon which to rest their philosophy of life when Charles Darwin gave to their dying cause "Evolution" and thereby secured a further temporary lease for their existence; so Modernism has become so insert, and even its administration of evangelical machinery so paralyzed that for some years now it has been looking in every direction for some method of galvanizing its corpse which would at least create the impression that it was living still!

This, the Oxford Movement provides. Unitarian ministers are heartily commending it; Modernist ministers are opening their pulpits to it; and those churches which have been brought to a state of spiritual death by hypnotizing D.D.s are hailing the apostles of this "another gospel" with joy!

In proof of this, one needs only to read the list of

pulpits that are open to them in Minneapolis. Unfortunately, one orthodox name appears; but one out of thirty is only a further illustration of the fact that some movements are so smooth and sinister that they occasionally deceive *"even the very elect."*

As Dr. Basil F.C. Atkinson of Cambridge University said:

"It is a mixture; a mixture of a few truly Christian people and others who can hold any sort of belief or doctrine."

It utterly ignores Paul's injunction to the Corinthians:

"Be ye not unequally yoked together with unbelievers: for what fellowship hath righteousness with unrighteousness? and what communion hath light with darkness? And what concord hath Christ with Belial? or what part hath he that believeth with an infidel?" (II Cor. 6:14-18)

The Perverted Gospel

The Oxford commission is a perversion of Christianity.

Captain James A. Campbell, president of the Bible League of England — the most orthodox organization known to that country — makes this exact charge against the movement:

"Tested by the infallible Word of God," he maintains, "it is an utter failure." He charges it with having a "lavender water" view of sin. He declares that it is utterly indifferent to the whole fact of sin as against God; and that while certain specified sins are confessed one to another, *"repentance toward God and faith toward our Lord Jesus Christ"* are not mentioned, nor have ruin, redemption, regeneration, any place.

Instead of considering man as being *"dead in tres-*

passes and sins," Buchman insists that in each man there is a divine spark that needs only to be kindled; and by the processes of "The five C's" he may remake himself — which, as Dr. A. C. Gaebelein remarks, is "another gospel" to such an extent that *"Christ is dead in vain."*

To me, however, the great danger from this Movement consists in three or four facts, all of which grow out of one false phase in its philosophy, namely the so-called "Quiet Hour."

In this "Quiet Hour" the mind is supposed to be vacant so that the Spirit of God may come in and dictate its thought.

Our first answer to that proposition is that just as the devil finds work for idle hands, so he has abundant suggestions for idle minds!

The natural fruit of this philosophy is the claim made by Dr. Russell for Buchman — that he is so Spirit-guided that his every word is dictated by the Holy Ghost; a claim which is in direct contradiction to John's plain declaration concerning the completeness of the Bible as a rule for faith and practice, namely: —

"I testify unto every man that heareth the words of the prophecy of this book, If any man shall add unto these things, God shall add unto him the plaques that are written in this book: And if any man shall take away from the words of the book of this prophecy, God shall take away his part out of the book of life, and out of the holy city, and from the things which are written in this book" (Rev. 22:18-19).

And still further evidence of its non-Scripturalness and also of its exceeding danger is given us in "The Indian Christian" of March 15, 1934, where it is said as herein quoted, as an illustration of where this method of obtaining guidance may lead to. It is an astounding conversation, and one which so far as we know has never been challenged, that Mr. J. C. Brown, a missionary, held with one of their men: —

Question: For what reason did Christ die?

Answer: To tell you the truth, I don't know myself.

Question: Has the group any list of sins?

Answer: No, we have no list of sins.

Question: Would you call adultery and murder sins?

Answer: Only if God told you they were.

Question: What would you do if you had a strong desire to commit adultery with another man's wife, or to murder some one?

Answer: I would go to God and get guidance about it.

Question: You mean that you would pray to God and ask Him to show you whether it was right or wrong?

Answer: No, I would not pray about it. I would just wait for God to give me guidance about it.

Question: And how would God give you this guidance?

Answer: I should get a strong impression what I should do.

Question: And if this strong impression was that you should murder that man, would you do it?

Answer: I should (!)

This brings us to another point —

The curse pronounced upon the proponents of a false gospel.

For fifty consecutive years in the ministry we have felt a justifiable degree of alarm for every evangelist who carried about the country a considerable company of women to aid him in his work. Not one in ten of these has escaped the severest criticism. I do not know how the public may feel about it; but I insist that the daily papers' report of the names of the Oxford Group visiting

Minneapolis did not impress one favorably. The constant travel together of Opera troupes has frequently proved to be necessary; but *Christians* should avoid suspicion.

A Man-Pleasing Gospel

This is a man-pleasing gospel!

That fact is stamped upon its very face. Its appeal to those Modernistic ministers who have worked their way into professorships and principal pulpits; its constant courting of the richest class in society; its use of their drawing-rooms for their social, hilarious and mutual confession meetings; its parade in full dress (so far removed from the simple, plain custom and attire of Christ and His apostles) — these are all a clear indication of its appeal to human pleasure. As Dr. F. C. Atkinson of Cambridge has said: "The movement is respectable in the wrong sense." It has secured the approval of such men as William James, Sherwood Eddy and others of like mind, who, as Dr. Gaebelein remarks, are "men who as to the Gospel of Jesus Christ, redemption by the blood, and salvation by the cross, are deniers."

Dr. Orchard, who some time ago left the Congregational ministry to unite with Romanism, has also paid it tribute.

The boast is that the great and wealthy, the educated, the so-called noble, princes, barons (and even a queen) belong to the group, and the extremely wealthy give it aid.

How different from the company about Christ! You will recall that it was asked *"if any of the rulers have believed on Him,"* and you will also remember that it was an astonishment of His ministry that *"the blind receive their sight, the lame walk, the lepers are cleansed, the deaf hear, the dead are raised up, and the poor have the gospel preached to them."*

Writing to the Corinthians, Paul said:

"For ye see your calling, brethren, how that not many wise men after the flesh, not many noble, not many mighty, are called: But God hath chosen the foolish things of the world to confound the wise; and God hath chosen the weak things of the world to confound the things which are mighty; And base things of the world, and things which are despised, hath God chosen, yea, and things which are not, to bring to nought things that are: That no flesh should glory in his presence. But of him are ye in Christ Jesus, who of God is made unto us wisdom, and righteousness, and sanctification, and redemption; That, according as it is written, He that glorieth, let him glory in the Lord." (I Cor. 1:18-31)

Little wonder that R. Wright Hay, secretary of the Bible League of England, quotes from a letter received from an earnest Christian worker this question:

"Has the dazzling and mighty Being Whom members of the Oxford Group call 'Christ' but seldom 'Lord' the print of the nails in His hands and feet and the spear wound in His side; and if so, why is so little significance attributed to His precious blood by members of that Movement?"

Then Dr. Hay remarks: "I had a three hours' talk a few years ago with Dr. Buchman, seeking to get at what he really believed himself and at what his purpose was in connection with this movement. I spoke very freely to him in regard to my own faith. . . . Never once during those three hours did Dr. Buchman mention the blood of Christ."

They ignore the fact that the Church of Christ was *"purchased with His own blood."* They forget the injunction: *"For as often as ye eat this bread, and drink this cup, ye do shew the Lord's death till he come,"* and Christ's plain statement: *"This is the New Testament in my blood."* They forget that it is written: *"In whom we have redemption through his blood, the forgiveness of sins, according to the riches of his grace."* And also the word to the Romans: *"Being now justified by his blood, we shall be saved from wrath through him."*

Any "gospel" that is a departure from the shed blood of the Son of God is as remote from the Gospel of Jesus Christ as darkness is remote from light, and is at best only a counterfeit.

Pursuing the apostle Paul further, we find that—

Such a "gospel" ignores the pleasure of Christ.

"If I yet pleased men, I should not be the servant of Christ."

It is a strange freak in a man which does not comprehend that a confession of sin one to another such as is advocated in this Movement is practically a surrender to the lusts of the flesh. There are only two instances in the Bible where man is asked to confess his sin to his fellow. First, where one has wronged the fellow, and one's gift is to be given to God, he must set the wrong right. The second is where one is sick and has called for the elders of the church to anoint him with oil and pray for him, that the prayer of faith may heal the sick, he is enjoined to confess his sin.

All other of the confessions are due to God, for it is true, as the Psalmist says: *"Against thee and thee only have I sinned and done this evil in thy sight."* John is his First Epistle generalizes upon this and says: *"If we say we have no sin, we deceive ourselves and the truth is not in us. If we confess our sins, He is faithful and just to forgive us our sins and to cleanse us from all unrighteousness."*

Christ is the only Great High Priest known to the Church of God and the only One Who has the power to put away sin!

The fact is that there are few sources of greater evil than the confession of sin when that confession is made to others rather than to the Lord. Our scandals, almost without exception, grow out of such confessions! The papers of less than a week ago had their pages stained by a story of such sort. A young Jew who had professed conversion and had even proffered himself as a student in a Bible School of the West, married a young actress, and the two travelled across the country. They fell in with a priest of Rome, and when they had sufficiently drunk to believe that the young husband was in slumber, the priest said to the wife; "Come to my room in the hotel for a confession."

But the Jew, with his accustomed astuteness, was more awake than they had imagined. He followed with his pistol, and killed them both!

How many priests have been defiled by opening their minds to such confessions, and what a multitude of them have both themselves fallen and carried down with them those making the same, so that, as Paul wrote to the Ephesians: *"It is a shame even to speak of those things that are done of them in secret."*

Years ago I read a book entitled "Old Chester Tales," published by the American Baptist Publication Society, and among its stories there was one of a young woman who had missed the way, joined herself to a travelling troupe, and night after night made her living in most questionable conduct and theatre performances. A farmer bachelor of 45, who had been so tied to his mother's apron strings that he had seldom gotten beyond the confines of his front yard, found himself in town one day, and being curious to see the sights of the city, he entered the theatre and ere long fell desperately in love with the blondined performer. Unfortunately for him, she fell suddenly sick, and when he next attended the theatre, she was not there. Upon inquiry he found that she was in a hospital. He sought her out and left a bunch of cheap flowers. She laughed at him and his meagre gift: but as he continued his daily attentions, she came to feel that here was genuine love — love of another sort from that which male sirens had whispered into her passionate ears; love that might *last*. So, upon her recovery, she stood with him at the marriage altar and promised him love and loyalty.

Five years later, when their little girl was four years old, the unstinted and unbroken affection of this man convicted her of her past sins. She felt that she had sinned against him as she thought of her immoral past life. So one day when she was in the city she consulted an old Presbyterian preacher as to whether she should confess all to her husband, make her life an open page.

The old man, wise from long experience and observation, replied, "Never! What good could come of it? It would grieve his soul, arouse in the man who has never had a suspicion questions that had never occurred to him! Confess your sins to God! Get His forgiveness, and go on gloriously in your present righteous relation."

I thought when I had finished that story that it was the acme of wisdom. Thousands — yea, tens of thousands — of individuals might have been saved from intense suffering, and an almost equal number of families would have remained intact, and reputations that have been sent to the gutter, might have been saved to the good of society had this preacher's sound counsel been followed by others!

I am thinking now of a young minister in my own city, whose "Oxford" confession of a lustful past reached the ears of his betrothed, and it sent her to bed brokenhearted and invalided in body — while the guilty one goes on brazenly seeking all the ministerial honors and offices possible!

The text that reads, *"Be not partakers of other men's sins,"* is said to be more literally translated,

"Be not sin-sharers" — the inspired prohibition of the very practice in which Oxfordites take pride and pleasure!

It is a sorry counterfeit of Christianity.

It departs from it in its view of sin; it departs from it in its idea of regeneration; it departs from it in its teaching concerning the Holy Spirit; it departs from it in its view of Bible inspiration; it departs from it in its practical rejection of the blood; it departs from it in making the confessional a matter of mutual unbosoming instead of a penitent acknowledgment to the Great High Priest; and it departs from it in supposing that when one has told his sins to the Group, he has secured the forgiveness and favor of God!

Wright Hay of England says:

"Non-Biblical! That ought to be enough for every one who has the privilege of living in a land Biblicized to the extent that ours is. Any movement that appears upon the scene as a religious movement and is non-Biblical is a movement that joins issue with the God of our salvation."

Dr. Burgess said:

"Christianity must be Scripture Christianity; Christian worship must be Scriptural worship; Christian zeal must be Scriptural zeal; so that, let a man have ever such sublime knowledge and such burning zeal, yet, if it be not according *"to the law and to the testimony, there is no light in him."*

"To say, 'It's upon my conscience; it's upon my spirit; I find much comfort and much sweetness in religion' — this is nothing, for all false religions can and do say this. But hast thou the Word of God to warrant thee? Doth that justify thee? All things else are but an empty shadow!" A counterfeit!

Doubtless Buchman and his confederates are honestly distressed by the disordered Christianity of the day. Doubtless they are worried at the fragmentary and disheveled condition among the churches. Doubtless they imagine that, like another writer who sent me his printed political program, they can make a model city of Minneapolis and easily renovate a wicked world if only men and women will give them attention.

But the simple fact remains that their Movement produces still further disorder, and will eventuate in still further divisions. Their movement breaks the churches into further fragments, and when their visit to the city is long forgotten, poor Minneapolis will move into the mould of prophecy and be more degenerate than ever, and the world itself will wag on to lower depths of immorality and even bestiality.

But all of that — assured as it is — does not even discourage a Scripture-instructed man. We know that there is a better time coming. We know that *"the Day of the Lord,"* the Millennium, will yet break. We know that when man has completed his demolition, God will then undertake and effect His perfect reparation.

There is a "Paradise Lost," but there will be a "Paradise Regained"!

A writer made a statement which would apply absolutely to our experience in the First Baptist Church of Minneapolis when a while ago we underwent our auditorium enlargement. The parts of our noble organ were all piled up, one upon another, in an out-of-the-way place. The whole wall against which it had rested had been torn away and the organ taken to pieces. To the thoughtless observer they must have seemed but a heap of dust-covered rubbish. Later, however, the parts were skillfully adjusted to one another, and the instrument stood in its new location complete in every way. "The hand of our artistic organist swept the keys, sending forth strains of noble music, electrifying, exalting, ennobling, spiritualizing the reverent congregations gathered."

He would be an utterly false critic who should judge the organ or the organ-builder by the dust-covered and disjointed pipes! Wait until the Master-hand has put them together, and from them brought forth music!

So it is with the church and the Christian life itself. They are not complete. But wait, O critics, until this glorious "organ" through which the breath of heaven pours has been set in the "cathedral" of eternity, with each portion of that perfected "Body" in its place! *Then* shall you hear the swelling music, the divine harmonies, the celestial choirs! Then will the carping critics be dumb with confusion and shame; then the tinkerers will see how, instead of correcting the church, they were simply increasing its confusion; and then they will pay their tribute to the Master under Whose hand (and Whose hand alone) salvation of the individual can be effected, and the salvation of society, the State, and the world accomplished.

VIII

Fundamentalism --- The True Coin Of The Christian Realm

DAILY newspapers frequently employ queer reporters. The man who is often interviewed must, almost as often, ask himself the question: "What are the requirements by which newspaper reporters are adjudged and employed?" They range all the way from ignorance to education, from dullness to keenness, from insufferable boors, to men of matchless tact; and the daily press reflects that fact.

Leading magazines commonly voice writers of talent, but they have a strange method of treating mooted questions. Either they propose to employ only the pens which harmonize with editorial prejudice, or they give place to the opinionated who enjoy a peculiar literary pull.

What could be stranger than the magazine course concerning "the war in the churches," or "the fight between Fundamentalism and Modernism"?

Twenty-five years ago, a great layman, Lyman Stewart of Los Angeles, placed in the hands of a competent Committee a fund of $300,000, requesting that the same be used to publish a series of books dealing with the Christian Fundamentals, and ordered that the entire Protestant ministry of the world be made a present of the same. The inspiration for this undertaking Lyman Stewart received as he listened to a great sermon from the lips of Dr. A. C. Dixon, then Pastor of the Metropolitan Tabernacle, London, England.

The publication and distribution of this series had been completed when Dr. Dixon and this writer were thrown together for several days in the Montrose, Pa. Bible Conference, together, we agreed to call the initial meeting that brought into existence *"The World's Christian Fundamentals Association."*

In its first meeting, held the last week of May, 1919, over sixty-five hundred fundamentalists gathered from different States, Provinces and Continents. Additional auditoriums had to be employed to accommodate the crowds. At the end of that week, the organization was a completed fact, and a volume — "God Hath Spoken" — was ready for the press. The Fundamentalist Movement was a new-born infant, but a lusty and promising one.

The frontispiece of the volume reporting that Convention week carries the pictures of Dr. George E. Guille, Extension Worker of the Moody Bible Institute; Dr. Lewis Sperry Chafer, President and Founder of the Dallas, Texas, Theological Seminary: Dr. A. B. Winchester, Pastor of Knox Presbyterian Church, Toronto; Dr. Reuben A. Torrey, then Dean of the Bible Institute of Los Angeles; Paul Rader, then Pastor of the Moody Tabernacle, Chicago; Dr. J. C. Massee, Pastor of the Tremont Temple, Boston; Dr. C. I. Scofield, Editor of the Scofield Reference Bible; Prof. W. H. Griffith Thomas of Wycliffe College, Toronto; Dr. Wm. L. Pettingill, Dean of the Philadelphia School of the Bible; Dr. John Roach Straton, Pastor of the Calvary Baptist Church, New York City; Dr. L. W. Munhall, Author and Editor of "The Eastern Methodist;" Dr. I. M. Haldeman, Pastor of the First Baptist Church, New York City; President Joseph Kyle of Xenia Theological Seminary, St. Louis, Missouri; Dr. P. W. Philpott, then of the Gospel Tabernacle, Hamilton, Ontario; Dr. George McNeeley, Pastor of the Elizabeth

Avenue Baptist Church, Newark, N. J.; Charles M. Alexander, the world-famous singer and President of the Pocket Testament League; and the writer, W. B. Riley, Pastor of the First Baptist Church, Minneapolis, Minn., founder and president of The Northwestern Bible and Missionary Training School, and Evangelical Seminary: and yet, will you believe it, in all the magazine discussions of twenty-five years, not one of these men was ever requested by a leading magazine in America to give to the public, through its columns, either a definition or a defense of Fundamentalism! On the contrary, they sought men to speak to this subject whose names were unknown to our circle, and palmed these off upon their readers as the exponents and even mouthpieces of Fundamentalism itself!

If the men prominent in this movement had not been men of the highest literary and scientific attainment, there would have been some excuse for this strange course: but in view of their outstanding eminence, it is up to the secular magazine world to make its own explanation.

When Luke sat down to write the Gospel which bears his name, by way of introduction he said: *"Forasmuch as many have taken in hand to set forth in order a declaration of those things which are most surely believed among us * * * it seemed good to me also, having had perfect understanding of all things from the very first, to write * * * that thou mightest know the certainty of those things"* (Luke 1:1,3,4).

That is at least one justification of my discussion of this subject — I have had to do with the Movement from its inception, and speak now from twenty years' thought, observation and participation.

To the question, then: *"What is Fundamentalism?"*

It would be quite impossible within the limits of a single article to so treat the subject as to satisfy all interested parties. There are too many features of this Christian faith for one to attempt a full delineation: but there are at least three major propositions which must appear in any adequate reply, and they are these: It is the Christian Creed; It is the Christian Character; It is the Christian Commission.

It Is The Christian Creed

Fundamentalism undertakes to reaffirm the greater Christian doctrines. Mark this phrase — "the greater Christian doctrines." It does not attempt to set forth every Christian doctrine with the elaboration that characterizes the great denominational Confessions: but it *did* lay them side by side, and out of their extensive statements, selected nine points upon which to rest its claims to Christian attention. These were, and are, as follows: —

"I. We believe in the Scriptures of the Old and New Testament as verbally inspired of God, and inerrant in the original writings, and that they are of supreme and final authority in faith and life.

II. We believe in one God, eternally existing in three persons — Father, Son and Holy Spirit.

III. We believe that Jesus Christ was begotten by the Holy Spirit, and born of the Virgin Mary, and is true God and true man.

IV. We believe that man was created in the image of God; that he sinned and thereby incurred not only physical death but also that spiritual death which is separation from God; and that all human beings are born with a sinful nature, and, in the case of those who reach moral responsibility, become sinners in thought, word and deed.

V. We believe that the Lord Jesus Christ died for our sins according to the Scriptures, as a representative and substitutionary sacrifice; and that all that believe in Him are justified on the ground of His shed blood.

VI. We believe in the resurrection of the crucified body of our Lord; in His ascension into heaven; and in His present life there for us, as High Priest and Advocate.

VII. We believe in "that blessed hope," the personal, premillennial and imminent return of our Lord and Saviour Jesus Christ.

VIII. We believe that all who receive by faith the Lord Jesus Christ are born again of the Holy Spirit and thereby become children of God.

IX. We believe in the bodily resurrection of the just and the unjust, the everlasting felicity of the saved, and the everlasting conscious suffering of the lost."

It seems absolutely clear that many of the "liberal" writers of recent years have never taken the trouble to ask for the basis of our belief.

Modernism, when it comes to deal with the Fundamentals Movement, is suddenly possessed of a strange imagination, and if you want to know what the movement is NOT and what its leaders are NOT, you should read the Modernists description of both! Certainly, as to what we believe the above declaration leaves no doubt; and only the man ignorant of the Bible or utterly indifferent to its teachings could ever call into question that these nine points constitute the greater essentials in the New Testament doctrinal system.

Fundamentalism insists upon the plain intent of Scripture speech. The members of this Movement have no sympathy whatsoever with that "weasel" method of sucking the meaning out of words and then presenting the empty shells with an attempt to palm them off as giving to the Christian faith a new and another interpretation. The absurdities to which such a "spiritualizing" method may lead are fully revealed in the writings of Mary Baker Eddy, and of Modernists in general.

When one is permitted to discard established and scientific definitions, and to create, at will, his own "glossary," language fails to be longer a vehicle of thought, and even inspiration itself may seem anything or nothing according to the preference of its employer. The late Prof. Machen of Princeton University properly exploited and exploded this procedure in his volume "Christianity and Liberalism." He showed that while Modernism still calls itself Christianity, it has nothing in common with the faith that for two thousand years has worn that great and honorable name; and that as a religion it does not even belong to the same family with Christianity. With keen discernment he said: "In trying to remove from Christianity everything that could possibly be objected to in the name of science, in trying to bribe off the enemy by those concessions which the enemy most desires, the (modern) apologist has really abandoned what he started out to defend."

The greater doctrines are not individual opinions that can be bandied about at pleasure. In the judgment of the Fundamentalist, they "are for ever settled in heaven." "*Holy men of God,*" who "*spake as they were borne along by the Holy Ghost,*" have told us the truth — God's truth — and truth is as unchangeable as it is imperishable. "Scripture cannot be broken." The "*truth of the Lord endureth for ever.*"

As an orator once said: "The empire of the Caesars is gone; the legions of Rome are moldering in the dust; the avalanches that Napoleon hurled upon Europe have melted away; the pride of the Pharaohs is fallen; the pyramids they raised to be their tombs are sinking every day in the desert sands; Tyre is a rock for bleaching fishermen's nets; Sidon has scarcely left a rock behind; but the Word of God still survives." And it not only endures for ever, but it remains for ever the same — the same in words, the same in meaning, the same in spiritual intent. God's work is incapable of improvement. The sun is old — but the world needs no new or improved one!

Fundamentalism is for ever the antithesis of Modernist critical Theology.

It is made up of another and an opposing school. Modernism submits all Scripture to the judgment of man. According to its method, he may reject any portion of the Book as uninspired, unprofitable, and even undesirable, and accept another portion as from God because its sentences suit him, or its teachings inspire him. Fundamentalism, on the contrary, makes the Bible the supreme and final authority in faith and life. Its teachings determine every question upon which they have spoken with some degree of fullness, and its mandates are only disregarded by the unbelieving, the materialistic, and the immoral.

Fundamentalists hold that the world is illumined, the church is instructed, and even science itself confirmed, when true, and condemned when false, by the clear teachings of the open Book; while Liberalism, as "The New York Nation" once said; "pretends to preach the higher criticism by interpreting the sacred writings as esoteric fables."

In other words, the two have nothing in common save church membership, and all the world wonders that they do or can remain together. The thinking world knows that but one tie holds them and that is, the billions of dollars invested. Nine out of ten of those dollars — if not ninety-nine out of every one hundred of them — spent to construct the great denominational Universities, Colleges, Schools of second grade, Theological Seminaries, great denominational mission stations, the multiplied hospitals bearing denominational names, the immense publication societies and the expensive magazines — which were given by Fundamentalists and filched by Modernists!

It took hundreds of years to collect this money and construct these institutions, but it has taken less than forty years for the Liberal bandits to capture them; and the only fellowship that remains to bind Modernists and Fundamentalists in one body (or a score of bodies) is the "Irish" fellowship of a "free fight" — Fundamentalists fighting to recover what they have founded and Modernists fighting to retain their hold on what they have filched!

It is a spectacle to grieve angels and amuse devils; but we doubt not that even the devils know where justice lies, and the angels from heaven sympathize with the fight, and trust that faithful men will "carry on."

But to our second assertion —

It Is The Christian Character

Creed alone is neither competent nor convincing. Creed, in the abstract, is cold and dead; but creed incarnate constitutes Christianity as positively as the Word incarnate constituted the Christ.

Christianity roots in a creed and fruits in character. "*As a man thinketh in his heart, so is he.*" It was that truth which the apostle James sought to set before his brethren many centuries ago, when he said: "*What doth it profit, my brethren, though a man say he hath faith, and have not works? * * * Faith, if it hath not works, is dead, being alone * * * A man may say, Thou hast faith, and I have works; shew me thy faith without thy works, and I will show thee my faith by my works.*" In fact that is the only faith which is ever seen! If the other exists at all, it is for ever invisible and ineffective. The longer one lives and the more closely he observes his fellows, the more profoundly is he impressed with this truth.

Years ago, I produced and employed in connection with the anti-saloon campaign an argument which I thought logical and effective. I now believe that it was extremely faulty. I used to say that "the true prohibitionist is the man who votes the prohibition ticket. He may be drunk the day before and drunk again the day after election; but if he sobers up enough to reach the polls and cast a vote against the infamous thing, he has proved himself a true prohibitionist. The man who votes against prohibition may never have tasted liquor in a lifetime, and yet his vote proves him a friend of intemperance." Both sides of the argument were faulty. The fact is that the true prohibitionist was the man who combined a vote against the saloon with sober living — who incarnated his creed in his daily conduct; for the first man, by his patronage of the saloon, proved his willingness to have it continued; while the second man, by his vote for the same, united his influence with the conduct of the first. Both of them proved that creed apart from conduct is not sufficient, and that conduct apart from creed is not adequate. He is not a true Christian, then, whose conduct is exemplary but who doubts or denies the Christ and disputes the revelation to be found in His Holy Word. He is merely a "Behaviorist," and in nine cases out of ten his good behaviour is the product of Christian principles and practices set before him by a faithful, Christian father or a godly mother. He is not a Christian who holds tenaciously to each and every one of the thirty-nine points of the Westminster Confession, or even adopts the ninety-seven Theses of Martin Luther, but who, in spite of this orthodoxy in creed, is heterodox and bestial in conduct. It has actually happened that the most loudly self-proclaimed Fundamentalist has been charged with lying, lust and murder!

The man who combines an unshaken faith in the authority and integrity of the Bible with an aggressive uprightness in conduct, is the man who approaches, in some human measure, the perfect pattern furnished in the Christ life; for in His words the most watchful of his enemies were unable to catch him, and against His works, no worthy objection was ever urged. Even His enemies were compelled to admit that *"never man spake like this man."* (John 7:46), and to raise the question, *"Whence hath this man this wisdom, and these mighty works?"* (Matt. 13:54)

Herbert Booth, the youngest son of General Booth, published a few years ago a book entitled "The Christian Confederacy," in which he pled as only a Booth can plead, for the combination of high conduct with correct creed. Of that combination Booth said: "The times are ripe for it, and nothing else will do. We must cry with the utmost boldness, 'This way for a fight to the finish, a fight that asks no quarter from the world, the flesh or the devil.' No cowards wanted here! No clever compromisers with the treacherous spirit of the age; no cunning contrivers who practise the art of 'holding the truth in unrighteousness'; no renegades who hold back their gospel weapons from attack while doing the 'popular' works which win the applause of men; none who doubt God or Jesus His only-begotten Son or His everlasting Gospel or His ever-present Spirit. Keep out, all of you! The object of this Confederacy is to raise up and gather a host whose faith shall be a challenge to the world's unbelief, whose happiness in the service of God shall put to shame the pleasures of the worldly Christians who go down to Egypt for their enjoyments — whose voices shall be raised in the churches and throughout the world as a protest against the cringing doubt which covers itself with ambiguous and plausible phrases because it is afraid to show its face in the open. These are the heroes we want!"

The proofs of Fundamentalism, then, are not in words but in deeds.

This has been the conception of Fundamentalists from the first; for while the "World's Christian Fundamentals Association," as an organization, is but twenty years old, Christian Fundamentalism has back of it two thousand years of glorious history.

It was Fundamentalism which produced the Book of Acts! You will find every essential feature of our creed in Peter's sermon at Pentecost — even to the Second Coming!

It was Fundamentalism which conquered the Roman Empire, and in one hundred years revised the conduct of men and brought in established laws of righteousness, including regard for the Sabbath, the rights of the Church in the State, and the recognition of law versus anarchy.

It was Fundamentalism which challenged corrupt Rome in Martin Luther's time, and called out a people whose clean and wholesome conduct became the condemnation of the foul papal practices, and turned the thought of the general public from the coercive measures of a corrupt church to the intelligent and voluntary service of the King of Glory.

It was Fundamentalism which faced the heresy of "Deism" one hundred and fifty years ago, and in an open and fair field fought the battle to the finish, and slew that infidel monster as effectually as Saint George was ever imagined to have trampled on the dragon.

And it was Fundamentalist Evangelists who so uniformly led the common people back to *"the faith once delivered"* as practically to bury atheism out of sight for one hundred years.

But to *battling*, Fundamentalism has for ever added

building. Of all the Colleges that Congregationalism, of one hundred years ago, contributed to America, commencing with Harvard in the East and dotting practically every State in the Union with at least one, Fundamentalism built the entire line. The same remark applies to the Baptist, Presbyterian and Methodist institutions known to the whole American Continent.

In Chicago a few years ago, Arthur Wells, then Vice-President of the Santa Fe Railroad system, handed me an excerpt from that memorable after dinner speech of James Russell Lowell when he had been both preceded and profoundly stirred by infidel utterances, and in the course of which he said: "Whatever defects and imperfections may attach to a few points of the doctrinal system of Calvin — the bulk of which is simply what all Christians believe — it will be found that Calvinism or any other 'isms' which claims an open Bible and proclaims a crucified and risen Christ is infinitely preferable to any form of polite and polished skepticism which gathers as its votaries the degenerate sons of heroic ancestors who, having been trained in society and educated in schools the foundations of which were laid by men of faith and piety, now turn and kick down the ladder by which they have climbed, and persuade men to live without God and leave them to die without hope."

Of what value is our boasted accomplishments in mechanical, electrical and chemical discoveries if while they are contributing to our material prosperity, they are more rapidly still undermining our morals? The whole doctrine of evolution not only lacks a single illustration in the processes of nature, but it is being disproved by the program of man; for mechanical invention resulting in moral decay is not even progress, but is degeneration instead! Babylon, Persia, Greece and Rome — each of them reached a climax of material development and then deliberately committed suicide by moral degeneracy.

Look now at the drift of modern nations. Certain advocates of evolution are beginning to fear the repetition of history, and even Henry Fairfield Osborn utters his warning that "our age needs the lofty moral teachings of the Bible," and follows it with the sane statement: "Our youthful confidence in the powers of reason has been shattered: like Icarus, we have taken our flight, and the wings of reason have ceased to sustain us."

The future of Fundamentalism is not with claims but with conquests. Glorious as is our past, history provides only an adequate base upon which to build. Fundamentalists will never need to apologize for the part which they have played in education — they have produced it! Nor for their relationship to colleges and universities and theological seminaries — they have created them!

Even the late Walter Rauschenbusch, famed higher critic as he was, pertinently asked: "Has the church not lifted woman to equality and companionship with man, secured the sanctity and stability of marriage, changed parental despotism to parental service, and eliminated unnatural vice, the abandonment of children, blood revenge, and the robbery of the ship-wrecked, from the customs of Christian nations? Has it not abolished slavery, mitigated war, covered all lands with a network of charities to uplift the poor and the fallen, fostered the institutions of education, aided the progress of civil liberty and social justice, and diffused a softening tenderness throughout human life?

"It has done all that, and vastly more. The influence of Christianity, in taming selfishness and stimulating the sympathetic affections, in creating a resolute sense of duty, a staunch love of liberty and independence, an irrepressible hunger for justice and a belief in the rights of the poor, has been so subtle and penetrating that no one can possibly trace its effects. We might as well try to count up the effect in our organism of all the oxygen we have inhaled since our first gasp for breath. In so far as humanity has yet been redeemed, Christianity has been its redemption."

Rauschenbusch dared not say what history demanded of him — that each and every one of these conquests had been the fruit of Fundamentalism.

But even that is not enough! Now that Modernism has come in to filch from us these creations of our creed, we must either wrest them from bandit hands or begin and build again. In the last few years — in fact since the Modernist highwayman rose up to trouble the Church and snatch its dearest treasures — Fundamentalism has shown itself as virile as the promise of Christ — *"The gates of hell shall not prevail against it."*

Today there are one hundred schools and colleges connected with our Fundamentalist Association, some of which have escaped the covetous clutches of Modernism, but most of which have been brought into being as a protest against Modernism itself. Their growth has been so phenomenal as to prove that the old tree is fruitful still, and that the finest fruit is to be found upon its newest branches, for we have orthodox churches, fundamentalist colleges, sound Bible-training schools, evangelical publication societies, multiplied Bible conferences, and staunch defenders of the faith in ever increasing numbers in each denomination. In fact, so fruitful is our movement that "The Christian Register," the mouthpiece of Modernism, was alarmed, and once complained: "Protestantism is in eclipse. Christianity enters a new dark age. The modernists who arose in the various denominations to fight fundamentalism and to bring new freedom to the churches have all retired; their movement has collapsed; victory rests with the fundamentalists."

Let us here remark that the greatest menace to Fundamentalism today is not the outright Modernist. It is that "middle-of-the-roader" who is milking his denomination with one hand and every wealthy fundamentalist approachable with the other, in behalf of what he claims will be "a new fundamentalist college or theological seminary," but who, when once the bucket is filled, will walk away with the same, to turn it over, again — as has been so often done — to the enemies of Christ. It is this course, employed by not a few in the last fifteen years, that makes it difficult for the sound fundamentalist institutions to secure help from those who believe with them.

Mark what I tell you! Five years more will fix theological affiliations to such an extent that these hypocritical pretenders will be branded for ever as they deserve, and the institutions over which they preside will be passing through the same Court procedure that Andover endured for years, to have the final and supreme decision rendered against their covert and cowardly course, and the cash of the fundamentalists, living and dead, turned again into those channels of education for which its donors really intended it.

It Is The Christian Commission

That commission is to preach the Gospel of Christ. and not "another Gospel."

Think of it, will you, — the head of a great denominational Mission Board producing and publishing a booklet on "The Great Commission," and while about the *apparent* defense of Matthew 28:19, 20, actually discrediting the inspiration of that passage, and writing an interrogation point into the middle of the very claim of inspiration itself!

Paul, nearly two thousand years ago, faced such foreign mission officials, and, having heard of their influence, wrote to his Galatian brethren: *"I marvel that ye are so soon removed from him that called you into the grace of Christ unto another gospel; Which is not another; but there be some that trouble you, and would pervert the Gospel of Christ. But though we, or an angel from heaven, preach any other gospel unto you than that which we have preached unto you, let him be accursed."* (Gal. 1:6-9) And in his Epistle to the Corinthians, Paul tells us exactly what that Gospel is: *"Moreover, brethren, I declare unto you the gospel which I preached unto you, which also ye have received * * * how that Christ died for our sins according to the Scriptures; And that he was buried, and that he rose again the third day, according to the Scriptures"* (I Cor. 15:1,3,4)

Imagine, if you can, a mission board willing to send out upon the foreign fields and fight for their retention and maintenance there, men who deny that declaration *in toto,* disputing alike the atonement made by Christ and His victory over the grave!

There is not a week but brings us some report from foreign fields of division on the field itself over the promulgation of "another gospel" which is "no gospel"; of foreign mission schools that scoff Moses and exalt Darwin; that reduce Christ to the level of a man and degrade Him to the descendant of a monkey, and of mission secretaries that hold to scorn the precious blood He shed, and denominate the declaration of it "the gospel of the shambles"!

Oh, the tragedy of it all! However, it takes hold of the heart of believers as they think of *"the cup of salvation"* sent to the Japanese, and learn that some man or woman has, while wearing the name of "missionary," put into that cup the deadly poison of Modernism, and made it to effect for those who drink of it, no redemption, but an epilepsy of Darwinism!

"The Bible Champion" once truly said: "The liberalistic movement in our Christian Churches is not a mark of normal and healthy growth. It is a case of pathology, and it threatens to become more and more virulent. If it is not cured, the disease will sap the very life of the Church.

Think of theological seminaries, endowed to the extent of millions and still pleading with fundamentalists to give them more, training the children of Trinitarian believers in the Unitarian philosophy, and sending them forth to pulpits at home and abroad! It is to this non-spiritual, anti-Christian and insane procedure that true believers object. Holding absolutely to the authority and integrity of God's Word, we believe ourselves commissioned by the risen Christ *"to teach all nations, baptizing them in the name of the Father, and of the Son, and of the Holy Ghost"* (Matt. 28:19) and *"to preach the gospel to every creature,"* baptizing them that believe as assuredly saved.

That commission is to make disciples and not denominationalists.

A "disciple" is a man taught—an instructed believer. We properly translate our commission; "Go ye, therefore, and disciple all nations."

The history of the rights of denominationalism might be an interesting study, but it would clearly demonstrate no divinity. There is nothing in the New Testament to advocate or even justify its existence.

The Bible is not a Book so difficult of understanding as to separate men into factions! The trouble is that they have come to it with their prejudiced opinions, with their fixed philosophies and heresies, and "denominationalism" has been the result. Is it any wonder that this modern "Diana" is now being discredited? And shall we marvel if she suffers the same fate that befell the Diana of the Ephesians? Should we be surprised if we find that ecclesiastical officials, who have profited financially at this false shrine, call together men of like occupation and salary with themselves, and say: *"Sirs, ye know that by this craft we have our wealth. Moreover, ye see and hear that not alone in Minneapolis, but throughout all America, and even to the end of the world, these fundamentalists are persuading and turning away much people, saying that denominationalism is not divine, so that not only our craft is in danger to be set at nought,* but even the great denomination itself may come to be *despised, and her magnificence destroyed."*

Strangest of all things, the very men who are now seeking to save denominationalism do not seem to realize that they have taken the very steps that lead the way to her destruction. The explosion of the Inter-Church World Movement was a blast that loosened every denominational foundation. By the wild attempt to combine in ONE people whose creeds were utterly antagonistic; to unite together those who held the Church authoritative and those who held the Bible authoritative and those who held their own inner conscience authoritative, they produced the elements which effected explosion. Just as chlorine and hydrogen when exposed to light produce an instant and destructive blast, so this Darwin-conceived attempt *to ignore the great fundamentals of the Christian faith and bind in one body the Unitarian, the Trinitarian and the Atheist,* when the light of God's truth was turned upon it, exploded the whole machine erected for the production of this combination: and while certain high officials found soft ecclesiastical positions on which to land, millions of dollars went up in that smoke — of which not one fragment has ever since been found!

It is practically the same men, ecclesiastical potentates, who have put their heads together and have agreed upon the division of fields at home and abroad, the cooperation of laborers irrespective of what views they might hold or what gospel they might preach, reducing even the gospel itself to a negligible quantity, and asking for nothing other than a co-operative endeavor in drawing salaries, enjoying offices, thinking out programs, pulling off feasts, and fleecing the uninformed in behalf of a world-scheme that gives no promise to the world itself! In nature and character such a scheme is a thinly disguised enemy of the Gospel of God's grace and of the true Church of Christ. It is the twentieth century counterfeit — away with it! Give us the *real* Gospel — God's true coin!

The Case Against Modernism

By Chester E. Tulga, D.D.

PRICE 25c

Published by
CONSERVATIVE BAPTIST FELLOWSHIP
352 Wellington Ave., Chicago 14, Ill.

*Copyright 1949 by
Chester E. Tulga*

Printed in USA

THE CASE
AGAINST MODERNISM

"Now the Spirit speaketh expressly that in the latter times some shall depart from the faith" (I Tim. 4:1).

"Heady" (II Tim. 3:4).

"Ever learning and never able to come to the knowledge of the truth" (II Tim. 3:7).

"For there are certain men crept in unawares, who were before of old ordained to this condemnation, ungodly men, turning the grace of our God into lasciviousness, and denying the only Lord God, and our Lord Jesus Christ" (Jude 4).

"But the natural man receiveth not the things of the Spirit of God; for they are foolishness unto him; neither can he know them, because they are spiritually discerned" (I Cor. 2:14).

"Their mouth speaketh great swelling words" (Jude 16).

INTRODUCTION

AT THE BEGINNING of the twentieth century modernism was at its height and bursting with self-confidence. The new theory of evolution became, for the modernists, the law of inevitable progress, which in turn guaranteed the upward progress of the race. The triumphs of the new science gave man unlimited confidence in his own power. The myth that education could solve most of our ills was widely held. The belief that war on a large scale was in the past was prevalent, and only disputed by a handful of premillennial fundamentalists. The belief in the magic powers of democracy was widely distributed. Modernism was utopian in spirit and as yet unchastened by the harsh judgment of history.

Modernism quickly penetrated to the strongholds of traditional orthodoxy, influencing all the schools and completely capturing most of the older seminaries. The conquest began with a plea for inclusivism; it ended in most cases with the fundamentalists excluded from the seminaries which their people had built and endowed. The emphasis upon the distinctive doctrines of the Christian faith was replaced by the increased emphasis upon the "Christian task." The faith of our fathers was replaced by "my task." The neglect of doctrine preceded the abandonment of doctrine. Modernism had arrived and now holds the strongholds of the Protestant world, its institutions, its vast endowments, its prestige. The men who "crept in unawares" are now masters of the house. We shall proceed to trace its devious course through the years.

I. MODERNISM: OLD MODEL

The older modernism, cock-sure in spirit, talked glibly of "the concensus of scholarship," the "assured results of Biblical criticism" and the "new scientific method," but modernism, deeply rooted in this world, was a child of its times. Let us examine its roots and its theology.

Its Roots

1. *The new theory of evolution.* Darwin published in 1859 the *Origin of the Species* and transformed an idle speculation into a world view and, unintentionally, a social philosophy. Although unproven, it quickly became to the credulous modernistic mind a scientific fact, for it confirmed what they wanted to believe—that human progress was on-

ward and upward. This unproven speculation was one of the roots of the older modernism.

2. *The new historical method of Bible study.* Rejecting the Scriptures as final authority in any subject, the older modernists spoke of the Bible as the story of man's developing religious experience rather than God's Word to men. They spoke of man's quest for truth, not God's revelation of truth. They spoke of Jesus as a spiritual pioneer in the realm of religious experience, rather than Jesus as the final revelation of God to man. The Bible, robbed of its supernatural origin and its authority, was subjected to all manner of historical criticism, both legitimate and illegitimate. Protestantism, having rejected the authority of the Church for the authority of the Bible, now rejects all authority unless verified in one's own mind and spirit.

3. *The new science.* Believing that the scientific method was an assured avenue to truth, modernism felt that it must present the Gospel in such a way as not to offend the scientific mind of the day. Supernaturalism gave way to naturalism; miracles were ruled out; the virgin birth of our Lord made an incredible thing; the miracles of our Lord reduced to legends; regeneration was reduced to religious education; the belief in the supernatural appearance of Christ the second time gave way to utopian dreams of a good society through the work of religious men. The new science, with its opposition to miracle, received the homage of the older modernists.

4. *The new interpretation of the Kingdom of God.* The

acceptance of the theory of evolution and the companion theory of the automatic progress of the race, the challenge of the rising tide of socialistic thought, the almost millennial faith in democracy, and the declining belief in the sovereignty of God called for the rejection of the Biblical teaching concerning the future Kingdom and the adoption of a new interpretation that would lend itself to the religious socialism of the times. The new historical method of Bible study, and the adoption of the scientific method with its rejection of supernaturalism combined to bring in the modernist version of the Kingdom of God, a form of regenerated Communism. A. C. McGiffert put the new spirit in a sentence when he said, "Democracy demands a God with whom men may cooperate, not one to whom they must submit" (Religious Education XLV 1919 pp. 158, 161). Modernist "scholars" boldly remodeled the Bible to suit the prevailing ideas of their times, and soon lesser modernists with their usual credulity were glibly repeating their stereotypes.

The Modernists Bring Forth a New Theology

1. *They created a sentimental God expressed in the slogan, "The Fatherhood of God and the Brotherhood of Man."* Having disposed of the troublesome doctrine of the sovereignty of God, the way was open to sentimentalize the relationship between God and man. God as a Father was acceptable to the lordly modernists; God as a Judge was not. God as a Father was pleasing; God as sovereign was incompatible with the democratic spirit. Man as a child of God was flattering, but man as a sinner and under judgment was

distasteful. God as Father was all love and no justice, all softness and no hardness, all sentiment and no discipline. It was felt that the new doctrine of the Fatherhood of God and the Brotherhood of Man was flattering to both parties. So popular religion forsook its God-centered basis and became man-centered; it forsook revelation for naturalism; it forsook realism for romanticism. God and man, with God as the junior partner set out to build the Kingdom. As an act of courtesy toward God who first thought of it, this supposed kingdom was to be called the Kingdom of God.

2. *They remodelled Christ, calling Him (falsely) the "Jesus of history."* This false Christ was the product of the vain imaginations of the day and the new Biblical "scholarship." Applying the methods of historical criticsm to the New Testament, they succeeded in remodelling Christ, thus fitting Him into the pattern they had selected for Him. They talked glibly about the "rediscovery of Jesus" whereas they had simply invented a false Christ who never existed outside their imagination. The real Jesus to them was a twentieth century modernist. They had created a god in their image. Man, the perpetual god-maker, had entered the ministry.

3. *They held an idealistic doctrine of the nature of man.* E. G. Homrighausen (Christian Century 4-12-1939) referred to those days when he saw that Jesus Christ as a prophet and leader "was a man full of that divinity of which I, as a human being was capable." Luther Wesley Smith, Baptist leader, tells his congregation, "Whether you are a disciple of Christ or not, can you not observe the evidences

of divinity within your common humanity?" (And So I Preached This, 1936) Washington Gladden, early prophet of the social gospel, said, "If God be the Father of us all—there can be no contrariety between our nature and His" (Present Day Theology 1913 p. 138). The deification of man began with Rousseau, with his doctrine of the natural goodness of man. The idea of man's growing goodness was given impetus by the spread of the popular concepts of Darwinian evolution—that man was on an escalator which was steadily carrying him higher and higher. Conversion then became gradual through religious education, rather than sudden through the conviction of the Spirit. Evangelism became natural instead of supernatural. The Biblical doctrine of human nature was abandoned for it is not flattering to the natural man. Later Bernard I. Bell (Religion for Living 1940 p. x) summed up this whole trend as "barely disguised self-adoration." Self-worshipping man ascribed his ills as "failure to live up to his possibilities." One said, "Men are what they are because of a fatal disbelief in their own divinity." No wonder no atoning blood was needed and no regeneration was necessary. Man had made himself a god, of the same nature as the Infinite God. No wonder the sovereign God permitted disaster to come upon this Babel-worshipping modernist.

4. *They had a millennial faith in the possibilities of religious education.* If man is already a child of God and of the same nature as God and with a latent divinity within him, he does not need the Pauline theology with its plan of salvation based upon redemption; he only needs ethical teaching and the development of his natural religious experience. So religious education conceived its task as educating the natural man to be a Christian and no supernatural evangelical conversion was necessary. The rallying cry of this new religious education came to be Bushnell's phrase, "The child is to grow up a Christian and never know himself as being otherwise." Sinners saved by grace were to be dreadfully old fashioned when this religious millennium arrived. Drinking deep at the springs of secular education, religious education in the words of Shailer Matthew was little more than "public education fitted out in a Prince Albert coat." Self-denying man now had a program that would bring out his inherent divinity. Intoxicated modernism, drunk on the new wine of the age, reeled on to its judgment.

5. *They rejected all belief in absolute truth and adopted the tentative attitude toward all professed truth.* It was held by many that no teacher of the past or present can be held a final authority in religion and ethics. The title "Lord" ascribed to Jesus was also an offense to the democratic ears of the modernism of the day. Why should a simple Galilean peasant lord it over a modernist bursting with his own divinity? Abandoning all authority, resting his faith only upon conclusions drawn from tested data, the older modernist held all truth tentative and subject to revision. So modernism, then and now, lacks that assurance of truth which expresses itself in a creed or a confession of faith. Rejecting the creeds as authoritative only in their own day and having no fixed truths of their own, the modernists rejected all attempts to restate the Christian faith in positive terms and frowned

upon every attempt of a Christian body to confess its faith in positive terms. Lacking any fixed points to steer by, modernists became wandering stars.

6. *They were enthusiastic advocates of a non-theological social gospel.* Given the theory of the inevitable evolutionary progress of the race; the goodness and even the divinity of man; a democratic God who has abdicated His sovereignty; a Christ who has been stripped of the medieval regalia of the creeds, the theological coloring of Paul, the apocalyptic trappings of the Gospels, and reclothed in the new fashions of the age of Rauschenbusch, emerging as a leader in the struggle for a better world; an amazing science which was turning poverty into plenty; an educational system which was turning fools into Solomons—all this gave the social gospel mighty impetus. How foolish seemed to be the old Gospel of "Christ and Him Crucified" and the old program of plucking brands from the burning. The social gospel was born and fathered by evolutionists and socialists, but with religious trappings to give it sanction. Given the natural goodness of man and the other false doctrines of modernism it had plausibility, but in the light of the Scriptures and history, it was sheer romanticism.

Weaknesses of the Older Modernism

1. *Its origin was in the human spirit, not the Holy Spirit.* Edwin McNeill Poteat (Christian Century 2-22-1939) addressing himself to disillusioned liberals said, "The cure for disillusionment is a return to the human spirit which is the

ground of liberalism . . . liberalism represents that disposition of the human spirit which is eternally restive in the presence of the mystery of the nature of things; which presses restlessly inward toward the sources of truth and the centers of power." Dr. Poteat is saying nicely, what the fundamentalists of that day were saying bluntly—that the source of modernism, with its rejection of the authority of Divine revelation and the Christ of the New Testament, was in the unregenerate mind and spirit of the natural man ("But the natural man receiveth not the things of the Spirit of God: for they are foolishness unto him: neither can he know them, because they are spiritually discerned" I Cor. 2:14). Fundamentalists insisted that modernism had substituted the religious experience of the natural man for the Christian experience wrought by the spiritual acceptance of the facts of Divine Revelation. Fundamentalists insisted that the freedom of interpretation insisted upon by the modernists, was the freedom asked by the natural man to place upon the Scriptures any interpretation dictated by his own mind and experience, even if it contradicted the writers. There is no evidence to disprove Dr. Poteat's claim—that liberalism is a product of the human spirit. It is evidently not the product of the movement of the Holy Spirit. It is the religion of the natural man; it interprets the faith by the criterions of the natural man; its religious experience is the religious experience of the natural man. It is one of the natural religions of the world. It only acknowledges Divine Revelation when it concurs with the tenets of the liberal.

2. *As the product of the human spirit, it expresses the*

egotism of the human spirit. Rollo May (Springs of Creative Living, 1940 p. 94) says, "It is significant that the chief religious movement in America in the last two decades has been the worship of ourselves." Bernard I. Bell (Religion for Living p. x) says, "To the liberal . . . religion largely consists of the admiration of human beings of themselves . . . When the liberal calls himself a son of God as he is fond of doing, there is virtually the assumption that it is God, not himself, who is the dependent relation." In the field of Biblical interpretation this egotistical "scholar" became the master of the text instead of the interpreter. In the field of theology, the egotistic modernist sinned the sin of Lucifer by the simple device of imposing limitations upon God. In the field of theological education, the egotist with his criticism of the sacred text reduced the giants of Biblical revelation to pigmies of inferior intellect to his own. In the pulpit self-worshipping clerics became purveyors of exegetical foolishness which emptied pews and killed prayer meetings. The modernist rejected that Christianity which strips him of self-righteousness and embraced a religion of his own devising which enabled him to retain his inordinate self-esteem, but hid behind a cloak of religiosity. He was religious but not Christian.

3. *The older modernism was the child of its times.* D. R. Davies, a chastened liberal, wrote later, "I belong to a generation which imbibed theological liberalism from the mental air of the times. Its basic and unspoken assumptions were accepted without challenge or criticism." He refers to "the passion for being up-to-date." He observes that "it was a

sign of intellectual inferiority to be orthodox . . . a mark of superiority to accept the liberal ideas" (On to Orthodoxy, 1939, pp. 9-10). So man found it easy to believe that which made him a superior person. Reinhold Niebuhr says, "Liberal Christianity quite obviously accepted the prejudices as well as the achievements of modern culture. It was pathetically eager to justify itself before the modern mind." The early modernists were children of their times.

4. *The older modernism accommodated itself to its age, not sensing its illusions and delusions.* Fosdick (Successful Christian Living, 1937, p. 155) referring to the older modernism, wrote: "Modernism . . . started by taking the intellectual culture of a particular period as its criterion and then adjusted Christianity to that standard." Georgia Harkness (The Resources of Religion, 1936, p. 75) commented in similar vein: "It became over-sentimental and too naively optimistic; it accommodated itself too much to contemporary culture, and paved the way for humanism." Another chastened liberal (God in These Times, 1935, pp. 30-31) H. P. Van Dusen says, "The life of the church has drunk deep of the enthusiasm of the secular world and fallen heavily under the spell of its assumptions and its ideals." They did not heed the truth so well put by G. K. Chesterton, "We need not a Church that is right when the world is right, but a Church which is right when the world is wrong." So instead of demanding that men conform to God's standards, they changed the standards. Instead of urging men to pass the test, they changed the tests. Instead of presenting the Christ of the New Testament as the solution of the prob-

lems of the world, they presented a Christ made in their own sinful image and announced him as a "rediscovery." The older modernism betrayed Christ but with a kiss of affection.

5. *The older modernism was not an interpretation of the Christian faith but a radical departure from it—apostasy.* This was freely admitted by many writers of that time. Lyman Abbott said, "The old orthodoxy is right in regarding the new (Biblical) criticism as revolutionary" (The Theology of an Evolutionist, 1897, p. 61). E. C. Moore of Harvard (The Spread of Christianity in the Modern World, 1909, p. 184) said, "The philosophy of religion has within the last generation undergone a revolution." Concerning the book, *The New Orthodoxy* by E. S. Ames, the Christian Register (2-20-1919) the official organ of the Unitarians said, "It advocates religious conceptions which differ in no wise from those of the Unitarians, and the 'new orthodoxy' has certainly nothing in common with what was formerly cherished under that name." Professor Errett Gates said, "Christianity is now being compelled to reshape its message and redefine its essence." (A Guide to the Study of the Christian Religion, 1916, p. 479) Dr. K. C. Anderson, a liberal, wrote: "Liberal Christianity is a radical departure from the creed of Christendom . . . The important question is whether the Christian church can make the great change of belief which the acceptance of the modern critics' Jesus would involve, and remain the Christian church. It is important that the churches of Christendom should realize the kind of Jesus the critics are presenting them with, and the vast revolution of belief which it involves . . . The triumph

of liberalism is really a defeat, for it means the destruction of Christianity as Christianity has been known in all ages of its history." (Hibbert Journal 8:314; The Monist, 1915, pp. 46, 55, 57) A. C. McGiffert pointed out that the doctrine of the Divine immanence, which was generally accepted by the liberals, ascribes divinity to man, since it is supposed that man's nature is one with God's and he needs simply to awake to the fact. "This means, of course," wrote McGiffert, "a revolution in the old conception of salvation. What a man requires is not regeneration in the old sense, or a change of nature, but simply an awakening to what he really is" (The Rise of Modern Religious Ideas, p. 206).

Dr. Fosdick writing in 1937 confessed, "The modernistic movement, adjusting itself to a man-centered culture, has encouraged this mood, watered down the thought of the Divine, and, may we be forgiven for this, *left souls standing, like the ancient Athenians, before an altar to an Unknown God*" (Successful Christian Living, p. 161). (Italics ours—CET.) No wonder the fundamentalist movement was born. Apostasy sits in high places in the Church of the Living God.

II. MODERNISM IN CRISIS

"Behold, the days come, saith the Lord God, that I will send a famine in the land, not a famine of bread, nor a thirst for water, but of hearing the words of the Lord" (Amos 8:11).

"There arose a mighty famine in that land, and he began to be in want. And when he had spent all..." (Luke 15:14).

"Where is the wise? where is the scribe? where is the disputer of this world? hath not God made foolish the wisdom of this world" (I Cor. 1:25).

"The foolishness of God is wiser than men" (I Cor. 1:25).

1. *A spiritual famine.* In 1927 R. Niebuhr wrote, "Religion is not in a robust state of health in modern civilization." (Does Civilization Need Religion, p. 1). In 1934 John A. Mackay, said, "Part of the crisis of religion today is that it lacks an adequate message for the times. It does not understand God, it does not understand man, and does not understand the times we are living in . . . Christian faith has been eviscerated, Christian life has become enervated, and a general despondency has set in" (Christian Message for the World today, p. 95). In 1935 H. P. Van Dusen (God in These Times, p. 29) said, "Something is wrong with men's faith in God today." In 1936 E. G. Homrighausen, a chastened liberal wrote, "Sincere lovers of the Church are disturbed by the state of the churches of our country . . . I am conscious of a theological flabbiness that is even now holding

our popular Christianity in its grasp . . . People do not know the simple fundamentals of what it means to be a Christian" (Christianity in America, pp. 7, 9). Georgia Harkness wrote in 1936, "Religion remains in an unhealthy state." In 1938 Adolph Keller (Five Minutes to Twelve, pp. 28, 32, 35, 36) struck a still more ominous note, saying, "The world is emptying visibly—like a leaky tank . . . Demons are conquering the territory formerly occupied by reason, intellect and morality . . . The ghosts whom Jesus permitted to enter the swine of the Gadarenes seem to be looking for new lodgings today." Modernism had spent its all in riotous living. It had betrayed its Christ. Its crisis hour had come. The world cried for bread; it had nothing to offer but a stone.

2. *Disillusionment with the evolutionary law of automatic progress.* Dr. Fosdick voiced the disillusionment of the older modernists in these words, "One of the predominant elements in the intellectual culture of the late nineteenth and early twentieth centuries, to which modernism adjusted itself was illusory belief in inevitable progress. How many elements in those romantic days seduced us into thinking that all was right with the world!" (Successful Christian Living, p. 157). Keller (Five Minutes to Twelve, p. 29) said sternly, "We had forgotten that the Bible does not speak of a world which would grow better and better, day by day, is an eternal process of evolution, but rather of a Judgment Day which would bring the world to an end. We took our civilization for granted and did not listen to the ominous trampling of the hoofs of the Apocalyptic steeds which cause the earth to tremble in fear and despair." Davies (On to Ortho-

doxy, p. 27) added, "The Great War caught liberal Christianity unawares ... It administered a nasty jar to its whole scheme and outlook ... It took the lid off that human nature of supposed fundamental goodness ... One thing stands out with tragic clearness: the complete and utter bankruptcy of Modernism and Liberal Christianity ... At long last the chickens are coming home to roost.'

3. *Disillusionment with the results of the new Biblical criticism.* The earlier Biblical critics had expected that the Bible, freed from the dogmatic presuppositions which seemed to them to conceal its meaning and to raise obstacles to the appreciation of its faith, would be more widely read and its teachings understood. The Bible, adjusted to the mind of modern man, would come unto its own. This proved to be an illusion. Bosley (On Final Ground, pp. 12-13) comments on the ignorance of the Bible. "Bruce Barton was overstating the fact when he entitled his book about the Bible, *The Book Nobody Knows.* But he comes too close for comfort. Biblical illiteracy is one of the startling facts in contemporary Christianity." Graduates of liberal seminaries know less about the Bible than the graduate of a first class Bible institute. Great Bible conferences are held—not by liberals, but by those who believe the Book. The result of the new Biblical criticism is "The Book Nobody Knows."

4. *Disillusionment with science and the scientific method.* This mood was well expressed in the title of a book issued a few years ago, "Science the False Messiah." Georgia Harkness, referring to the older modernism, said: "We were in danger of selling out to science as the only approach to truth,

of trusting too hopefully in man's power to remake his world" (Christian Century 3-15-1939). H. P. Van Dusen asks, "Why, then, do we list theology's servitude to science as one of the principal causes of the loss of vital faith in God in our times?" (God in These Times, p. 40). Science had indeed proven to be the false messiah of the modernists.

5. *Disillusionment with the socialized Kingdom of God of the critics.* After their romantic adventures in utopianism, the modernists belatedly "discovered" the Kingdom of God as taught by Jesus. How did the modernists happen to lose these teachings of Jesus concerning the Kingdom, teachings proclaimed by fundamentalists in every city? Possibly H. J. Cadbury (The Peril of Modernizing Jesus, p. 27) has the explanation. He says, "Men are too prone to operate unconsciously by modern presuppositions. Thus the apocalyptic element in the Gospels has been frequently laid almost exclusively to the account of the evangelists, not because there is any real evidence that Jesus did not share it, but mainly because it is uncongenial to the present day critic." Concerning these teachings he says, "We have found in the Gospels—it would not be too strong to say, rediscovered—an expectation of future world events so catastrophic and supernatural that they jar with our modern easy conception of slowly evolving historical processes." How did the modernists "rediscover" this truth? By the new Biblical criticism? No. By the "scientific method"? No. By examining their prejudices and squaring their thinking with the Word of God? No. World events had mercilessly shattered their former conception of the Kingdom. A modernist seldom changes his

mind in response to Divine Revelation but often by the pressure of human events, for he is generally a child of his times.

6. *Disillusionment with their sentimentalized version of God.* Harold A. Bosley (On Final Ground, p. 3) refers to "a generation like ours which has literally treated the idea of God like a toy, an intellectual plaything, instead of the moral structure of life and the universe." Dr. Fosdick put it this way, "Modernistic Christianity largely eliminated from its faith the God of moral judgment . . . and created the general impression that there is nothing here to fear at all" (Successful Christian Living, pp. 57-59). The Modernists have now "re-discovered" God. The older modernists were idolators for men can make a god out of ideas as truly as the heathen make a god of wood or stone.

7. *Disillusionment with the "rediscovered" Jesus of history.* A. C. McGiffert (Christianity as History and Faith, p. 302) said, "The greatest fact in modern Christian history is the rediscovery of Jesus." He referred to the Jesus of the higher critics, not the Christ of the New Testament. History, again, has dealt harshly with this synthetic Jesus of the modernists. This ersatz Jesus did not satisfy either the mind or the heart of man.

John A. Mackay (The Christian Message for the World Today, pp. 101-102) writing of his disillusionment with the "Jesus of history" says, "I later came to feel the insufficiency of the approach through the Jesus of history. It tended to produce ethical but not religious fruits; it created religious interest, but not religious faith . . . The Jesus of history has not redeemed the world." Homrighausen says truly, "The historical Jesus is a Jesus who has been largely *read into* the New Testament by men living in a romantic and rationalistic modern world" (Christianity and America, p. 184). In 1937, writing on the brink of a world catastrophe, Adolph Keller (Five Minutes to Twelve, p. 70) gives us a picture of the Christ presented at the Oxford and Edinburgh conferences by Continental speakers for the most part. It was not the Christ of "scholarship" or the "rediscovered" Christ of the modernist. The times were too serious for such a false Christ to serve. He said, "The Christ who rose above the conference was not the Good Man, the Moral Hero, the Social Reformer, the Great Proletariat, the Best Councilor, the Religious Philosopher, the Skillful Educator, the Idealistic Pacifist, but the Son and Revealer of God, the Saviour of Mankind, the Redeemer and Sovereign of our lives, the Lord of the Kingdom to come." Liberalism, scared by world events always witnesses a neo-orthodox movement in its ranks. The harsh events of history forced the abandonment of the false Christ on the Continent.

8. *Disillusionment with the optimistic view of human nature.* D. R. Davies, a chastened liberal (The Two Humanities, Preface) refers to the "peril of suffering the curse of him who 'trusteth in man'." He says, "I have no hope whatever in unregenerate human nature. None! None!" H. C. Phillips (Christian Century, 8-2-1939) strikes the new note when he says, "Now I can preach about sin with great unction! Sin has returned to good and regular standing in my homiletical equipment. This is due, no doubt, to the

fact that one of the outstanding revelations of the past decade has been the sheer wickedness of the human heart. No beast is capable of the deviltry of man." Jeremiah could have told Phillips this same truth had he been listening to the Eternal Word. The liberal sits at the feet of current events and learns by shock and disillusionment what others learn from the Word of God. Sinful men are not sons of God and do not act like it.

9. *Disillusionment with religious education.* Salvation by religious education has failed. Religious education as a substitute for the gospel of salvation through the blood of Christ has failed to produce the desired results. The considered judgment of one liberal writer is this: "The thought patterns of modern religious nurture have largely exhausted their vitality, and that failure to reconstruct them in terms of a more adequate faith will ultimately result in the collapse, or at least the slow death, of the twentieth century movement of religious education" (Faith and Nurture by H. Shelton Smith, p. vii). C. E. Conover (Christian Century 7-13-1938) points the way to a more realistic approach, saying, "I believe that bringing religion up-to-date requires a realistic view of human sinfulness, as against the optimism of the liberal repudiation of the doctrines of sin and redemption; God-centered rather than primarily pulpit-centered, what is distinctively Christian in contrast to secularism and to a vague emphasis upon 'religious experience'." The program of religious education, still influenced deeply by the older modernism, has fully manifested its spiritual sterility. Bernard I. Bell defines religious education as "the art of im-

parting to others the moral and devotional implications of a dogmatic religion no longer existent."

10. *Disillusionment with the tentative approach to truth.* Homrighausen says bluntly, "Liberalism . . . never finds anything, although it has been clearing the fields a long time" (Christianity in America, p. 14). Again, "Young preachers emerged from theological halls with a gospel of the interrogation point" (p. 45). Again, "It's inquiry into the Biblical, the person of Jesus, or Paul, the rise of the early Church and kindred realms, has failed to answer any of our urgent questions with positive conviction . . . *With a cynical smile, it has murdered revelation in cold blood, and has triumphantly 'explained away' what it has destroyed*" (Italics ours—CET). Such strong language indicates the depth of the disillusionment with the intellectual approach of liberalism.

11. *Disillusionment with the social gospel.* Hear W. M. Horton (Christian Century, 5-17-1939): "Time was when I thought myself a radical because I was a believer in socialism, pacifism and other drastic proposals for the amendment of the status quo. Now I realize I was not radical enough. The disease of modern civilization has revealed itself in the last ten years as a deadly illness, which superficial remedies can only augment, like a mustard plaster on the chest of a man suffering from agina. I have become increasingly skeptical of mustard plasters—among them certain types of socialism and certain types of pacifism."

H. P. Van Dusen (God in These Times, p. 180) points out that "it was the delusion of the early advocates of the

Social Gospel that the holders of privilege would be won to justice and sacrifice by lofty persuasion and confrontation with spoken truth. We have been delivered from the delusion by the realistic analyses of contemporary social prophets, as well as by the teaching of events."

Adolph Keller again strikes the realistic note, "The helplessness of mankind is a striking contradiction to the idealistic assumption that we can easily mold the world with our hands and our will. This world is not clay, but granite—nay, harder! Our chisels and hammers break on the inconceivably resistant material which we are trying to shape. It is far less plastic than we thought in our "constructive idealism". (Five Minutes to Twelve, p. 33). The disillusionment with the social gospel is widespread but many "belated minds" are still following its false gleam.

12. *Disillusionment with trying to make Christianity acceptable to the "modern mind."* Rollo May (Springs of Creative Living, p. 95) pays his respects to this unholy scramble to please the natural man. "Religious leaders fell over each other in a kind of panic to explain and re-interpret Christian truths in forms which would flatter a self-worshipping epoch. Innumerable books were written to show that religion was 'intellectually respectable,' which actually meant a cutting of the cloth of religion to suit the pattern of the temporary whims of our mental life."

Edwin T. Lewis (Christian Century, 5-4-1939), after wandering in the wilderness of the older modernism for years saw the error of changing the essence of Christianity to appease a sinful world. He says, "I saw with devastating clarity that speculative philosophy whether it got as far as supernaturalism or whether it stopped with naturalism, could never accommodate itself to Christianity. Instead, it required Christianity to do the accommodating and that was something which could not be, if Christianity as represented in the New Testament, was to be taken seriously." To make new applications of Christianity to contemporary events is one thing, to change the very essence of Christianity to please an unbelieving and sinful world is a betrayal of Christianity into the hands of its foes. Modernism is dead but its spirit lives on in what modernism is now pleased to call liberalism.

III. THE MODERNISTS BECOME LIBERALS

"Intellectual systems have the knack of surviving their own death" (On to Orthodoxy by D. R. Davies, p. 25).

"Modernism is the half-and-half religion. It is half revelation and half science, half under authority and half free, half theism and half humanism . . . I cannot be halved or hyphenated. It is abhorrent for me to straddle or muddle" (Dieffenbeck, Editor of the Christian Register, Christian Century, 8-23-1939).

"The devout Modernist is the best example in the contemporary religious field of the type of person who desires to eat his cake and still have it. It is this attempt of the devout Modernist to render compatible two bodies of thought that are actually incompatible which has led to the notorious intellectual confusion characteristic of devout modernist apologetics. The devout Modernist may not unfairly be likened unto a group of sportsmen solemnly insisting on planning and executing a season of hunting and fishing in the American Museum of Natural History. Having killed Cock Robin, they expect him to chirp and flit with all his former animation" (Harry Elmer Barnes, The Twilight of Christianity, p. 331).

Dr. Fosdick, after repudiating the older modernism, said "We must go beyond modernism." So modernists abandoned a discredited modernism in large numbers and called themselves liberals. Others abandoned liberalism for neo-orthodoxy, which is neither new nor orthodox. Others went into humanism. Any attempt to appraise the theological situation today must take into account the divisions of thought within liberalism. However, they have certain principles in common, which we shall discuss systematically.

1. *The new liberalism does not believe in an authoritative Bible.* Georgia Harkness (Understanding the Christian Faith, p. 28) says, "The authors who wrote the Bible . . . were human beings like ourselves and as prone to make mistakes . . . Many of their own erroneous ideas naturally got mixed in with the truth that came to them from God." Nels Ferre of Andover-Newton (Pillars of Faith, p. 96) says that "God wants to write new and even better scriptures, both in life and in books." Homrighausen of Princeton says, "The Bible contains much history, some of it faintly embedded in age-old myths, folk tales, battle songs, camp fire recitals, and the like" (Christianity in America, p. 121). C. C. Morrison, commenting on "Dr. Niebuhr's (Reinhold) Unorthodox Orthodoxy" (Christian Century, 3-17-1943) says of this noted liberal theologian: "He is orthodox in his faithful devotion to the biblical ideology, for he sees that there is no approach to the revelation save through these biblical ideas, and he reverently recognizes the 'authority' which they possess as the original media through which the revelation came. But he is unorthodox in the freedom of spirit with which he deals with these biblical concepts. He refuses to be bound by their literal or even their historical meaning. They are symbols of the revelation, and as such are open to critical examination, but always in the light of the revelation

which poured through them." Thus the Scriptures may not mean what sound interpretation would make them mean but what the liberal scholar wants them to mean. This is the key to understanding the present "vogue of standardless interpretation" in liberal circles. Touch liberalism wherever you will, it rejects the Scriptures as final authority even in religion.

2. *The new liberals do not accept the full New Testament stature of Christ.* They frequently question the authority of the New Testament records concerning Jesus. Georgia Harkness (Understanding the Christian Faith, p. 67) insists that "We do not have in the Gospels a biography of Jesus, but a portrait drawn by first-century Christians." These, she asserts, wrote their interpretations into the story, thus coloring the picture. Concerning the virgin birth of Christ her conclusion is that the stories of the virgin birth are traditional rather than authentic (p. 76). R. H. Beaven, President of the Baptist Missionary Training School (In Him Is Life, p. 126) says of Jesus, "We shall never understand the deity of Christ unless we recognize that it is not an idea. It did not begin as an idea. It began as an experience, out of which an idea grew. Men experienced a new and immediate relationship to God in Christ . . . Just as soon as we lose sight of this fact and interpret Christ's deity as an intellectual truth, just so soon does Christianity become another source of division. That is why so many liberals reacted— and RIGHTLY—against many who took Christ as *the* revelation to the heathen. For they were proclaiming Christ's deity as an intellectual truth and were thereby dividing

themselves by pride from others who did not share that belief" (p. 123). It is evident then that the liberals place an interpretation upon "deity" other than that of the New Testament. It is also evident that the deity of Christ as set forth in the New Testament is not a basis of fellowship for liberals. There is a thin line—and often none at all—between liberalism and Unitarianism. The liberals do not accept the full New Testament stature of Christ. E. C. Colwell, formerly Dean of the Divinity School of the University of Chicago (Unitarian, Baptist, Disciples and Congregational) belongs to that school of radical critics which still has many liberal followers. He says, "In the Fourth Gospel Jesus is proud, powerful, and glorious. Through its pages Jesus walks as a self-conscious god sure of the fact of his divinity" (An Approach to the Teachings of Jesus, p. 59). Again, "It is unfortunate for the understanding of Jesus in modern times that the interpreters have followed in the path of the Fourth Gospel rather than the first three" (p. 51). Liberalism like modernism is Unitarian in its view of the person of Jesus.

3. *The new liberal has hazy views concerning the Holy Spirit.* The literature of liberal theology today, indicates by its lack of emphasis upon the Holy Spirit, or even the absence of mention, that it does not give to the Holy Spirit the place the New Testament assigns to Him. The liberals do not believe in the Trinitarian conception of the personality of the Holy Spirit. Some confuse Him with religious experience, others think of the Spirit as simply a manifestation of God, or even God's influence in the world. Liberalism has no clear

cut doctrine of the Holy Spirit, other than the Unitarian conception commonly held by liberals. Many liberal books do not even mention the Holy Spirit.

4. *The liberals still reject the stories of the virgin birth of Jesus as untrue, or, at the best, not relevant today.* The examination of scores of liberal books confirm this statement. It is very unusual to find a liberal who professes to believe in the virgin birth of Christ. The naturalistic position of liberalism forbids it and the new psuedo-Biblical criticism rejects it on flimsy grounds. This position is also that of many large denominational foreign mission boards who will not require their missionaries to believe in the virgin birth. Dryden L. Phelps, a missionary under the American Baptist Foreign Mission Society in West China, writes, "Jesus' father was a Jewish carpenter called Joseph" (Jesus by Dryden L. Phelps, Leslie E. Wilmott and Lewis C. Walmsley p. 1). Writing to Rev. H. U. Fisher (Christian Beacon 7-24-1947) Dr. Fosdick, an acknowledged spokesman for liberalism said, "Of course I do not believe in the virgin birth . . . I do not know any intelligent Christian minister who does." Dr. Fosdick, with an arrogant statement, rules out of the ranks of intelligent ministers those who disagree with him on this point. Dr. John W. Bowman (The Intention of Jesus) a Presbyterian writer, says of the virgin birth, "It was the Church that added these mundane traditions to its Gospels" (pp. 183, 184). While there is no evidence for this statement, that does not deter a liberal determined to get rid of the virgin birth of Christ. Touch liberalism at any point: it denies the

authority of the Scriptures, the veracity of the birth narratives, and undermines the deity of Christ.

5. *The new liberal still has a sentimental and optimistic view of the nature of man.* While the neo-orthodox movement has tended toward a more realistic view of human nature, all liberals still regard the natural man as a child of God, thus breaking down that sharp distinction between the natural man and the spiritual man as set forth in the Scriptures. This conception of the essential divinity of man permeates all liberal thought today. Cady (Liberal Theology, 1942 p. 150) says, "The basic liberal belief that the God and Father of our Lord Jesus Christ is also and inevitably the Father of all men and the source of every form of good wherever it appears has been fully incorporated in the Findings of all three of these great World Missionary Church gatherings. This is convincing evidence of the leavening work of liberal Christian thought." That liberal thought has leavened the great missionary enterprise is evident in a thousand forms.

However, some realists in the world are revolting from "the angelic fallacy." Stanley High (Time, August 1947) gets down to the basic facts of human nature when he says, "Ever since my Sunday School days I've had it dinned into my ears that I am a child of God, that I'm made in His image. It means that those who lay so much emphasis on my bearing such a resemblance to the Almighty are not only mistaken about me, they're also mistaken about history. Man was made in the image of God in the first chapter of Genesis. He didn't stay that way very long." This basic fallacy concerning man's true nature and relationship to God is the fatal defect in the liberal gospel, the liberal approach to other religions, the liberal approach to social problems, the liberal approach to war and many other things. The liberal is still more of a romanticist than a realist.

6. *The new liberal doctrine of the Church.* Modernism first raised the cry, "Back to Christ," rejecting the Pauline presentation of Christ. But the new Biblical scholarship which set out to "rediscover" Jesus bogged down in disagreement. In the first World War we heard much about "making the world safe for democracy" and modernists brought forth a democratic religion suitable (as they thought) for the times. This was a lost cause. Then we heard a great deal about "the teaching Church" and the world was to be saved through religious education. It resulted in more Biblical illiteracy than before. Now the liberals have "rediscovered" the Church. Brown (Liberal Theology p. 225) says, "The most significant change which has taken place in the consciousness of the American liberal Christians has been the change in their attitude toward the Church. . . . They had little faith in the ability of the Churches, as at present organized, to make any significant contribution." What sort of a "Church" is this Church which the liberals are so enthusiastic about?

(a) *Most liberal writers speak of the "body of Christ" as the universal world Church.* (H. P. Van Dusen in Towards a United Church; Georgia Harkness in Understanding the Christian Faith and many others). So, while the ecclesiastical leaders are building the world Church, the liberal theologians are laying the intellectual foundations for the new catholicity, that the visible religious structure of Christendom is the body of Christ, the continuation of the incarnation and should be revered as such. Consequently schism becomes a mortal sin and to remain outside of it is to be in religion's "outer darkness." In fact, the World Council of Churches has frankly stated that some sects are not wanted, by indirection making them schismatics (World Council of Churches p. 77).

(b) *This universal Church (with Rome "regrettably absent"), identified as the body of Christ, becomes what liberals are now fond of calling "a redemptive fellowship," a new addition to the developing Protestant catholicity.* It is a trend toward the Romish doctrine that salvation is through the Church and not independent of the Church. It is an attempt to give a redemptive value to a worldly organization that does not inherently have it. It is significant that, as the redeeming work of Christ fades more and more into the background, when salvation through Christ and Christ alone is seldom mentioned, that the Church as a "redemptive fellowship" is emphasized. There is a thin line today between the new catholicism and the Romish conception of the Church as a redemptive fellowship outside of which there is no salvation. This conception is closely akin to that eastern orthodox catholicity which is more and more influencing the liberals.

(c) *This Christendom, spiritually and doctrinally a "mixed multitude," now equated with the "body of Christ," given the sanctity of a "redemptive fellowship" is now identi-*

fied more and more as a vehicle of God's continued revelation to men. Nels Ferre lays the groundwork (The Pillars of Faith p. 96) when he claims that God never closed the canon of Scriptures, insisting that "fearful men who no longer dared to live in the Spirit froze the records of the past."

The push toward the Church as the organ of continuing revelation is given by these words, "Even now the Holy Spirit wants to write Gospels. . . . Even now there can be letters written to the Churches which speak with authority" (p. 96). So the way is being paved for the new liberal catholicity, thus providing an ideological approach to Rome. In 1939 (Christian Century 8-23-1939), Dr. Dieffenbeck, editor of the *Christian Register,* wrote: "These repentant liberals or modernists would have a single Protestant Church that in solidarity, and it is to be presumed in authority, would vie with the Roman Catholic Church. 'Nothing less than a corporate and Catholic Christianity' these theologians say, 'is an adequate expression of religion in the modern world.'" Readers of liberal books today will agree with this prediction.

7. *The new liberal doctrine of ecumenicity.* The old evangelical basis of ecumenicity was the acceptance of the fundamental doctrines of the Christian faith, as set forth in the doctrinal basis of the World's Evangelical Alliance. Rejecting this evangelical framework, liberals pioneered in the formation of the Federal Council and later the World Council, based only upon the acknowledgment of Jesus as Saviour and Lord, and that to be interpreted as the constituent denominations saw fit. The liberal doctrine of ecumenicity is, in effect, a non-doctrinal ecumenicity, with unity given priority

over fidelity to the doctrines of the Christian faith. C. C. Morrison, a high priest of liberalism, stated it in these words: "doctrine is not prior to unity but unity takes precedence over doctrine" (Christendom Autumn 1935 p. 51). Here is liberal ecumenicity in a nutshell. Here is briefly stated the difference between fundamental interdenominationalism and liberal interdenominationalism.

The liberal doctrine and practice of ecumenicity is not based upon a common faith in the great doctrines of the Scriptures. It includes Trinitarians and Unitarians, free churches and state churches, catholic churches and Protestant churches, churches which pray to God alone and those who also pray to the Virgin Mary and the saints. It includes Baptists, both believing and unbelieving, and state churches and corrupt ecclesiasticisms against which the Baptist faith is in perpetual conflict. It is that corrupt ecclesiasticism which reformers in every age have opposed. It's chief Biblical text, "That they all may be one" (John 17:21) presupposes a oneness in Christ which does not exist. It includes those churches which insist upon regeneration and those who do not. The liberal doctrine and practice of ecumenicity is a departure from the New Testament (II Cor. 6:14-15; Gal. 1:8 and II John 9-11).

8. *The new liberalism rejects the Biblical doctrine of the atonement.* In a letter to H. E. Fisher (Christian Beacon 7-24-1947) Dr. Fosdick said, "Of course I do not believe in the Virgin Birth, or in that old fashioned doctrine of the atonement, and I do not know any intelligent Christian minister who does." In this statement, we have the position

of liberalism today, for the new liberal does not believe in the substitutionary doctrine of the atonement so clearly set forth in the New Testament. The new modernism does not believe that "Christ died for our sins according to the Scriptures" (I Cor. 15:3). The new modernism does not believe that God set forth Jesus "to be a propitiation through faith in His blood" (Rom. 3:25). The new modernism does not believe that "the blood of Jesus Christ His Son cleanseth us from all sin" (I John 1:9). The new modernism does not believe in Him "who His ownself bare our sins in His own body on the tree" (I Peter 2:24). The new modernism does not accept, but emphatically rejects the Biblical teaching that "He hath made Him (Christ) to be sin for us, who knew no sin: that we might be made the righteousness of God in Him" (II Cor. 5:21). Dr. George A. Buttrick, Presbyterian leader, says, "If God dealt with Him as if He were a sinner and the greatest sinner, then we must say of God (as a cynical Frenchman did say of the God of these penal theologies): 'Your God is my devil'." (Great Themes of the Christian Faith p. 18). We prefer Paul to Buttrick. Nowhere in the liberal books of the day do we find belief in the Biblical teaching concerning the atonement of Christ. Modern liberalism, conceiving of all men as children of God, sees no need of the atonement as presented in the New Testament.

In consequence, the new liberalism's doctrine of salvation is religious but not Christian; it is psychological but not supernatural; it is human rather than a new creation in Christ Jesus. Since it is not based upon the plan of salvation as set forth in the New Testament, it is counterfeit rather than genuine.

Its gospel, rejecting the gospel as set forth in the New Testament is "another gospel" (Gal. 1:8) and must not be accepted. Rejecting the Biblical basis of atonement, it is not the power of God unto salvation (Rom. 1:16) for it rejects the only basis upon which the power of God will act: the atoning blood of His Son. The salvation doctrine of modern liberalism is the psychological re-integration of personality, by reorganizing the personality around an uplifting concept, and not salvation through the blood of Christ.

9. *The liberal view of evangelism.* When evangelism was still largely carried on by gospel preachers and on Scriptural lines, the modernists had little use for it. It is only since they found a way to "reinterpret" the cross, to change the gospel, and to translate salvation into psychological terms, that liberals have been interested in it. An evangelism based upon the new naturalism, is acceptable. J. C. Massee, writing in the days of modernistic hostility to evangelism (Watchman-Examiner 11-6-1930) said of the new evangelism, "The propagandists of the so-called 'visitation evangelism without preaching' are in revolt against the old methods and the old message of evangelism. They do not see the necessity for regeneration. Their aim and end seems to be to corral people into church membership free from any preaching of the gospel. The method is mechanical, the spiritual preparation inadequate, and the result disastrous. If these men could combine their methods with the other half of the Scriptural methods and use their machinery to bring as many men within the hearing of the gospel preaching, they would at once lose their hostility to evangelism and accomplish much more

for the kingdom." Liberalism, however, is hostile even toward the New Testament gospel, consequently they do not care for New Testament evangelism. Their evangelism looks like the real thing at times, but it lacks the saving vitamin of salvation through the atoning blood of Jesus Christ.

Some Weaknesses of the New Liberalism

1. *The new liberalism is non-intellectual in its nature.* Dr. Randall, writing of the older modernism pays tribute to the superior logic of orthodoxy: "Orthodoxy has, moreover, an intellectual power that liberalism has so far lacked. In the face of uncertainty and confusion, the muddled thinking and mingling of contradictory ideas, that so abound in modernist circles, its theological tenets stand out with clarity and precision" (Religion and the Modern World p. 145). Writing of the straightforwardness of orthodoxy, James B. Pratt (Religious Liberals Reply p. 99) says, "It is a doctrine which one respects for its clarity and its honesty."

Concerning the neo-orthodox liberals, Pratt, in the same volume (p. 113) says of this type of liberal, "They have an extraordinary appetite for paradox and a fondness for using familiar English words in an unusual and, to most unwary readers, misleading sense." Again, he accuses the neo-orthodox of "inventing new and ever more extreme and snappy paradoxes. These are the firecrackers with which they celebrate their Declaration of Independence from the restrictions of reason." Professor Wieman rightly points out, "evasive ambiguity by which problems are concealed instead of solved, and by which reason is said to be confounded and surpassed, are among the most dangerous practices in the world today" (The Growth of Religion p. 433). Neibuhr's "principle of comprehension which is beyond our comprehension" sounds brilliant but it murders logic in cold blood (Religious Liberals Reply p. 29).

The liberalism of today, rejecting such objective criterions of truth as the teachings of the Scripture, the creeds, confession of faith, or anything outside the experience of the liberal, is always on the verge of polytheism and idolatry in its doctrines of God and Christ. Boasting of its vast intellectualism, liberalism has divorced religion from theology; faith from belief, and, abandoning creeds, has embraced creedlessness, and revolted from confessions of faith so far that it no longer has a faith to confess. J. Gresham Machen, a conservative scholar (What is Faith p. 13) calls attention to the widespread tendency in his day to "disparage the intellectual aspect of the religious life. Religion, it is held, is an ineffable experience; the intellectual expression of it can be symbolized merely; the most various opinions in the religious sphere are compatible with a fundamental unity of life; theology may vary and yet religion remain the same."

The liberal opposition to creeds and its refusal to state its own creed; liberalism's opposition to confessions of faith and its refusal to confess its faith in logical terms: these are indications of the basic non-intellectual nature of its philosophy. Finding its final authority in religious experience, it becomes the victim of its own anarchic subjectivism. Liberalism is always pursuing but never finding ultimate truth. Failing to attain to truth, they glorify the "quest." The oft repeated statement that liberalism is a method rather than a position adds confirmation to this summary of its non-intellectual nature.

2. *The new liberalism is anti-intellectual in its approach.* Roland Turnbull (Shurtleff College Bulletin 7-1947) begins an article with these words, "Let me follow orthodox procedure by defining my use of the terms." Liberalism, however, is hostile to precise definitions. Indeed, nothing makes a man more unpopular in the controversies of the present hour than insistence upon the definition of terms. "Men discourse very eloquently today upon such subjects as God, religion, Christianity, atonement, redemption, faith; but are greatly incensed when they are asked to tell in a simple language what they mean by these terms. They do not like to have the flow of their eloquence checked by so vulgar a thing as a definition" (What is Faith by J. Gresham Machen pp. 13-14). Humanists are right in pointing the finger of scorn at the boasted intellectualism of liberals, who unlike humanists and fundamentalists, shrink in mortal fear from stating their faith in logical terms. Their opposition to creeds is in reality opposition to stating their faith in logical terms.

Both humanism and orthodoxy are intellectual systems, but differing fundamentally on their basic presupposition. Humanists begin with reason, with naturalism, and rejecting all supernaturalism, attempt to reason logically from there. Fundamentalists begin with revelation (God has spoken authoritatively, intelligibly and finally) and then endeavor to raise a logical theological structure thereon. Modernism or liberalism, an illogical combination of revelation and naturalism, of mysticism and logic, uses as its foundation the "religious experience" of the individual and the result is intellectual anarchy, spiritual confusion and a deep resentment against those who would confess ANY FAITH in logical terms. The revolt of the humanists and the atheists against creeds is a revolt against their CONTENT or meaning. The revolt of the liberals against creeds and confessions, is not only a revolt against their content but also against any attempt to state the Christian faith in intellectual terms. Modernism is not only a revolt against the authority of the Church (Romanism), against the authority of the Scriptures (Protestantism), but against the authority of reason, as represented in creeds and confessions—the attempt of the intellect to comprehend and make intelligible the Divine mysteries. Liberalism is primarily anti-intellectual in spite of its boasts and its feverish intellectual activities which discover nothing, and simply "rediscovers" what the simple Bible student knew all the time.

3. *The new liberalism has divorced faith from belief.* James B. Pratt, criticizing neo-orthodoxy (Religious Liberals Reply, by Seven Men of Philosophy p. 114) says, "'Faith' for example, is a word like the Japanese 'Degozaimes' that can apparently mean anything you happen to want it to." Dr. Pratt goes on and on exploring the illogical character of neo-orthodoxy on this important matter of faith. He decides that "The careful reader must conclude that faith does not mean what the English tongue has regularly meant by it." Evidently, believing does not involve believing the great Christian facts of revelation. In the Scriptures, Christian faith is

always associated with belief in the Christian facts as set forth in Divine Revelation. In the thinking and preaching of present day liberals faith is independent of the the fundamental doctrines of the New Testament, the historic basis of the Christian faith. Men are urged to have faith in God whether they accept the teachings of His Word or not, and men are urged to accept the Lordship of Christ without necessarily accepting the New Testament basis of that claim to Lordship. Faith has been divorced from belief.

Christianity is a religion founded upon facts which must be accepted as a basis of faith. These facts are the redemptive acts of God in history, in Christ, in the establishment of the Church. The doctrines growing out of these facts are essential elements in the structure. The moral principles are derivatives of these acts and doctrines. Liberalism is non-factual. In some cases the historicity of the redemptive acts as set forth in the Scriptures is denied. In others, they are accepted but the doctrines based upon these acts are denied. In still other cases both the redemptive acts and the doctrines are ignored and religion is based entirely upon moral principles, with a religious veneer.

R. H. Beaven, President of the Baptist Mission Training School, shows how the nonfactual character of liberalism influences evangelism. Evangelism is not "an attempt to convert others to our beliefs" but an invitation to share God's fellowship in response to Him (In Him is Life p. 185). While it is true that we have no right to ask people to share OUR beliefs, it is also true that evangelism to conform to the Christian pattern must require the acceptance of CERTAIN

FACTS which everywhere in the New Testament are set forth as the basis of saving faith. Liberalism, would attempt to save apart from the acceptance of Christian beliefs. The same non-factual basis is revealed in the liberal statement, that the deity of Christ is not an intellectual truth to be accepted but an experience (Beaven, p. 123). Statements could be multiplied from liberal sources indicating this divorce of faith from belief. The New Testament position is well stated in the Westminster Shorter Catechism, "Faith in Jesus Christ is a saving grace, whereby we receive and rest upon Him alone for salvation, AS HE IS OFFERED TO US IN THE GOSPEL."

4. *The new liberalism continues its anti-intellectual course by divorcing religion from theology.* This is well illustrated by the words of a noted liberal who saw this weakness in the older modernism. "Not long ago a well known teacher gave a talk to some theological students about religion . . . He told them . . . and he was quite serious in doing so—that belief is negligible in matters of religion. Religion, he said, is a certain attitude of the spirit, an emotional mood which is compatible with every conceivable belief; and whether we choose one theology or another, or dispense with theology altogether, is as far as the social effect of the choice are concerned, a matter of indifference. In saying this, he was only putting into words a view held, more or less consciously by many people" (Beliefs That Matter, W. A. Brown 1938 p. 7). Humanists and some Unitarians carry this to its logical end—you can be religious and not even believe in God.

The recent emphasis upon theology in liberal circles indicates some recognition of this weakness, but it is not a return to Christian theology. Liberal theology is that theology which begins with human experience. Christian theology is that theology which begins with Divine Revelation. Frank B. Fagerburg (This Questioning Age pp. 97-98) says, "So theology is a description of religious experience, an attempted explanation of spiritual realities." The majority of the liberals interpret the Bible, not as God's progressive revelation of Himself to man, but as the record of man's progressive discovery of God. Christian theology is the attempt of the human mind and heart to explore the riches of a Divinely given, authoritative revelation, and then proceeds to study its impact upon the life of men. Christian theology begins with God; liberal theology begins with man. The neo-orthodox, while acknowledging the priority of Divine Revelation, accept the claims of Biblical criticism thus destroying its authority for all practical purposes, also claiming a liberty of interpretation which makes the Bible mean what the neo-orthodox want it to mean. The liberals who ground theology primarily in religious experience instead of Divine Revelation; the neo-orthodox who set aside the literal meaning of the Scriptures and place upon them arbitrary symbolic and mystic meanings, both part company sharply with that intellectual apprehension of Divine Revelation which distinguishes true Christian theology. Liberalism has divorced faith from belief and consequently religion from theology.

5. *Liberalism casts off all intellectual restraints in its doctrine of soul liberty.* Soul liberty, as held by liberals generally, is that form of religious liberty guaranteed by the state

to skeptics and others. Liberals claim the right of unlimited religious liberty within the framework of the word Christian, and within the framework of their ecclesiastical organization. The most glaring statement of this was editorially stated in *Missions Magazine* (December 1943). Commenting on the decision of the Supreme Court concerning the refusal of Jehovah's Witnesses to salute the flag, the editor quoted this statement, "If there is any fixed star in our constitutional constellation, it is that no official, high or petty, can prescribe what shall be orthodox in politics, nationalism, religion or any other matter of opinion, or force citizens to confess by word or act their faith therein." Then Editor Lipphard says, "There is a lesson in this historic paragraph for Baptists whenever periodically they are tempted to forget their historic position on religious freedom and efforts are made to impose creedal tests of fellowship and service. Whenever such situations arise, a Baptist adaptation of the Supreme Court's decision might read: *'If there is any fixed star in our denominational constellation, it is that no official, high or petty, no secretary, no board, no group, no association or convention, not even the Northern Baptist Convention, can prescribe what shall be orthodox in polity, denominationalism, doctrine, or other matters of opinion or force Baptists to confess by word or act their faith therein'*" (Emphasis ours CET). The conduct of the liberals in the great denominations indicate that Editor Lipphard has stated a fundamental principle of liberalism. This is not the liberty within the Christian fellowship which our fathers allowed, this is not liberty within the framework of the Christian faith, but liberty to accept or deny and remain in the Church, liberty to believe or refuse to believe in Christianity and still call oneself a Christian. Tom Paine fought for the right to be an atheist in the political state. Liberals, as in the case of some Unitarians and humanists, want the right to be an atheist and remain in the Church of God. Liberals resent all intellectual curbs on their liberty and all ecclesiastical restraints upon their freedom. This is anarchy.

6. *The new liberalism abandons all intellectual standards in Biblical interpretation.* Even such a radical liberal as President Colwell of the University of Chicago revolts from what he calls the "vogue of standardless interpretation" (An Approach to the Teachings of Jesus 1947 pp. 40-41). Dr. Earle V. Pierce says rightly, "Correct interpretation depends upon the correct use of the five great forms of exegesis: the historical, grammatical, rhetorical, logical and practical. Disagreements in interpretation come through failure, at some point, to follow correctly the laws of interpretation." Liberalism insists upon liberty to interpret the text, regardless of the circumstances, or the context. It deliberately places interpretations upon the text totally unrelated to it. The admonition of Peter that "no prophecy of the Scripture is of any private interpretation" (I Pet. 1:20) goes unheeded, in spite of its common sense.

The modernist doctrine of soul liberty (to the modernist) justifies him in taking unlimited liberties with the meaning of the sacred text, consequently, the "vogue of standardless interpretation." This is surrealism in exegesis. It often insists upon using the text regardless of the context. It insists that revealed truth can be found in the disreputable literary framework manufactured by the higher critics. It insists that the intellectual and moral integrity of a Biblical author can be preserved and his truth regarded as sacred after his literary work has been thoroughly discredited. It insists upon liberty to deny the text under the pretext of interpreting the text. Its "reconstructions" of Jesus are many and confusing. Its "reconstructions" of Jesus run the gamut from the sublime to the ridiculous. Its "ersatz Jesus" is made to be anything that a passing religious fad requires him to be. The Christian faith is interpreted to mean what its twentieth-century interpreters think it should mean, not what its original interpreters knew it to mean. Even John, who wrote the Gospel to prove that Jesus Christ is the very Son of God, has been made, by an exegetical sleight-of-hand performance to be the chief supporter of a Unitarianized Jesus—a mystical incarnation of God in man apart from a virgin birth. Liberalism has rejected the authority of logic as utterly as it has rejected the authority of the Word of God. Its claim to be THE intellectual peak of Christian thought is absurd.

7. *Knowing its indefensible position, the liberal frowns on creative controversy: the sword of true intellectualism.* It may be freely admitted at the outset that some controversies do more harm than good. It must also be admitted that history testifies to the fact that controversies which have been the most creative were bitterly opposed at the outset by entrenched systems of thought which considered them unnecessary. Liberals of today, grown fat with intellectual

pride fear the ordeal by logic. They prefer to assert their views, not defend them. This is safer for the weak.

Conservative Christians believe that creative controversy stimulates intellectual growth; it stimulates fresh study of the Word of God; it brings out neglected truths; it presents all sides of a question; it exposes the fallacies of accepted sophistries; it holds up to ridicule pious cant; it reveals the hollowness of empty shibboleths. Liberalism today is the liberalism of the closed mind; controversy is unnecessary in the thinking of the liberal for they have all the answers. Selah!

Controversy has always been a service to the Christian faith, oftentimes releasing it in new power from dead forms and ecclesiasticisms which God could no longer use. Conservatives, knowing Church history, appreciate the necessity for creative controversy in the Church to save it from stagnation and corruption. Conservatives, realizing the necessity of interpreting God's Word correctly welcome creative controversies which challenge erroneous interpretations and the heresies of men.

8. *Liberalism, entrenched in modern ecclesiasticism insists upon an inclusivism which promotes an anti-intellectual middle-of-the-roadism.* Liberalism, entrenched in most of the great denominations, is fostering that anti-intellectualism which glorifies the God of love at the expense of the God of truth, that produces the Church of the Least Common Denominator. The darkest hours of Church history have been those when the Church has been too inclusive. Unity around an easy minimum is not a prelude to victory for the

Church but the forerunner of apostasy. A united front based upon adherence to secondary truths is too soft to split but it will also be too soft to win in a world where evil is like granite. A liberal writer, Elton Trueblood (Foundations for Reconstruction, 1946, p. 27) calls attention to the fact that "great advances come in culture, not when all distinctions are blurred in a hazy and jovial good will, but when sharp distinctions are made, dictated by the truth." He says, very pertinently, that "power comes not by supposing that one view is as good as another, but by finding, in honest inquiry, what the objective truth seems to be, and then following it with stubborn courage tempered by humility ... The new spirit we need in our time will not come by some vague thing called 'religion'." The shallow sentimentalism, "Agreed to differ, resolved to love" is the magic which discourages any religious distinctions between revealed truth and the vain speculations of the natural man. The non-doctrinal middle-of-the-roadism so sedulously cultivated by the denominational cheer leaders of liberalism is fundamentally anti-intellectual in its nature and effects.

Liberal denominationalism today has gone further and encouraged that blind denominational loyalty which is the worst form of sectarianism; it has encouraged a subtle glorification of the denominational leadership, a hero worship of the "king can-do-no-wrong" variety; it has substituted loyalty to a man-made denominational program for loyalty to the Christian faith; for the old loyalty to creeds it has substituted the new loyalty to an ecclesiastical machine. It has encouraged and used for political purposes a great group of non-doctrinal organizations which have no intellectual basis for their activities. It has encouraged that hybrid denominationalism which attempts to plow the world with the ox of truth and the ass of unquestioning faithfulness to denominational leadership. It has encouraged a vague religiosity, unrelated to the historic Christian doctrines. It has played upon sentimental humanitarianism and played up "world need" for the purpose of financing all sorts of dubious ecclesiastical projects. Liberalism has demonstrated completely its anti-intellectual character by using every device in its power to hide its real doctrines from the common people. Modernism, miscalled liberalism, dare not take its chances in the arena of free and openly stated ideas. The bulwark of modern theological liberalism in the great denominations is not a great multitude convinced of the validity of their ideas, but the blind denominational loyalty which a decadent liberalism uses as a substitute for its own lack of vitality and integrity. Liberalism, bankrupt intellectually and impoverished spiritually, lives by that mass inertia and that unthinking loyalty to sanctimonious leadership that often permits regimes to remain in power who cover up their fruitlessness by the enormous output of "great swelling" words and pious cant. Liberalism is non-intellectual, anti-intellectual and fundamentally unethical in its conduct within the so-called evangelical denominations. It is not open honest thinking, for it dares not be open, it cannot afford to be honest, and stands in fear of someone outside their group who dares to think.

9. *The new modernism proceeds to the logical end of its*

anti-intellectualism by substituting religion for Christianity.
In the days before the advent of modernism, religion and Christianity were often used interchangeably, meaning in every case, Christianity. We often heard of people "getting religion" or "the Christian religion" but now, religion as interpreted by the liberals, is a substitute for Christianity, but cleverly disguised. Many liberals, who have no ecclesiastical axe to grind or special interest to serve, admit this. Kirsopp Lake (The Religion of Yesterday and Tomorrow, 1925, pp. 61f) says of the older modernism, "No, the fundamentalist may be wrong; I think he is. But it is we who have departed from the tradition, not he, and I am sorry for the fate of anyone who tries to argue with a fundamentalist on the basis of authority. The Bible and the corpus theologium of the Church is on the fundamentalist side."

Another liberal, speaking of liberalism today, says pretty much the same thing (Harvey McArthur in Religion in Life, 1945, p. 540), "The liberal stultifies his own thinking if he deludes himself into believing that his reinterpretations are the original teachings of Jesus or the New Testament. He has departed from the original form of the teaching and must expect to be so charged by the fundamentalists. Fundamentalism is in line with the creeds and doctrines of historic Christianity through the centuries." Modern liberalism is not Christianity.

IV. MODERN LIBERALISM IS NOT CHRISTIANITY BUT ANOTHER RELIGION

"But there were false prophets also among the people, even as there shall be false teachers among you, who privily shall bring in damnable heresies, even denying the Lord that bought them and bring upon themselves swift destruction.

"And many shall follow their pernicious ways; by reason of whom the way of truth shall be evil spoken of.

"And through covetousness shall they with feigned words make merchandise of you; whose judgment now of a long time lingereth not, and their damnation slumbereth not" (II Peter 2:1-3).

"Beloved, when I gave all diligence to write unto you of the common salvation, it was needful for me to write unto you, and exhort you that ye should contend earnestly for the faith which was once delivered unto the saints.

"For there are certain men crept in unawares, who were before of old ordained to this condemnation, ungodly men, turning the grace of our God into lasciviousness, and denying the only Lord God, and our Lord Jesus Christ." (Judge 3-4).

We are contending, not with those who differ with us on the teaching of the Scriptures but with those who sweep aside Divine Revelation and build their structure on the shifting sands of human speculation. The fundamental contradiction between these two systems of faith was recognized many years ago by the liberal Christian Century. The editorial was entitled, "Fundamentalism and Modernism: Two Religions," and the editor said: "*Christianity according to Fundamentalism is one religion. Christianity according to Modernism is another religion. Which is the true religion is the question that is to be settled in all probability by our generation for future generations. . . . There is a clash here as profound and as grim as between Christianity and Confucianism. Amiable words cannot hide the differences. 'Blest be the tie' may be sung till doomsday but it cannot bind these worlds together. The God of the fundamentalist is one God; the God of the modernist is another. The Christ of the fundamentalist is one Christ; the Christ of modernism is another. The Bible of fundamentalism is one Bible; the Bible of modernism is another. The church, the kingdom, the salvation, the consummation of all things—these are one thing to fundamentalists and another thing to modernists. Which God is the Christian God, which Christ is the Christian Christ, which Bible is the Christian Bible, which church, which kingdom, which salvation, which consummation, are the Christian church, the Christian kingdom, the Christian salvation, the Christian consummation? The future will tell*" (Christian Century, January 1924).

V. MODERN LIBERALISM HAS NO SONG

"How shall we sing the Lord's song in a strange land" (Psa. 137:4).

"Take thou away from me the noise of thy songs" (Amos 5:23).

"And be not drunk with wine, wherein is excess; but be filled with the Spirit; speaking to yourselves in psalms and hymns and spiritual songs, singing and making melody in your heart to the Lord" (Eph. 5:18-19).

"But how can the Church expect to have the power of apostolic days and go forth bright as the sun and terrible as an army with banners; how can she expect to have seasons of refreshing from on high and to have the song of the Lord in her heart as long as many of our ministers are preaching from a mutilated Bible, and are contending for the Christ-dishonoring teaching of a brute ancestry for one who bears the image of God, and seeks to remove the Virgin Birth and the supernatural in general from the Revelation of God, as we find it in the Bible?" (When the Son of the Lord Began by W. E. Biederwolf, pp. 9-15).

The new liberalism has no song! Someone has said of modern religious liberalism, "It can neither reason with Aristotle nor sing with Homer." Edwin McNeill Poteat (Christian Century, 2-22-1939) voices the uneasiness of the liberals when he asks, "But can the liberal interpreters of the gospel warm the fire of the heart, and kindle the flame of the imagination as once the literalists did? Fundamentalists say they cannot; and the voice of our affirmative sometimes sounds strangely like timidity touched with deference?" Let the abandoned Sunday evening meetings, the deserted prayer meetings and the cold services of the average liberal Church give Dr. Poteat his answer.

The humanist, Harry Elmer Barnes, goes to the heart of the problem when he says of the liberals, "The Devout Modernists may not unfairly be likened unto a group of sportsmen solemnly insisting on planning and executing a season of hunting and fishing in the American Museum of Natural History. Having killed Cock Robin, they expect him to chirp and flit with all his former animation" (Twilight of Christianity p. 331).

Richard Hoiland (Ministry of Friendly Guidance 1931 p. 53) senses the absence of abounding vitality in the new evangelistic methods. "Despite all its limitations and weakness, however, the old time form of evangelism did engender a spiritual dynamic that seems to be lacking in so much of our religious activity today. One has only to make a very superficial study of many of our modern Church programs to discover the absence of that earnestness of purpose and 'burden for souls', as our fathers expressed it, which characterized both the Church and the Sunday School of a generation ago." Mr. Hoiland fails to see, however, that the crucial difference between the evangelism of old and the liberal evangelism of today, is that the evangelism of the past was based openly upon the great evangelical doctrines of the New Testament and the liberal evangelism of today does not believe those doctrines. Our fathers believed that men were lost eternally without Christ and no wonder they had a burden for souls! No wonder they spent hours in intercessory prayer! Liberalism has no such a burden for it has no such conviction. Liberalism has embraced a subtle form of Universalism which has destroyed these precious values of the past. Liberals yearn for the fervor of the past, but no longer believe in the doctrines and experiences which produced that spiritual fervor. They are continually wondering why liberalism is so spiritually dead. They speak much about their concern for the masses, but liberalism has no message that will move the masses. Professing to speak the language of young people, they wonder why the young people by the thousands flock to the banner of fundamentalism and crowd its colleges and Bible institutes. Liberalism has no song.

Modern liberalism has no song because it has forsaken the Christian faith. Modernism quotes "thus saith the Lord" but its own Biblical criticism has robbed that noble and powerful admonition of any authority. Modernism attempts to find authority in religious experience but bogs down in confusion. Modernism attempts to construct a rational faith only to hear the mocking laughter of the new psychology with its accusations against human rationality. Modernism rebels against the attempt of logic to formulate its faith, preferring its own confusion (misnamed liberty) but embraces logic in ecclesiasticism to the destruction of liberty. It mourns over the ex-communicated heretics of the past who denied the faith, while it excommunicates the heretics of today, not for denying the faith but for rebelling against autocratic authority. Modernism has no song for it has nothing to sing about.

Fundamentalism, true to the Word of God, seeking the guidance of the Spirit of God, preaching the unsearchable riches of Christ, has a singing heart. From its presses flow a living stream of gospel song, singing choruses, stately anthems. The multitudes sing its gospel songs and the hosts of young people in the land sing its choruses, and the radio sings over and over again the old gospel songs which seem to live forever. Fundamentalism has a singing heart and sings the songs of living fundamentalists. Liberalism has no song, and every one of its churches must depend for its music on the songs of dead fundamentalists. Modernism uses the songs of dead fundamentalists for modernism has no song. Their predicament is well illustrated by a recent Sunday morning service (Peoples Church of Chicago) when that Unitarian congregation sang lustily, "Faith of Our Fathers Living Still." Modernists sing of a God whom they have deserted, a Christ whom they have discredited, a Holy Spirit whom they do not know, a Gospel they no longer believe, an atonement they have not experienced, a Christian hope which has been reduced to philosophical speculation. In singing the songs of dead fundamentalists, Liberalism exhibits its own inherent hypocrisy and displays its loss of integrity. Fundamentalism has a singing heart, singing the songs of Zion, which, like the manna of old, comes fresh from the hearts of the newly redeemed. Modernism has, in the words of Jeremiah: "Forsaken me the fountain of living waters, and hewed them out cisterns, that can hold no water" (Jer. 2:13). Modernism has no song, but the songs of dead fundamentalists.

TITLES IN THIS SERIES

The Evangelical Matrix
1875-1900

■ 1. William R. Moody
D. L. Moody,
New York, 1930

■ 2. Joel A. Carpenter, ed.
The Premillennial Second Coming:
Two Early Champions
New York, 1988

■ 3. - 6. Donald W. Dayton, ed.
The Prophecy Conference Movement
New York, 1988

■ 7. Delavan Leonard Pierson
Arthur T. Pierson
New York, 1912

■ 8. Helen Cadbury Alexander Dixon
A. C. Dixon, A Romance of Preaching
New York, 1931

■ 9. Amzi C. Dixon
The Person and Ministry of the Holy Spirit
Baltimore, 1890

■ 10. Arthur T. Pierson, ed.
The Inspired Word: A Series of Papers and Addresses Delivered at the Bible Inspiration Conference, Philadelphia, 1887
London, 1888

■ 11. Moody Bible Institute Correspondence Dept. *First Course — Bible Doctrines, Instructor— R. A. Torrey; Eight Sections with Questions,*
Chicago, 1901

The Formation of A Fundamentalist Agenda 1900-1920

■ 12. Amzi C. Dixon,
Evangelism Old and New,
New York, 1905

■ 13. William Bell Riley
The Finality of the Higher Criticism; or, The Theory of Evolution and False Theology
Minneapolis, 1909

■ 14.-17 George M. Marsden, ed.
The Fundamentals: A Testimony to the Truth
New York, 1988

■ 18. Joel A. Carpenter, ed.
*The Bible in Faith and Life,
as Taught by James M. Gray*
New York, 1988

■ 19. Mark A. Noll, ed.
*The Princeton Defense
of Plenary Verbal Inspiration*
New York, 1988

■ 20. *The Victorious Life:
Messages from the Summer Conferences*
Philadelphia, 1918

■ 21. Joel A. Carpenter, ed.
Conservative Call to Arms
New York, 1988

■ 22. *God Hath Spoken: Twenty-five Addresses
Delivered at the World Conference on
Christian Fundamentals, May 25- June 1, 1919*
Philadelphia, 1919

Fundamentalism Versus Modernism 1920-1935

■ 23. Joel A. Carpenter, ed.
*The Fundamentalist -Modernist Conflict:
Opposing Views on Three Major Issues*
New York, 1988

■ 24. Joel A. Carpentar, ed.
*Modernism and Foreign Missions:
Two Fundamentalist Protests*
New York, 1988

■ 25. John Horsch
*Modern Religious Liberalism: The Destructiveness
and Irrationality of Modernist Theology*
Scottsdale, Pa., 1921

■ 26. Joel A. Carpenter, ed.
*Fundamentalist vesus Modernist
The Debates Between
John Roach Stratton and Charles Francis Potter*
New York, 1988

■ 27. Joel A. Carpenter, ed.
*William Jennings Bryan on
Orthodoxy, Modernism, and Evolution*
New York, 1988

■ 28. Edwin H. Rian
The Presbyterian Conflict
Grand Rapids, 1940

Sectarian Fundamentalism 1930-1950

■ 29. Arno C. Gaebelein
Half a Century: The Autobiography of a Servant
New York, 1930

■ 30. Charles G. Trumball
Prophecy's Light on Today
New York, 1937

■ 31. Joel A. Carpenter, ed.
*Biblical Prophecy in an Apocalyptic Age:
Selected Writings of Louis S. Bauman*
New York, 1988

■ 32. Joel A. Carpenter, ed.
*Fighting Fundamentalism:
Polemical Thrusts of the 1930s and 1940s*
New York, 1988

■ 33. *Inside History of First Baptist Church, Fort
Worth, and Temple Baptist Church, Detroit:
Life Story of Dr. J. Frank Norris*
Fort Worth, 1938

■ 34. John R. Rice
*The Home — Courtship, Marriage, and Children: A
Biblical Manual of Twenty -Two Chapters
on the Christian Home.*
Wheaton, 1945

■ 35. Joel A. Carpenter, ed.
*Good Books and the Good Book: Reading Lists by
Wilbur M. Smith, Fundamentalist Bibliophile*
New York, 1988

■ 36. H. A. Ironside
Random Reminiscences from Fifty Years of Ministry
New York, 1939

■ 37 Joel A. Carpenter, ed.
*Sacrificial Lives: Young Martyrs
and Fundamentalist Idealism*
New York, 1988.

Rebuilding, Regrouping, & Revival
1930-1950

■ 38. J. Elwin Wright
*The Old Fashioned Revival Hour
and the Broadcasters*
Boston, 1940

■ 39. Joel A. Carpenter, ed.
*Enterprising Fundamentalism:
Two Second-Generation Leaders*
New York, 1988

■ 40. Joel A. Carpenter, ed.
Missionary Innovation and Expansion
New York, 1988

■ 41. Joel A. Carpenter, ed.
*A New Evangelical Coalition: Early Documents
of the National Association of Evangelicals*
New York, 1988

■ 42. Carl McIntire
Twentieth Century Reformation
Collingswood, N. J., 1944

■ 43. Joel A. Carpenter, ed.
The Youth for Christ Movement and Its Pioneers
New York, 1988

■ 44. Joel A. Carpenter, ed.
*The Early Billy Graham:
Sermons and Revival Accounts*
New York, 1988

■ 45. Joel A. Carpenter, ed.
*Two Reformers of Fundamentalism:
Harold John Ockenga and Carl F. H. Henry*
New York, 1988

DATE DUE

JUN 12 89			
OCT 5 '90			
SE 22'93			
DE 18 98			

BT
82.3
.F54
1988

30734

Fighting fundamentalism.

HIEBERT LIBRARY
Fresno Pacific College - M. B. Seminary
Fresno, Calif. 93702